The Guided Reader to Teaching and Learning

Featuring extracts from some of the most influential education writers in recent times *The Guided Reader to Teaching and Learning* is an essential compendium providing insight, guidance and clarity about key issues affecting practitioners at every level.

All extracts have been carefully chosen to represent education issues that affect every practising teacher. Each extract is accompanied by an introduction to the passage, key words and phrases and a summary of key points. In addition, there are questions to prompt discussion, suggestions about areas for possible investigation, and reference to other key readings to extend thinking. Uniquely, the book provides cross-referencing between extracts to facilitate a more complete understanding of how different issues overlap and how competing arguments have to be evaluated.

Combining both theoretical and practical dimensions into one handy and engaging volume, *The Guided Reader to Teaching and Learning* includes extracts, summaries and discussions about the following:

- the teacher
- effective teachers and teaching
- motivating learners
- teaching approaches
- teaching younger children
- managing teaching and learning
- other adults in the school
- child development
- ways that pupils learn
- learning climate
- learning styles
- thinking and learning
- assessment and learning.

The book will be of considerable interest to trainee and newly qualified teachers who are seeking to gain a higher qualification, notably at Masters degree level. More experienced teachers and teaching assistants wishing to upgrade their qualifications will also find the book an invaluable source of information and guidance.

Denis Hayes worked in both primary and secondary schools before moving into higher education. Until recently he was Professor of Education at the University of Plymouth, and he has published extensively about a wide range of education issues affecting teachers, teaching and learning.

The Guided Reader to Teaching and Learning

Denis Hayes

Routledge
Taylor & Francis Group

LONDON AND NEW YORK

This first edition published 2011
by Routledge
2 Park Square, Milton Park, Abingdon, Oxon OX14 4RN

Simultaneously published in the USA and Canada
by Routledge
270 Madison Avenue, New York, NY 10016

Routledge is an imprint of the Taylor & Francis Group, an informa business

© 2011 Denis Hayes

Typeset in Helvetica and Bembo
by Keystroke, Tettenhall, Wolverhampton
Printed and bound in Great Britain
by TJ International Ltd, Padstow, Cornwall

British Library Cataloguing in Publication Data
A catalogue record for this book is available from the British Library

Library of Congress Cataloging-in-Publication Data
Hayes, Denis, 1949–
    Guided reader to teaching and learning / by Denis Hayes. — 1st ed.
        p. cm.
    Includes bibliographical references.
    1. Reading (Early childhood)—United States. 2. Language arts (Early
    childhood)—Social aspects—United States. 3. Language policy—United States. I.
    Title.
    LB1139.5.R43H395 2011
    372.1102–dc22   2010012320

ISBN13: 978–0–415–58121–9 (hbk)
ISBN13: 978–0–415–58122–6 (pbk)
ISBN13: 978–0–203–84270–6 (ebk)

Contents

The Guided Reader to Teaching and Learning consists of seven sections, though there is overlap across the range of articles, and most of the extracts span several areas of interest. The numbers in parentheses refer to the extracts.

Introduction

The Guided Reader to Teaching and Learning is for serious students of education who have a professional involvement with children and young people at any stage from the nursery to the post-compulsory phase. The book is especially relevant to those who teach or aspire to teach in schools or colleges and will be of particular value to qualified teachers responsible for in-service training and those seeking to gain a higher qualification, such as a Master's-level degree. It will also be of considerable interest to teacher trainers and to students registered for Foundation degrees and HEFCE courses located within Education departments, such as Education Studies; Inclusive Studies; Family and Lifelong Learning; and Childhood Studies.

The Guided Reader seeks to raise significant education issues for practitioners and theorists who are interested in the general study of education, the learning process, teaching as a profession, the role of teachers, pedagogy, behaviour issues and the politics of education. In compiling the Reader, I have tried hard to avoid passages that contain an excessive amount of complex terminology, though some extracts require concerted effort to grasp the main points. The guidance I have provided with each extract should, however, make the task of understanding the authors' intentions in writing more straightforward. Website addresses are correct in 2010 but should be checked before disseminating.

For consistency, I have tended to employ the word 'pupils' in the additional information unless the word 'student' or 'child' has particular significance in the extract. It is worth noting that whereas writers from North America and other areas of the world tend to use 'student' for learners of any age, it is more common in Britain to employ 'child' or 'pupil' for learners in the primary phase (up to eleven or twelve years) and 'student' for those aged about twelve years and above. I have been scrupulously careful about accuracy, though there are occasions when minor adjustments to punctuation have been necessary to improve the clarity of expression. For consistency, all spelling has been adjusted to conform to UK English style. Also, please note that the word 'school' is used as a catch-all term in referring to education institutions for children and young people up to the age of eighteen.

The extracts in this Reader are taken from a variety of sources and their selection has been challenging. I have used a wide range of journals from the large number available through the Taylor & Francis organisation, which also publishes books under the Routledge and David Fulton imprints. In researching suitable material, I have become acutely aware of how much high-quality material is around and, I suspect, read by far fewer people than it deserves to be. If you find one of the extracts particularly enthralling it makes sense, of course, to obtain a copy of the book or journal article.

In selecting extracts from journals, there have been numerous occasions when I have been obliged to omit sections that I suspect the author(s) would ideally like to have been included; indeed, the act of assembling fragments of a carefully written piece sometimes felt like an act of literary and academic desecration. In truth, I would love to have used complete portions of text but the constraints of book length required me to exercise a lot of self-discipline in this regard. Similarly, there were numerous topics that I was itching to include because I knew that some readers would be disappointed by their omission. Perhaps another time! Regardless of any misgivings that authors may entertain about my interpretation of their work, I hope that they will be consoled in the knowledge that I have chosen their piece ahead of other excellent examples.

To make the task more manageable, I have avoided examples that focus *solely* on single subjects, ICT, leadership or management, special educational needs, national testing, 'school improvement' literature and brain research, though all of these areas receive mention. I have also tended to select more recent articles for the simple reason that education is always in a state of flux, such that even skilfully written and worthwhile publications can soon look dated – though you will find a few outstanding exceptions listed. The majority of the articles are set in a UK context; however, a proportion of them draw from Europe, North America, Australasia and elsewhere. Each extract is accompanied by additional information as follows:

- full details of the *source*;
- an *introduction* to the passage;
- *key words and phrases* from the extract;
- a *summary* of key points;
- *questions to consider* based on points arising from the extract;
- three suggested areas for *investigation*;
- further relevant sources and references allowing you to *think deeper*;
- related sources and references encouraging you to *think wider*.

The 'Investigations' sections offer starting points for further study, writing dissertations, completing a research project or carrying out in-service work. The suggestions are not, however, intended to be a substitute for a properly constructed research proposal or project description. Before embarking on any of the suggested studies, it is essential that you read the section 'Research advice' (p. ix) and seek advice from a suitably qualified tutor about preparing and undertaking the work. There are all sorts of pitfalls awaiting the unwary researcher, not least gaining permissions from and maintaining good relationships with the people who provide the focus for your study. Schools and colleges are usually tightly knit communities and susceptible to gossip and rumour, so although you must be transparent about the purpose and intention of your study, you must also be extremely careful that you don't unintentionally betray a confidence, disclose personal details, imply that someone is failing or inadequate at the job or otherwise cause disquiet. Maintaining the transparency/confidentiality balance is never easy and is made much harder if you are a member of the community that forms the object of your research.

The sections headed 'Think deeper' are means of extending your knowledge about the key issues raised by the author(s) of the extract. The 'Think wider' sections embrace related issues of relevance that spring out of the extract. Both the 'Think deeper' and the 'Think wider' additions contain details of interesting perspectives and/or results from research projects that provide you with insights and direction for expanded study. In preparing them, I have drawn freely from my previous publications, notably the *Encyclopedia of Primary Education* (Routledge, 2010).

The Title Key Words list (p. 261) allows you to trace and explore specific themes across the extracts. The Author List (p. 257) consists of some 300 names of principal authors whose works are cited.

Research advice

If your course of study involves undertaking a research project, you will receive guidance from your supervisor or tutor about the ethics and practicalities of doing so. In the meantime, it is worth noting the following:

- Research tends to be broadly classified as *quantitative* (involving numbers) or *qualitative* (involving descriptions). In practice, however, almost every study in education involves a degree of both quantitative and qualitative research, with one or the other dominating.
- Whatever research project you decide to undertake, it is certain that someone somewhere has already spent time researching the area. Don't be discouraged when you make this discovery because it provides you with the all-important context for your own research to which you can refer and from which you can shape your project.
- There are many different ways of gaining information (or 'data', plural), but the most commonly used are (1) through interviews; (2) by closely observing a situation; or (3) by distributing a questionnaire. It may be, of course, that you employ more than one method; for example, you may distribute a questionnaire and invite respondents to contact you if they wish to discuss matters further – thereby employing interview technique as a second source of data.
- Make sure from the start that you keep a detailed log of your research 'journey', including *full* details of each book, journal and online reference. Maintaining accurate references is a particularly important consideration as it is hugely frustrating to find that you failed to make a note of (say) the page number of an article and have to spend precious time hunting it down when the deadline for submission of your work is approaching.

- It is sometimes appropriate to keep a record of your own emotions and responses throughout the research. Remember that research is not just about 'them'; it is also about 'you' as the researcher. One of my education students was determined to interview young people who were considered to be failures at school about the factors contributing to their demise. While she was conscientious in setting up the research and following correct ethical procedures, she had not taken sufficient account of the profound *emotional* impact on the interviewees or on herself as they recounted their experiences. The trauma proved so distressing for this caring young woman that she abandoned the study and chose something more manageable to investigate.

- It is important to be *realistic* about what you can achieve in your project. Think carefully about practical issues, such as gaining permissions (notably where studying children is concerned), travel time, availability of the participants, ways to record conversations and, as noted above, the emotional impact of the study – especially if it unearths previously suppressed frustrations and hurt. It is also worth bearing in mind that data have to be analysed, so don't spend ages accumulating masses of information that you don't have time to evaluate and write up. A project that is modest in scope but properly organised and thorough is likely to be more successful than an over-ambitious one.

- Think of the people with whom you have contact as collaborators, participants or respondents, rather than as 'subjects' who are having the research 'done' to them. Most people are only too happy to cooperate with you and give of their time freely, which makes it even more important to show them respect and courtesy.

- Research that involves direct contact with children and young people requires particularly careful handling. There are protocols that must be observed, about which your supervisor will advise you. In the meantime, here are a few basic points of which you should be aware: (1) You must always have written permission from the relevant adults (teacher, parent, carer, social worker, or a combination of these) to observe, interview or (especially) film children or young people aged sixteen years and under. (2) Your presence in the room or educational setting will affect behaviour, so several visits are nearly always necessary to gain a true picture of what is happening. (3) You must never be alone with a child or small group 'in private'; always ensure that another adult is within sight. (4) Do not agree to keep secrets; make it clear to pupils that what is said to you is confidential but *not* secret. (5) All data should be destroyed at the end of the project.

- Confidentiality is a vital consideration in all research, especially if it is an *ethnographic* study in which you are focusing on a definable social context where people interact, such as a classroom, staff room, governors' meeting, waiting room, hospital ward, nursery unit, home, prison, etc., because of the intimacy and close human relationships. For instance, imagine that you were interviewing a group of teachers about their views concerning a recent school innovation; it is likely that there would be some respondents critical of the idea, the leadership or the implementation who would want to register their views with you but would *not* want to be identified (for fear of reprisal) and would trust you completely in this regard. Such considerations are sharpened when you are dealing with sensitive situations, such as parental involvement or child protection.

■ Respondents are usually very interested in what you have found as a result of your research, so plan opportunities to offer feedback. However, this process is not straightforward, as it takes time to assemble conclusions and produce a summary report, by which time many participants have lost interest.

Most research projects necessitate the production of an 'ethics protocol' or similar, as a way of spelling out the procedures and safeguards that characterise the project. Such a protocol will contain safeguards, such as ensuring that respondents are not identified; stating unambiguously that a participant has the right to withdraw from proceedings at any point without giving a reason; the way that conversations will be recorded; and how data will be used. Your supervisor will give you a template that will form the basis of the protocol or agreement, which you can personalise for the specific circumstances of the study.

Maintaining confidentiality

■ Never discuss with another person what a respondent has said to you.
■ From the start of the project, use pseudonyms, or numbers or letters, to identify each participant.
■ Keep your notes, recordings and other data in a secure place; don't leave them lying around.
■ Avoid using someone's job title or description when referring to a respondent, as this could make the person traceable.
■ Encrypt or otherwise disguise information held on your computer.

How to use *The Guided Reader*

There are four principal ways to use this Reader:

1. Use the *title key words* search facility to track words and phrases in the titles of the extracts.
2. Take the *introductions* and *summaries* from each extract as a shorthand method to elicit information, then follow up in depth the extracts of most immediate interest.
3. Find the general area of education in which you are interested and use the *extract cross-references* to identify related passages and information.
4. Use the *author list* to gain information about the views and research findings of writers in whom you have a particular interest.

Extract references

Every effort has been made to contact all the copyright holders of material included in the book. If any material has been included without permission, the publishers offer their apologies. We would welcome correspondence from those individuals/companies whom we have been unable to trace and will be happy to make acknowledgement in any future edition of the book.

Extract 1   5

Broadhead, P. (2009) 'Conflict resolution and children's behaviour: observing and understanding social and cooperative play in early years educational settings', *Early Years*, 29 (2), 105–18.

Extract 2   9

Coltman, P. and Whitebread, D. (2008) 'Organising the whole curriculum: enterprise projects in the early years', in Whitebread, D. and Coltman, P. (eds) *Teaching and Learning in the Early Years*, Abingdon: Routledge.

Extract 3   13

Baines, E., Rubie-Davies, C. and Blatchford, P. (2009) 'Improving pupil group work interaction and dialogue in primary classrooms: results from a year-long intervention study', *Cambridge Journal of Education*, 39 (1), 95–117.

Extract 4   16

Galton, M., Hargreaves, L. and Pell, T. (2009) 'Group work and whole-class teaching with 11- to 14-year-olds compared', *Cambridge Journal of Education*, 39 (1), 119–40.

Extract 5 21

Drummond, M.J. (2003) *Assessing Children's Learning*, second edition, London: David Fulton.

Extract 6 24

Newton, P.E. (2007) 'Clarifying the purposes of educational assessment', *Assessment in Education*, 14 (2), 149–70.

Extract 7 29

Wallace, B., Cave, D. and Berry, A. (2009) *Teaching Problem-Solving and Thinking Skills through Science*, London: David Fulton.

Extract 8 33

Costello, P.J.M. (2000) *Thinking Skills and Early Childhood Education*, London: David Fulton.

Extract 9 37

Jeffrey, B. and Woods, P. (2003) *The Creative School: A framework for success, quality and effectiveness*, London: RoutledgeFalmer.

Extract 10 41

Fisher, R. (2004) 'What is creativity?', in Fisher, R. and Williams, M. (eds) *Unlocking Creativity: A teacher's guide to creativity across the curriculum*, London: David Fulton.

Extract 11 45

Humphries, S. and Rowe, S. (1994) 'The biggest classroom', in Blatchford, P. and Sharp, S. (eds) *Breaktime and School: Understanding and changing playground behaviour*, London: Routledge.

Extract 12 48

Casey, B., Casey, N., Calvert, B., French, L. and Lewis, J. (2002) *Television Studies: The key concepts*, London: Routledge.

Extract 13 55

Smidt, S. (2006) *The Developing Child in the 21st Century: A global perspective on Child Development*, Abingdon: Routledge.

Extract 58 246

O'Quinn, E.J. and Garrison, J. (2004) 'Creating loving relations in the classroom', in Liston, D. and Garrison, J. (eds) *Teaching, Learning and Loving: Reclaiming passion in educational practice*, London: RoutledgeFalmer.

Extract 59 250

Addison, R. and Brundrett, M. (2008) 'Motivation and demotivation of teachers in primary schools: the challenge of change', *Education 3–13*, 36 (1), 79–94.

Extract 60 253

Day, C. (2004) *A Passion for Teaching*, London: RoutledgeFalmer.

EXTRACTS

Pupil learning

Early learning

Extract 1

Source

Broadhead, P. (2009) 'Conflict resolution and children's behaviour: observing and understanding social and cooperative play in early years educational settings', *Early Years*, 29 (2), 105–18.

Introduction

This paper draws from continuing research into the growth of sociability and co-operation in young children across the three to six years age range. The research has underpinned the development of an observational tool, the Social Play Continuum (SPC), drawing on play observations of nursery children (aged three to four years) and reception class children (aged four to five years) in one school, with particular attention given to conflict and its interpretation. Broadhead considers stress in children's lives and its potential impact on playful learning needs. (Based on article abstract)

Key words & phrases

Action, age, child-directed play, children's play, conditions of stress, conflict resolution, cooperative play, effective pedagogy, friendship building, interaction, intervention, joint learning, nursery, observations, peer conflict, peers, playful activity, playful pedagogies, reception, skills, social, use of language

---

Extract

"Over time, the SPC was developed to illustrate children's uses of language and action/interaction with peers as a progression along four domains – the *Associative domain*, the *Social domain*, the *Highly Social domain* and the *Cooperative domain*, in keeping with the inherent and implied progression of a personal ZPD [zone of proximal development] . . .

Conditions of stress affect the quality of life for all family members and whilst young children may not directly understand the economic consequences of low income, they do register and live amidst the associated conditions of adult stress that accompanies poverty; they bring these realisations, concerns and uncertainties into the classroom as integral to their identity. Conflict resolution is not therefore merely a matter of 'skill level' but exists within a broader frame of human experience whereby stress and conflict may be intertwined; they are natural conditions which all adults and children experience to some degree but which are experienced at especially high levels for children whose families live with poverty, low income and high levels of day-to-day stress . . .

School and classroom environments can also be stressful. There is nothing inherently natural in children being together in large groups with few adults and in sometimes cramped conditions. The only amelioration between such conditions and stress is the teacher's capacity for implementing effective pedagogy wherein the child's sense of self, identity and purpose might find voice amidst the crowds, clutter and demands of the given curriculum . . .

Our observations and reflections noted, and the above findings confirmed, that age was not a key determinant in attaining cooperative play with its higher levels of cognitive challenge. The play was also influenced by:

- the children's familiarity with the play materials and the play potential of the materials;
- regular and sustained access to the play materials where play themes could be developed and deepened over time;
- flexibility within the play resources to accommodate the children's own prior learning and their thematic interests;
- opportunities for the children to work though their instances of conflict and return to their play materials and play themes . . .

Intervention programmes might seem to address concerns regarding perceptions of poorly developed social skills and heightened conflicts amongst young children. However, this paper advocates an increase in the amount of child-initiated and child-directed play available to children in educational settings to resonate more fully with child-initiated play themes. Through the use of the SPC it also proposes that playful activity can be cognitively challenging through problem-setting and problem-solving and through complex uses of language and that often these behaviours are 'hidden' amongst seemingly more boisterous activity . . .

The paper has illustrated the value of extended and well-focused observations in relation to adult perceptions of what might, from just a quick glance, be defined as 'misbehaviour, chaos and conflict'. Detailed observations and opportunities for post-observation reflection allow educators to explore the potentially multiple meanings and purposes of children's play, just as play allows children to make meanings that can inter-connect the potentially disparate worlds of home and school . . .

Creating and sustaining playful learning requires a facilitative pedagogical climate and a clear understanding of the potential young children have to take control of their play, to resolve their difficulties and to intellectually engage within a community of learners. Pedagogies of interaction and intervention need to be informed by a deep understanding of the purposes and meanings of play. Let us give play back to children rather than compensating them for its loss through intervention programmes."

See also Brooker, L. (2002) *Starting School: Young children learning cultures*, Buckingham: Open University Press.

Summary

Broadhead's work demonstrates that understanding the nature and purpose of play is complex and requires studied consideration rather than basing conclusions on superficial observations of children. Play is a medium that links home and school; experiences in school should offer children opportunities not only to develop their social skills but also to be empowered as a means of combating stress, resolving issues and intellectually engaging within a community of learners.

Questions to consider

1. What factors inhibit children's social development and interaction with peers? How might educators ameliorate such tendencies?
2. What should adults take into account when deciding whether to intervene or to stand back and allow children to resolve conflicts themselves?
3. How might play relieve stress?

Investigations

Note: With the sensitivities attached to child protection, it is particularly important to ensure that you have gained all the necessary permissions to conduct research.

Close observations of children at play (1). Spend a few minutes each day for (say) one week observing specific children and noting their involvement using Broadhead's four domains (the *associative domain* – 'looking on'; the *social domain* – 'passive involvement'; the *highly social domain* – 'active involvement'; and the *cooperative domain* – 'initiating action and talk'). See appendix 1 in the original article for full details.

Close observations of children at play (2). Spend a few minutes each day for (say) one week observing specific children and noting episodes of conflict, instances of adult intervention and children's subsequent behaviour.

Close observations of children at play (3). Spend a few minutes each day for (say) one week observing specific children, together with at least one other adult, someone who knows the children well. Discuss the children's behaviour with the adult(s) to gain multiple perspectives on their actions, motives, social skills and learning.

Think deeper

Cohen (2006) states that if learning is to occur, it is necessary for play to translate from the 'pretend' (or 'playful') state to a 'serious' state. He argues that play is not always beneficial; for example, initial 'messing about' can turn into something more threatening, and adults need to be alert to occasions when children's natural liveliness deteriorates into bullying. He distinguishes between a playful state of mind, in which the individual is able to explore and elaborate a variety of skills and test them to the limits in a free and imaginative way; and a serious state of mind, which is goal orientated. Cohen claims that in the playful state the child is able to build up a stockpile of habits, skills and knowledge that is more extensive than it would have been in the goal-orientated state alone. When in the 'serious' state, a child selects from this playful agenda and begins to articulate the ideas. The synergy between the two states is where learning takes place. See also Wood (2007), who suggests that contemporary research highlights the effectiveness of mixed pedagogical approaches, including child- and adult-initiated play. She argues that while early childhood specialists recognise these approaches as central to high-quality curricula in early childhood settings, the place and significance of play continues to pose challenges to teachers and other practitioners. **Play: see also Extracts 2 and 11.**

Cohen, D. (2006) *Social Skills for Primary Pupils*, Birmingham: Questions Publishing.
Wood, E. (2007) 'New directions in play: consensus or collision?' *Education 3–13*, 35 (4), 309–20.

Think wider

A study by Gmitrova *et al.* (2009) in the Slovak Republic found that girls significantly preferred pretend play, whereas boys favoured constructive play. The most preferred pretend play, acceptable for both genders, came from the family environment, comprising a potentially effective 'carrier' of the cognitive skills. They conclude that an emphasis on 'academic readiness' through concentrated and direct teaching of skills such as the alphabet, number and colours is adversely affecting the amount of time allocated for play in preschools. Yet cognitive skills that are demonstrated in pretence are as important (or even more important) for academic readiness and later school success than the officially prescribed early childhood competencies. **Gender issues: see also Extracts 16, 19 and 56.**

Gmitrova, V., Podhajeck, M. and Gmitro, J. (2009) 'Children's play preferences: implications for the preschool education', *Early Child Development and Care*, 179 (7), 949–68.

Extract 2

Source

Coltman, P. and Whitebread, D. (2008) 'Organising the whole curriculum: enterprise projects in the early years', in Whitebread, D. and Coltman, P. (eds) *Teaching and Learning in the Early Years*, Abingdon: Routledge; see pp. 66–77.

Introduction

The extract below focuses on ways to organise the whole curriculum. The book is based on the premise that children need to become independent learners and that an effective early years curriculum must start with the children's needs and potential. Teaching must have a strong element of fun, wonder and excitement, and play is viewed as a particularly important learning medium in the process.

Key words & phrases

Content and organisation, early years curriculum, early years educators, enterprise projects, explore, first-hand experiences, imaginative play and talk, investigate, lack of forethought, learn effectively, make more sense, muddle, opportunities, play as a learning medium, problem-solve, provision for play, topic-based approach, turmoil in education, understandings

---

Extract

"There is no doubt that the last few years have been ones of considerable turmoil in education, and that teachers and other educators have been pulled in different directions, often as a consequence of muddle and lack of forethought among those in positions of power. However, now that the dust has settled to some extent, a clearer picture is emerging, and it is not one that is entirely compatible, in the present authors' view, with early years principles. One example of this might be the role afforded to play as a learning medium in early years classrooms. The important role of 'active' self-directed modes of learning, often in the form of one or other kind of play, has long been recognised by early years educators. There appears to have been a decline in the provision for play within early years classrooms, however, possibly under the pressure referred to above to 'prepare' children for the national curriculum, and the literacy and numeracy strategies . . .

Through all this debate, in the view of the present authors, there remain a number of important principles which should guide the content and organisation of the early years curriculum. These principles derive from the evidence about children's learning and from the collective experiences and views of early years educators . . . Despite

9

the dangers, the national curriculum is not necessarily incompatible with these principles, but they should guide the way it is taught and managed . . .

Young children need a curriculum which starts with what they understand and can do already, and that helps them make more sense of their world by providing them with meaningful tasks which require their active engagement, and which give them opportunities to express their understandings in a variety of media, principally through imaginative play and talk. Young children's natural curiosity can be stimulated to help them learn effectively by providing novel first-hand experiences and opportunities to explore, investigate and problem-solve.

From these principles we have derived four principles that we believe should guide the organisation and management of the early years curriculum. These principles are as follows. Young children's learning will be enhanced when:

1. The content of the curriculum is 'meaningful' to them and related to their existing knowledge and interests.
2. They are active participants in their learning rather than just passive recipients – they should have opportunities to make their own decisions about their learning.
3. They are encouraged to indulge their natural inclination to engage in imaginative play related to significant life experiences.
4. They are emotionally secure because there is continuity and good communication between the worlds of home and school.

These principles clearly support an integrated, topic-based approach, and this can be carried out in a whole variety of ways . . . This approach consists of what has been called 'Enterprise' projects. In essence these consist of using some kind of adult 'enterprise' or place of work as a starting point and enabling children to explore and investigate it, partly by carrying out a similar kind of enterprise themselves."

Summary

The authors argue strongly for the centrality of play as a focal point for learning, especially among the younger pupils in school. They regret the decline in play taking place in the early years of schooling and describe how a combination of adult direction (to comply with curriculum requirements) and pupil spontaneity produces a powerful combination. Furthermore, they suggest that enterprise projects might provide the solution to achieving a balance of compliance and child-initiated active engagement.

Questions to consider

1. To what extent can play be described as a 'learning medium'?
2. In what ways can play (in its broadest sense) be utilised in other phases of education, including work with secondary and adult learners?

3.   How can teachers achieve a balance between pupil-initiated and adult-initiated activities, while satisfying the demands of an externally imposed curriculum?

Investigations

Types of play. Through observation of children playing and discussions with teachers and helpers, draw up a provisional theory about types of play that occur in the classroom. Share your ideas with practitioners to gain further comment and insights. See Sharman *et al.* (2004) and Hobart and Frankel (2004) for practical suggestions about observing and assessing children.

Early years curriculum. Identify and contrast the references to play in curriculum documents from a variety of educational settings.

Enterprise projects. Using an action research approach, investigate the potential benefits and challenges of using an enterprise project approach. **Action research: see also Extract 37 under 'Think deeper'.**

Hobart, C. and Frankel, J. (2004) *Child Observation and Assessment*, London: Nelson Thornes.
Sharman, C., Cross, W. and Vennis, D. (2004) *Observing Children*, London: Continuum.

Think deeper

Singer *et al.* (2006) argue that the creation of imaginary situations, characters and events lays the foundation for abstract thinking. Play assists children in utilising spoken and other non-verbal forms of language ('body language') effectively. It offers pupils in school opportunities to converse meaningfully with other children and understand that their words and actions can evoke a variety of responses in their peers. There is considerable evidence to support the view that play helps to develop a child's imagination and ultimately helps them to distinguish between fantasy and reality. **Body language: see also Extracts 25 under 'Think wider', 41 ('Think wider') and 42 ('Think deeper').**

Goouch (2008) suggests that an environment or play space designed and defined for young children's development and learning reflects broad educational ideologies and that of the designers, as well as of the teacher who is using and controlling the space. In doing so, she considers the way in which teachers' values and principles have a key role to play in making and shaping pedagogical choices: using space; how and where adults are located; issues of power and control; the resources and ways that interactions with resources and others take place. One key factor is that children choose to play and cannot be coerced to do so, yet 'play' is becoming a statutory element of the early years curriculum. Goouch concludes that attention needs to be given to cultures of power and the use of language to symbolise that power in the classroom, claiming that intuitive teachers are able to lead by following the interests, desires and intentions of the children.

Goouch, K. (2008) 'Understanding playful pedagogies, play narratives and play spaces', *Early Years*, 28 (1), 93–102.
Singer, D.G., Golinkoff, R.M. and Hirsh-Pasek, K. (eds) (2006) *Play Equals Learning: How play motivates and enhances children's cognitive and social–emotional growth*, New York: Oxford University Press.

Think wider

Adults responsible for young primary-age children take account of the different forms of play when organising and monitoring activities. For instance, *parallel play* describes a situation where pupils play side by side but with little or no interaction. A desire for isolation during play is normal, provided it is not excessive, as a balance between social and solitary play is necessary for all children. Pupils benefit from the social learning that is gained through sharing and cooperating with other children during *group play* and it may signal a problem if children insist on playing on their own for most or all of the time. See Casey (2005) for suggestions about inclusive play. Elements of *imaginary play* are also significant for older primary pupils engaged in producing spontaneous drama sequences and acting out contrived scenes. Experienced teachers learn to judge when to become involved in children's play and when to observe and allow children to take the initiative (see Call 1999). When left alone, children normally play unprompted and create imaginative situations out of ordinary conditions (Duffy 1998).

Ahn and Filipenko (2007) documented the ways in which the spontaneous narratives of a focus group of six 'kindergarten' children reflected the ways in which they constructed meaning about their world and their place in it by engaging in extended episodes of imaginary dramatic play and producing drawings, paintings and three-dimensional objects. Three themes emerged from the qualitative analysis of the data: (1) *Engendering* emerged from observations of the ways in which children's narratives focused on *self* or *I* and revealed the ways in which children construct (*engender*) their identities as moral, social, cultural and gendered beings. (2) *Crossing texts and reconfiguration* emerged from the ways in which children negotiate their roles (*self*) with others (*reconfiguring* the 'I' to 'We'). (3) *Reconstruction/re-imagination* emerged from the ways in which children used narrative with others to grapple with abstract scientific, philosophical and moral questions, building hypotheses about themselves and their world which, during subsequent narrative interactions, were challenged and reformulated (*re-imagined*). Brock *et al.* (2008) explore, debate and further develop the theory of play, relating theory to examples of practice that are taken from a broad range of multidisciplinary perspectives.

Ahn, J. and Filipenko, M. (2007) 'Narrative, imaginary play, art and self: intersecting worlds', *Early Childhood Education Journal*, 34 (4), 279–89.

Brock, A., Dodds, S., Jarvis, P. and Olusoga, Y. (2008) *Perspectives on Play*, London: Longman.

Call, N.J. (1999) 'The importance of play', online at www.acceleratedlearning.co.uk.

Casey, T. (2005) *Inclusive Play: Practical strategies for working with children aged 3 to 8*, London: Paul Chapman.

Duffy, B. (1998) *Supporting Creativity and Imagination in the Early Years*, Maidenhead: Open University Press.

Group work and collaboration

Extract 3

Source

Baines, E., Rubie-Davies, C. and Blatchford, P. (2009) 'Improving pupil group work interaction and dialogue in primary classrooms: results from a year-long intervention study', *Cambridge Journal of Education*, 39 (1), 95–117.

Introduction

Findings in this article are based on a year's evaluation of the effectiveness of the SPRinG (Social Pedagogic Research into Group-work) programme relative to a control group in classes at Key Stages 1–3 (ages 5–14). The project aimed to address the hiatus between the potential of group interaction to promote learning and its limited use in schools. It involved working with teachers to develop strategies for enhancing pupil group work and dialogue, and to implement a pupil relational and group skills training programme.

Key words & phrases

Behavioural interactions, discussion, free-riding, group blocking, group maintenance, group planning, groups, inferential talk, off-task talk, procedural talk, reasoning, relational skills

---

Extract

"This study examined whether pupil groups in classrooms where the SPRinG group work programme took place changed their behavioural interactions in predicted ways, in comparison with a control group . . .

We found, in line with predictions, that involvement in SPRinG increased the amount of time pupils spent working together as a whole group. By contrast, control groups were more likely to split into subgroups, while remaining on task, and also more likely to have a portion of the group not involved in the group work activity and thus free-riding on the back of other group members' efforts to do the task. However, these students were not just passively free-riding, rather they were actively engaged in non-task related activity which in many circumstances may function to disrupt group on task activity and also create bad feeling within the group. Free rider behaviour is an oft-cited problem (Slavin *et al.*, 2003) and a main reason teachers give for not undertaking group work . . . Group blocking was more prevalent in control groups . . .

Findings showed . . . little difference in the amount of explicit group maintenance (for example encouraging others to participate), which was unexpected . . . However, it was the observers' perception that, as a result of the SPRinG training and practice with group work, participation and facilitation of others was so built into the fabric of interactions (for example by addressing each other's comments and explanations) that there was little need to make encouraging verbal gestures to others . . .

SPRinG groups produced more high-level inferential talk involving speculative reasoning that went beyond the information provided for the task. There was, however, little sign of a difference between SPRinG and control groups in levels of high level text based reasoning. Control groups were more likely to engage in talk that involved the sharing of information with less effort to reason or explore ideas or evidence further. These results indicate that overall involvement in SPRinG training encouraged students to engage in higher order talk and reasoning in groups.

As the term indicates, higher order inferential talk is more than using available evidence as part of an argument but involves participants using available information to speculate and explore alternate possibilities and to co-construct inferences that go beyond the boundaries of the task to examine implications and arrive at more considered conclusions. Because of the open ended nature of the group tasks, text based higher order reasoning will only allow the discussion to go so far in the decision making process. In order to make a final (and logical) decision in such tasks, group members must go beyond the evidence available. Higher order inferential talk therefore reflects the use of important critical thinking skills . . .

Findings in relation to levels of procedural talk were in line with predictions with SPRinG pupils producing less than control pupils, though levels were low in both groups . . . A similar finding was found in relation to disputes between peers . . . Overall, disputational talk was very low but was in greater evidence in control group members' interactions . . .

We also found that SPRinG pupils were more likely to sustain topics under discussion . . . group members considered at length the arguments both for and against making a particular decision and may imply a more systematic approach to reasoning."

Slavin, R., Hurley, E.A., Chamberlain, A., Reynolds, W.M. and Miller, G.E. (eds) (2003) 'Cooperative learning and achievement: theory and research', in *Handbook of Psychology: Educational psychology* (vol. 7), pp. 177–98, New York: Wiley.

Note: the authors define 'group blocking' as ranging from acts of aggression and ridicule against other members to mild behaviour designed to disrupt the task and prevent group progress.

Summary

Baines *et al.* found that SPRinG groups displayed higher levels of participation, engagement, active and sustained discussion. They also showed higher levels of inferential joint reasoning and lower levels of group disruptive blocking behaviours than the control group. The authors argue that if teachers take time to train pupils in relational and group working skills, group work can be successfully implemented as a part of regular classroom activities to improve pupil interactions and enhance the quality of discussion.

Questions to consider

1. What are the potential advantages of group work over individual work or pairs?
2. What skills do pupils need to possess before group work can achieve optimal effectiveness?
3. How can teachers effectively monitor and assess the contribution and learning of each group member?

Investigations

Comparing two groups (1). Give the same investigative task to two groups: for one group, spend time inculcating relational and group working skills; for the other group, leave them largely to their own devices. Ask an assistant to 'listen in' to both groups and observe progress without intervening.

Comparing two groups (2). Give the same investigative task to two groups: intervene in the one group; offer minimal support to the other group. Ask an assistant to 'listen in' to both groups and observe progress without intervening.

Comparing two groups (3). Give the same investigative task to two groups: in the one case, spend time inculcating relational and group skills; in the other case, do not. Record or observe the nature of interaction in terms of the types of talk described in the Baines *et al.* extract. **Group work and social skills: see Extract 14.**

Think deeper

Researchers led by Peter Kutnick in England found that effective use of pupil groupings within classrooms for pupils at the top end of the primary school and lower secondary school (up to age fourteen years) was often limited by conflicts between pupil group size and composition, assigned learning tasks and interpersonal interactions. The study concluded that there was only limited evidence that pupils or teachers had received training or support to work effectively within their classroom groups (Kutnick *et al.* 2005; see also DfES 2006).

DfES (2006) Pupil Grouping Strategies and Practices at Key Stage 2 and 3, Brief no. RB796, Nottingham: DfES Publications.

Kutnick, P., Sebba, J., Blatchford, P., Galton, M. and Thorp, J. (2005) *The Effects of Pupil Grouping: Literature review*, Nottingham: DfES Publications.

Think wider

Hallam *et al.* (2004) conducted a major study into primary school pupils' perceptions of the purposes and practices of ability grouping, their experiences of these practices, and how their attitudes, behaviour, self-esteem, social interaction and feelings towards school were affected. Results showed that pupils were aware of the purposes of ability grouping and most of them were in favour of its use. Children saw the main advantage of ability grouping as having their work set at an appropriate level for them; they saw the main disadvantage as being the stigmatisation of pupils in the lower-level groups. Over 40 per cent of pupils reported being teased or having witnessed teasing connected with levels of ability in the classroom. The study's findings suggested that whether or not they were grouped by ability was of less importance to pupils than being in a supportive school ethos. For a wholly different perspective, see the article by Gordon (2009), in which he argues that constructivist teaching has often been misinterpreted and misused, resulting in learning practices that neither challenge students nor address their needs.

Gordon, M. (2009) 'The misuses and effective uses of constructivist teaching', *Teachers and Teaching*, 15 (6), 737–46.

Hallam, S., Ireson, J. and Davies, J. (2004) 'Grouping practices in the primary school: what influences change?', *British Educational Research Journal*, 30 (1), 117–40.

Extract 4

Source

Galton, M., Hargreaves, L. and Pell, T. (2009) 'Group work and whole-class teaching with 11- to 14-year-olds compared', *Cambridge Journal of Education*, 39 (1), 119–40.

Introduction

In this third strand of the SPRinG (Social Pedagogic Research into Group-work) project, research was conducted with eleven- to fourteen-year-old pupils in Key Stage 3 classes, making comparisons of their attainment in English, mathematics and science. Pupils were also observed using a specially designed structured observation schedule. Initially, fourteen English and sixteen science teachers were recruited but in the second year of the study a further cohort of twelve mathematics specialists were added.

Key words & phrases

Conceptual and metacognitive learning, context, debriefing, demonstration, feedback, group work, group work training, pedagogic repertoire, peer relationships, scaffolding, shortage of time, supporting cues, thinking time

---

Extract

"This comparative study was not intended to sustain an argument that group work should replace whole-class teaching and indeed these findings in themselves do not constitute an overwhelming case for the use of group work rather than whole-class discussion. Rather we argue that group work should be a complementary organisational strategy in promoting conceptual and metacognitive learning, and our results support this claim. When the academic outcomes of group work, as demonstrated in this study, are coupled with the widespread evidence that use of this teaching approach also promotes better peer relationships, then the case for ensuring that group work no longer remains a 'neglected art' in English classrooms becomes an exceptionally strong one . . .

First, as part of training pupils to work effectively in groups it is vital that teachers brief and debrief the class so that they can begin to gain metacognitive awareness of what it means to be part of a group. Debriefing sessions therefore are particularly important because they not only evaluate how individuals responded in the groups but also call for participants to make suggestions about suitable strategies for improving the situation on future occasions . . . It was noticeable, however, particularly in science, that teachers rarely found time for these debriefing sessions . . . More often teachers preferred to use an evaluation sheet, which they handed to pupils as they left the class. Thus the exercise tended to take the form of an additional homework task rather than generate a debate on the consequences of the previous classroom activity . . .

A second factor concerns the context of the group work training. Some teachers admitted that they had skipped parts of the training, again on the grounds of time, and justified this action by arguing that similar training procedures were also part of the personal, social and health education (PSHE) programme . . .

A third factor which tended to diminish the effectiveness of the groups involved the quality of feedback which often emerged during the 'reporting back' session . . . Given the limited available time, these reporting-back sessions by the various groups tended to be short and to consist mainly of reporting what had been done and the results of this activity, rather than giving explanations for the group's chosen approach since this would have taken considerably longer . . . Part of the value of group work is therefore lost if this kind of reasoning is not present and not shared by all the pupils during the reporting-back and debriefing stages . . .

The fourth factor which inhibited greater progress within the groups concerned the manner of scaffolding the various activities . . . Within the present teaching culture, however, teacher-directed scaffolding such as demonstration and guided discovery are promoted as the most effective means of support rather than the building supporting cues within the task, an approach often advocated in the cognitive developmental literature . . . When cues are incorporated into the task instructions, on the other hand, it becomes possible to maintain the task's ambiguity while reducing the risk of failure by framing tasks in such a way that pupils feel that their initial efforts have some relationship to what is ultimately required . . . teachers gave pupils very little thinking time before they intervened within the groups and during subsequent interviews pupils often complained about this, saying that they wanted to be left 'to work things out for themselves' until they had arrived as a group at some initial consensus . . . when teachers intervened too early, to give some guidance, pupils tended to see this as a sign of 'teacher take-over' in which he or she were seeking to impose certain of their own ideas. This was strongly resented."

Summary

Classroom observations indicated that there were more sustained, higher cognitive level interactions when pupils worked in groups than during whole-class discussions. It is argued in conclusion that the group work results could be improved still further if teachers gave more attention to training pupils to work in groups and if more time were given to debriefing after group work.

Questions to consider

1. What are the key organisational and management issues for teachers in promoting group work?
2. What sorts of 'cues' do teachers need to ensure they include in their task explanations?
3. How can teachers balance pupil thinking time and greater autonomy with lesson time constraints and the pressure of establishing predetermined outcomes?

Investigations

Quantifying group work. Observe a number of lessons, taking particular note of the use of individual, pairs and group work. Try to quantify the proportion of each type.

Effective use of explanation. Observe a number of lessons, taking particular note of the explanations that teachers use and the subsequent clarification resulting from pupils' questions about procedures or their incorrect assumptions about the teacher's requirements.

Use of feedback. Observe a number of lessons, taking particular note of the type of feedback from the teacher during the lesson (formative assessment / assessment for learning); the use of pupils' feedback to other pupils (peer mentoring); and the nature of general feedback at the end of the session (summative assessment / assessment of learning).

Think deeper

Kelly (2006) asserts that how teachers organise their classrooms says a great deal about the way that they view children's learning; thus:

> The areas of the curriculum you choose to link and focus on, the lessons and activities you plan, the roles you ascribe to other adults in your classroom, how you group and seat the children, the decisions you allow children to take, the resources you provide and the ways in which you make them available, your use of display and of opportunities to learn outside the classroom and school.
>
> (p. 137)

Black and Varley (2008) examined children's understanding of the role and purpose of whole-class discussions in supporting learning and also considered children's perceptions of their own participation in such discussions. They found that pupils identified as being of 'low ability' referred to the learning process as something beyond their control – a practice in which they participated as a stepping stone to getting a job or going to college at some point in the distant future. By contrast, high-ability pupils recognised the immediate value of participation in enhancing both their understanding and ability status in the classroom.

Black, L. and Varley, D. (2008) 'Young children's perspectives on whole class discussions', *Education 3–13*, 36 (3), 207–21.
Kelly, P. (2006) 'Organising your classroom for learning', in Arthur, J., Grainger, T. and Wray, D. (eds) *Learning to Teach in the Primary School*, Abingdon: Routledge.

Think wider

Hargreaves (2007) explored the features relating to the validity of assessment for learning, in particular the features of a *collaborative* assessment because of the learning benefits frequently claimed for collaborative learning. Hargreaves concludes that learning is particularly valuable if it includes learners making their own meanings in a particular area of knowledge, constructing knowledge of participating and communicating socially and reflecting critically on their learning in diverse contexts, as well as retaining, using and applying information appropriately. **Assessment: see also Extracts 5 and 6.**

Hargreaves, E. (2007) 'The validity of collaborative assessment for learning', *Assessment in Education*, 14 (2), 185–99.

Assessment and learning

Source

Drummond, M.J. (2003) *Assessing Children's Learning* (second edition), London: David Fulton; see pp. 175–7.

Introduction

Mary Jane Drummond has written extensively about assessment, especially with regard to younger children. She explains her position earlier in the book in challenging the simple notion that assessment is a three-stage process of accruing evidence to inform a judgement, which translates into outcomes. Thus, 'Assessment is essentially provisional, partial, tentative, exploratory and, inevitably, incomplete' (p. 14).

Key words & phrases

Appreciate the past, assessment practice, children's learning, core values, courageous responses, lovingly, make choices, make sense, understanding, values, welcome the future

---

Extract

"In this book I have identified three crucial questions that teachers and other educators must, I believe, ask themselves as they set about assessing children's learning. These questions are, when we look at learning:

- What is there to see?
- How best can we understand what we see?
- How can we put our understanding to good use?

I have tried not to suggest that there is only one possible set of answers to these questions. We could be deluding ourselves if we thought that these questions could ever be answered once and for all, or that assessment is a practice that can ever be perfected. But this lack of finality, this imperfection in our practice, should not cause us to feel shame or despair . . .

Children's learning is so complex and various that the task of trying to understand it is necessarily complex too. The task entails trying to see and understand the whole, as well as the minutest parts; it requires us to appreciate the past and analyse the present, as well as envisage and welcome the future; it obliges us to look for and attend to differences as well as similarities, individuals as well as groups, the unexpected as well as the intended outcome, absence as well as presence. It demands a broad vision and a narrow focus.

Above all, effective assessment requires educators to make choices, in the interests of children, that are based on a coherent set of principles, which are themselves an expression of each educator's core values. As these choices are made and translated into daily classroom practice, teachers are exercising . . . their responsibility for children's learning, their right to act in children's interests, and their power to do so wisely and well.

In effective assessment, teachers recognise the disparity of power between adults and children in school classrooms . . . I believe that a full understanding of what it might mean for teachers, parents and children if we learned to use our power to educate *lovingly* (as well as effectively or efficiently) would transform our practice in assessment . . .

For all the ferocity of the debate about assessment and the passion of the arguments on either side, it would be foolish to suggest that the teaching profession has been facing an issue of recent invention, a new and unlooked for addition to their heavy load of responsibilities. Of course, assessment is no such thing. Teachers are not dumb beasts of burden; they have always been interested in learning and struggled to make sense of it . . . And in our cautious and anxious and, I hope, courageous responses to demands on us that *are* new, we will do well to turn back to earlier educationists working within a very different set of values from those of today's legislators. Their work may help us to be clearer and more articulate about the values that permeate our chosen practices and what we must do to live up to them."

Summary

Drummond promotes the need to approach assessment from a principled position, rather than unthinkingly employing a set of techniques. She recognises that assessment cannot be an exact science but urges practitioners to strive for excellence, while acknowledging that we have much to learn from the experience of educators in the past.

Questions to consider

1. In what respects can assessment never be perfected?
2. What are the assessment implications of educating 'lovingly'? **Loving relations: see also Extract 58.**
3. What principles and values might underpin assessment today that were less relevant in the past, and vice versa?

Investigations

Principles that guide assessment. By using questionnaires or short interviews, carry out a survey of teachers to ascertain the principles that underpin their assessment approach. Draw up a set of categories under headings as appropriate and discuss your findings with each of them.

Types of assessment. Conduct an observation of two teachers over (say) five lessons each in which you note each occasion that a form of assessment interaction takes place. Present your results to the teacher and discuss their implications.

Alternative perceptions. Ask your teaching assistant or a trusted colleague to pay particular attention to the nature of your feedback and the way that the pupils appear to receive and interpret it.

Think deeper

Black and Wiliam (2006) are among educationists to challenge the notion that assessment and its impact on learning should be the teacher's sole responsibility. They refer to treating the classroom as a 'black box', whereby certain external *inputs* are fed in and make particular demands, such as those from pupils; teachers; other resources; management rules and requirements; parental anxieties; and tests, with pressure for children to score highly. The authors completed the model by noting that some *outputs* invariably follow, such as pupils who are more knowledgeable and competent; better test results; teachers who are more or less satisfied; and teachers who experience varying degrees of exhaustion.

Black, P. and Wiliam, D. (2006) 'Developing a theory of formative assessment', in Gardner, J. (ed.) *Assessment and Learning*, London: Sage.

Think wider

Where the purpose of the feedback is to help pupils make an evaluation of their own work quality, the child is encouraged to reflect on his or her progress and suggest strategies for improvement. The pupil then becomes supported by, but not dependent on, an adult's direction and approval (Gipps *et al.* 2000). Teachers commonly find that less confident children prefer to be told what to do rather than trust their own judgement, and have to exercise fine judgement when offering feedback to children about their work and effort. At one level there is a need for them to explain to children how things can be improved. At another level there is a pressing need to encourage, praise and celebrate small achievements.

Webb and Jones (2009) found that differences in formative assessment practices were associated with the activity system of the class and its teacher, rather than the teacher alone. When a teacher who was experienced in formative assessment approaches had 'embedded' formative assessment (see below) with one class, the formative classroom practice reverted to a less sophisticated level unless the pupils were already used to this approach with their previous teacher. The authors identified three levels of classroom practice associated with formative assessment that they refer to as 'trialling', 'integrated' and 'embedded'. Thus, (1) *Trialling:* Teachers were using and evaluating formative assessment tools and strategies in some parts of their practice but not in an integrated or systematic way. They were evaluating the effects on their students and thinking about other changes that they needed to make in order to use formative assessment successfully. (2) *Integrating:* Classroom practice had changed and a range of formative assessment strategies were operating effectively. Both teachers and students felt comfortable with their new ways of working but, typically, formative assessment strategies were used more frequently and successfully in some curriculum areas than others. (3) *Embedded:* Formative assessment was integrated throughout all the teaching and learning in the class, and both teachers and students made use of a wide range of strategies.

Gipps, C., McCallum, B. and Hargreaves, E. (2000) *What Makes a Good Primary Teacher?* London: Routledge.

Webb, M. and Jones, J. (2009) 'Exploring tensions in developing assessment for learning', *Assessment in Education*, 16 (2), 165–84.

Extract 6

Source

Newton, P.E. (2007) 'Clarifying the purposes of educational assessment, *Assessment in Education*, 14 (2), 149–70.

Introduction

Newton argues that a simple separation of assessment types into 'formative' (assessment for learning) and summative ('assessment of learning') and evaluative ('quality of') is unhelpful. He suggests that the phrase 'assessment purpose' can be interpreted in at least three ways: (1) the judgement level; (2) the decision level; and (3) the impact level. In the article, Newton also illustrates the wide range of uses to which assessment results might be put.

Key words & phrases

Assessment judgements, categories, certification, competence, decision level, evaluative, formative, grading, legitimate and illegitimate uses, messages, monitoring, policy-makers, prioritisation of purposes, summative

Extract

"Since the earliest days, most commentators have assumed that there *is* a meaningful distinction to be drawn between summative and formative. At least to my mind, though, no one has yet managed to nail a definition. I believe that there is a simple reason for this: the term 'summative' can only meaningfully characterise a type of assessment judgement (i.e. it operates at the judgement level of discourse), while the term 'formative' can only meaningfully characterise a type of use to which assessment judgements are put (i.e. it operates at the decision level of discourse). The terms belong to qualitatively different categories; to attempt to identify characteristics that distinguish them – within a single category – is to make a category error . . . It is not simply the case that results which are fit for one purpose (e.g. selection) may not be fit for another (e.g. placement), it is even the case that results which are fit for one instance of a particular purpose (e.g. short-term system monitoring) may not be fit for another (e.g. long-term system monitoring). We need to convey the complexities of assessment design and fitness-for-purpose; we should not allow those complexities to be over-simplified. The following discussion aims to draw clearer distinctions between assessment purposes and to emphasise that the different uses to which results are put often require substantially different assessment processes, even when those uses appear to be quite similar . . .

There are very many purposes for which educational assessment judgements might be used, of which the following is merely a selection . . .

Social evaluation uses
Formative uses
Student monitoring uses
Transfer uses
Placement uses
Diagnosis uses
Guidance uses
Qualification uses
Selection uses
Licensing uses
School choice uses
Institution monitoring uses
Resource allocation uses

Organisational intervention uses
Programme evaluation uses
System monitoring uses
Comparability uses
National accounting uses

Some might be surprised by the omission of 'certification' from this list of purposes. However, unlike the others on the list, its use often fails to implicate a specific decision, action or process. Sometimes 'certification' is used as loosely as 'grading' and fails to refer to a specific purpose for the reason described earlier. Other times it is used somewhat more precisely to indicate – and to testify to – the attainment of a general competence or profile of competencies. This is when it begins to hint at a specific use, although none is made explicit; even so, it is not clear that the implicated use(s) would be distinct from others on the list . . .

Since different purposes require different assessment design decisions it is important for the system designer, in collaboration with policy-makers, to define the *primary purpose* for which results are intended to be used. Where there is an aspiration for the assessment system to support a number of different purposes (assuming that they are not logically incompatible) an explicit *prioritisation* of purposes should be defined."

Summary

Newton is keen to reinforce the view that two major obstacles to effective communication in educational assessment have become apparent. First, the term 'assessment purpose' can be interpreted in a variety of different ways; second, the uses to which assessment results are put are often categorised misleadingly. He also concludes that the fact that 'assessment purpose' can be interpreted in a variety of different ways is, perhaps, the most basic point for assessment professionals to appreciate to ensure that their advice is not misunderstood.

Questions to consider

1. What are your definitions of 'formative', 'summative' and 'evaluative forms of assessment'? How do you define 'assessment of learning' and 'assessment in learning'?
2. Which of the educational assessment judgements are relevant to your situation?
3. How should different assessment results be used?

Investigations

Views about definitions. Carry out a survey of colleagues' definitions of the three commonly used assessment categories – formative, summative and evaluative – and contrast their responses. Consider the implications of the differing definitions for practice.

Educational assessment judgements. Convene a discussion about the use and limitations of Newton's classification of educational assessment judgements, as a means of drawing up a workable system for the institution.

Literature survey. Examine the available literature and collate the variety of definitions and uses for assessment judgements. Use your results to create a schema of assessments types and their operation.

Think deeper

Meyers and Nulty (2009) claim that in order to maximise the quality of student learning outcomes, curriculum design must ensure that students are provided with teaching and learning materials, tasks and experiences that (1) are authentic, real-world and relevant; (2) are constructive, sequential and interlinked; (3) require students to use and engage with progressively higher-order cognitive processes; (4) are all aligned with each other and the desired learning outcomes; and (5) provide challenge, interest and motivation to learn. The authors claim that the effect of applying these principles is to manipulate the learning system in ways that require students to adopt a deep learning approach in order to meet the course's assessment requirements, which, in turn, meet the desired course learning outcomes. They found that the students' enhanced enjoyment of their learning corresponded with improved learning outcomes; furthermore, evaluations of their summative assessment tasks demonstrated responses that featured deeper and more sophisticated understandings, and holistic and well-differentiated knowledge structures, together with high levels of synthesis and integration.

Meyers, N.M. and Nulty, D.D. (2009) 'How to use five curriculum design principles to align authentic learning environments, assessment, students' approaches to thinking and learning outcomes', *Assessment and Evaluation in Higher Education*, 34 (5), 565–77.

Think wider

Cowan (2009) surveyed the implementation of formative assessment strategies ('Assessment is for Learning', AifL) during school placements by three cohorts of final-year Bachelor of Education students at a Scottish university. The use of formative assessment by one cohort of Professional Graduate Diploma in Education (Secondary) student teachers at the university was compared with that of the most recent BEd cohort. For both groups the greatest barrier was a perceived lack of time, but significantly more of the primary students cited this as a factor. Within both student groups a few students were in schools that had not really begun to focus on AifL. Another negative issue cited by a small number of students related to attitudes expressed by teachers against the initiative. Overall, primary students were more confident and consistent in using classroom strategies than their secondary counterparts. One of the key factors in explaining this disparity was that more primary than secondary students were placed in schools already implementing formative assessment; primary students were also more experienced in the classroom (four years compared to one year for the postgraduates) and more easily able to accommodate new initiatives.

Cowan, E.M. (2009) 'Implementing formative assessment: student teachers' experiences on placements', *Teacher Development*, 13 (1), 71–84.

Thinking skills

Source

Wallace, B., Cave, D. and Berry, A. (2009) *Teaching Problem-Solving and Thinking Skills through Science*, London: David Fulton; see pp. 1–2, 8, 146.

Introduction

Wallace *et al.* base their approach to learning on the 'Every Child Matters' agenda and 'inclusion with differentiation'. Their premise is that although teachers must plan carefully, pupil involvement in what is learned and how it is learned creates a vibrant learning environment that increases motivation, independence and engagement. The authors claim that other benefits of teachers and learners working interactively to construct knowledge include heightened self-esteem, enjoyment and success, with the inevitable improvements in behaviour and social cohesion.

Key words & phrases

Asking questions, caring mentorship, celebration, correcting, creativity, curiosity, differentiating learning, engaged children, gifts, motivated learners, no mistakes, nurturing, personalising, problem-solving, re-think, role of teacher, self-esteem, self-reliance, strengths, support and care, thinking actively, thinking skills, weaknesses, whole brain activity

---

Extract

"The TASC [Thinking Actively in a Social Context] Framework develops whole brain activity, and the more we learn about brain activity through neuro-science, the more validity is given to the TASC Framework for developing problem-solving and thinking skills . . . it confirms that 'research' into teaching and learning must start with *reflective living research* that involves teachers, parents and, most importantly, the children, as equal partners. The very beginnings of the TASC Framework grew from discussions with learners about the problem solving and thinking skills they were using successfully; and then listening carefully to what skills they felt they needed to learn more effectively. The role of caring mentorship was essential in these discussions because often the learners were unaware of the strategies they could develop to improve their thinking. The role of the 'teacher' was one of listening, praising and making suggestions that the learners used, and then afterwards discussing the usefulness of these strategies.

Learners are often more perceptive than we often realise. Of course they know when they are interested and excited about their learning, and happy, engaged children are motivated learners. Hence an important aspect of the TASC Framework is to say to learners: What do you find interesting? What questions would you like to research? How can I help you to do this? This is the very foundation of personalising and differentiating learning – the teacher is the guide and inspiration; the learner has ownership and is involved in decision-making . . .

Another vital element of the TASC message is that there are no mistakes, only re-thinks. How empowering it is to know that everyone makes mistakes and that everyone is capable of correcting those mistakes! The role of the teacher is to praise every effort and then to ask those questions that allow children to re-think. In addition, the skill of the good teacher is to identify what skills the children need to make progress and to directly teach those skills, discussing with the learners why such skills are necessary . . .

All children are born with the gifts of curiosity and creativity – and the potential, usually insatiable, gift for asking questions to find out about the world in which they live. Fostering these questions and developing inquisitive and investigating minds is one of the essential roles of parent and teacher, and scientific enquiry is a wonderful route for nurturing and developing all children's potential for thoughtful discovery . . .

The greatest gifts we can give to any learner are the gifts of self-esteem, self-reliance and the confidence to solve problems in the belief that learning for life is a process of continual re-thinks until a suitable answer or solution is found . . . The essence of the TASC Framework is the celebration of *all* pupils' gifts and talents . . . All children are more efficient learners when they have opportunities to celebrate their strengths; and when they can confidently discuss their weaknesses, knowing that everyone has weaknesses, but there is support and care at hand to strengthen them."

Summary

The authors argue that the principles of pupil involvement, collaboration and open-mindedness towards solutions have general applicability. It is noteworthy that they make a number of strong statements, including 'learners were unaware of the strategies they could develop to improve their thinking' and 'learners are often more perceptive than we often realise' and 'the role of the teacher is to praise every effort' and 'all children are born with the gifts of curiosity and creativity'. You may like to go through the extract to list and evaluate the other assertions.

Questions to consider

1. In what ways can pupils be seen as 'equal partners' in learning? How is such a state of working attainable?
2. What are the implications for teaching and learning of an educational philosophy involving 'no mistakes', only 're-thinks'?
3. How is the role of the teacher as described above different from that which pertains in a more formal situation?

Investigations

Involving pupils in planning. For a set period (one week, say), spend a few minutes each session in explaining to pupils the purpose of the lesson and inviting their comments, questions and suggestions. At the end of the week, discuss with them the impact that this approach has had on their attitude. **Pupil involvement: see also Extracts 14 under 'Think wider', 46 under 'Think wider' and 47.**

No mistakes philosophy. For a set period (one week, say), make a conscious effort to implement a philosophy of 'no mistakes, only re-thinks'. Ask a colleague or assistant to take note of any perceived changes. Discuss with the class the implications for learning and relationships.

Celebrating pupils' wider interests. Invite pupil volunteers to spend a set period of time (five to ten minutes, say) in the lesson sharing with their classmates an interest lying outside the main school curriculum. Consider ways in which this knowledge links with the regular curriculum.

Think deeper

The concept of 'learning styles' gained considerable impetus after David Kolb published his Learning Styles Model (Kolb 1984), which in turn gave rise to the experiential learning theory (ELT) and learning styles inventory (LSI). Kolb's learning theory sets out four distinct learning styles (or preferences), which are based on a four-stage learning cycle: (1) concrete experience (CE); (2) reflective observation (RO); (3) abstract conceptualisation (AC); and (4) active experimentation (AE). The theory holds that this cycle leads to a four-type definition of learning styles, each representing the combination of two preferred styles: diverging (CE/RO); assimilating (AC/RO); converging (AC/AE); and accommodating (CE/AE). Furthermore, Kolb argues that people have a preference for a certain single learning style, influenced as they pass through three stages of development: *acquisition* – birth to adolescence; *specialisation* – school and early adulthood; and *integration* – mid-career to later life. He also suggests that our propensity to reconcile and successfully integrate the four different learning styles improves as we mature through our development stages. Given (2000) offers an historical overview of learning styles. **Adult learning: see also Extracts 39 and 40.**

Cook (2008) argues that there are four main ways in which children learn: visual, auditory, kinaesthetic and also *tactile* (relying on touch). He claims that all children learn best – though not exclusively – through one or more of these learning channels, and adults can help them to be successful by teaching each child through his or her primary learning style or learning styles. A teaching approach can be described as 'multi-sensory' if the method of instruction utilises all or most of these channels in each lesson. Cook describes each learning preference in terms of their characteristics listed, noting that some descriptors (e.g. 'field trips') apply to more than one category. Thus: *Auditory:* reading aloud; debates; panel discussions; informal discussions; interviews; lectures and speeches; recorded books; text-to-speech; plays; radio broadcasts; music and songs. In the typical classroom, auditory activities that involve reading, listening and hearing tend to dominate proceedings. *Visual:* films, movies, DVDs and videos; television; pictures; posters; murals; maps, charts, graphs; field trips; computer software; demonstrations; drama; experiments. Cook also claims that all children with dyslexia are strong visual learners. *Kinaesthetic:* for example, games; models; letter tiles, computer software; arts and crafts; hands-on practice; experiments; field trips. *Tactile:* for example, arts and crafts; clay modelling; gardening; dressing up; painting; sewing. **Teaching approaches: see also Extracts 26, 40 and 56.**

Cook, S.L. (2008) 'Learning styles', online at www.learningabledkids.com/home_school_info/learning_styles.html.

Given, B.K. (2000) *Learning Styles*, Fairfax, VA: Learning Forum Publications.

Kolb, D. (1984) *Experiential Learning: Experience as the source of learning and development*, Englewood Cliffs, NJ: Prentice Hall.

Think wider

Rogers (2009) asked further and higher education students from a number of different class groups to complete a questionnaire that related to learning style categories represented by VARK (visual, audio, read/write, kinaesthetic) to assess their awareness of their learning style preference techniques. The study also evaluated how students responded to the use of a variety of different teaching methods to accommodate students who do not respond well to the traditional read/write style of learning and revision. The author also found that using a range of teaching techniques encouraged student participation in the course and in some cases enhanced their assessment performance.

Studies suggest that pupils' satisfaction with their education experience decreases with age and drops considerably when they reach secondary school (see, for example, Woods 1990; Cullingford 2002). Thus, a large majority of primary pupils think that school is a positive experience; this contrasts with about one-quarter in secondary schools who feel similarly enthusiastic. When one measures pupils' views about the relevance of what they learn and retain while in school, the motivation gap between the primary and secondary phases is even more pronounced.

Cullingford, C. (2002) *The Best Years of their Lives? Pupils' experiences of school*, London: Kogan Page.

Rogers, K.M.A. (2009) 'A preliminary investigation and analysis of student learning style preferences in further and higher education', *Journal of Further and Higher Education*, 33 (1), 13–21.

Woods, P. (1990) *The Happiest Days? How pupils cope with school*, Basingstoke: Falmer.

Extract 8

Source

Costello, P.J.M. (2000) *Thinking Skills and Early Childhood Education*, London: David Fulton; see pp. 103–4.

Introduction

Costello states that teachers need to be encouraged to place strong emphasis on moral values and facilitate opportunities to question and reason through an approach commonly referred to as 'philosophy for children'. He argues that such an aim can be achieved by teaching pupils the skills of thinking, reasoning and argument, assisted by adults who are skilled in doing these very things. In this way, pupils and adults can discuss rather than simply accept the conventional wisdom. The author concludes that 'reasoned enquiry' lies at the heart of education. As a means of introducing primary school pupils to philosophical ideas, Costello has written four short stories, of which the one below is the first.

Key words & phrases

Bad rules, children, fed up, happy, live together sensibly, no rules, real work, rules, teachers smiled, terrible school

Extract

"There were once three children. They were called Knowlittle, Knowless and Knownothing. They lived in the kingdom of a very harsh king, King Extrawork.

Now, King Extrawork was always imposing rules on his subjects. For example, if they wore black shoes in public, he would remind them of his rule: 'No wearing of black shoes in public' and give them a heavy fine and extra work. So it went on: 'No reading books on Saturdays', 'No riding bicycles on Wednesdays' and 'No "quarter pounders" or milk shakes on any day of the week'.

At last Knowlittle, Knowless and Knownothing got fed up and decided to leave the Kingdom of Extrawork and to live on their own completely, without rules . . . So they set up home together in the kingdom of King Eversonice, where there were no rules whatsoever. When they went to Eversonice Primary School, there were no rules to be obeyed . . . Some children played marbles all week long. The teachers never gave tests or extra work, and they never marked books. There were no exams because the children in the school said that they did not like them. In class discussions, all the children shouted at once and all the teachers smiled because there was no rule which said that children should be polite.

For a couple of days, Knowlittle, Knowless and Knownothing thought their school was a very good school but then they grew tired of playing marbles and longed for some real work to do. But when they tried to tell the teacher this, they could not be heard because the other children were shouting. And all the time their teacher smiled.

One of the children in the class saw that Knowlittle had a big red apple, and he grabbed it and ate it in one mouthful. Knowlittle ran to his teacher and told him, but the teacher said this was allowed because there was no rule forbidding stealing. When it came to lunch time, several children pushed in front of Knowless in the dinner queue. Knowless complained to the dinner lady but she told him that there was no rule which said that pushing in was forbidden. And when it came to home time and the school bell rang, all the children rushed for the door without waiting to be told, and Knownothing was crushed in the battle which took place to get out.

'That's a terrible school', said Knowlittle. 'Everyone does what they want.'

'I think the kingdom of King Eversonice isn't as good as we thought', said Knowless. 'To have no rules is as bad as having bad rules. I wish there was a kingdom where the people had some good rules to live by, so that they could live together sensibly.'

'But where can we find such a place?' said Knownothing.

'I know one thing', said Knowless, 'I'm not going back to that school. Let's leave this kingdom and look for somewhere new to live right away.' So they did."

Summary

Costello uses stories as a vehicle for introducing children to thinking in a deeper and more meaningful way. The story is intentionally absurd but uses images and expressions that are sufficiently familiar to render the piece believable. Certainly the majority of younger children are used to hearing fables, allegories and myths. It is noteworthy that the author adopts a simple storyline, which is devoid of extraneous detail, to encourage pupils to concentrate on the issues rather than the minutiae.

Questions to consider

1. What advantages and disadvantages are attached to using stories to promote philosophical thinking?
2. What are the key issues in the story?
3. What sort of stories would be appropriate for older pupils?

Investigations

Views of older and younger pupils. Read the story to a group of younger and older pupils. Invite them to share their perceptions and reactions.

Older pupils write a story. Ask a group of older pupils to write their own short story to highlight the need for sensible rules and regulations.

Writing rules. Discuss with pupils the relationship between rules, right and wrong, and rewards and punishments. **Rules: see also Extract 46.**

Think deeper

Philosophy for children – sometimes referred to as P4C – promotes questioning, reasoning and dialogue. It has its origins in the early 1970s with the publication of Matthew Lipman's philosophical novel for children, *Harry Stottlemeier's Discovery*, where Harry and his friends discover several basic concepts and rules of logic and puzzle over questions about the nature of thought, mind, causality, reality, knowledge and belief, right and wrong, and fairness and unfairness. Further work by Lipman (e.g. 1991, 2003) was highly influential in promoting the popularity of this approach by offering a strategy for building on the inquisitiveness that children display. The dialogue between child and child, and between adult and child, is promoted by setting up the classroom in such a way that every person can see everyone else (a 'circle time' approach), and a community of enquiry is fostered through oral (spoken) means. In this environment, all opinions are welcomed and the teacher discourages the concept of a 'right' or 'wrong' viewpoint. As a result, support is given to minority views as well as to mainstream ones, and disagreements are presented as natural and tension-free rather than as a source of conflict (see also Haynes 2007).

SAPERE (the Society for Advancing Philosophical Enquiry and Reflection in Education, online at www.sapere.org.uk) is an educational charity that promotes philosophical enquiry with children and communities throughout the United Kingdom. Through P4C the society aims to encourage children (or adults) to think critically, caringly, creatively and collaboratively. It helps teachers to build a 'community of enquiry' where participants create and enquire into their own questions, and 'learn how to learn' in the process.

Haynes, J. (2007) 'Thinking together: enjoying dialogue with children', in Hayes, D. (ed.) *Joyful Teaching and Learning in the Primary School*, Exeter: Learning Matters.
Lipman, M. (1974) *Harry Stottlemeier's Discovery*, Upper Montclair, NJ: Institute for the Advancement of Philosophy for Children.

Lipman, M. (1991, 2003) *Thinking in Education*, Cambridge: Cambridge University Press.

Think wider

Introducing a philosophy programme is not without its challenges, notably the pressures of an already crowded curriculum and the demands it places on teachers as they step aside from their more traditional role and have to inculcate unfamiliar practices and behaviour into children. In addition, teachers are required to demonstrate that their pupils are performing at satisfactory levels in the national tests, which do not incorporate philosophical reflection. Test results have implications for the school's reputation and funding, which is not an issue that teachers can take lightly, whatever their personal priorities and educational beliefs (Pritchard 2008). Supporters of the philosophy for children approach counter-argue by claiming that the development of reason, sound judgement, balanced argument and thinking skills positively influences academic work across the curriculum, so that time spent on philosophy for children is amply justified. See also Burke and Williams (2009) for evidence about ways in which younger children conceptualise specific thinking skills.

Burke, L.A. and Williams, J.M. (2009) 'Developmental changes in children's understandings of intelligence and thinking skills', *Early Child Development and Care*, 179 (2), 949–68.

Pritchard, M. (2008) *Philosophy for Children*, Stanford University, online at plato.stanford.edu/entries/children.

Creativity

Source

Jeffrey, B. and Woods, P. (2003) *The Creative School: A framework for success, quality and effectiveness*, London: RoutledgeFalmer; see pp. 1–3.

Introduction

For a number of years, Jeffrey and Woods studied school life at 'Coombes' in considerable detail. Their research included interviews with teachers, support workers, parents, children and visitors. This extract relates to a time in which they were especially interested in children's perspectives about the move towards creative teaching taking place across the school. In the account that follows, note the new definition of 'child-centredness' and the tensions that the authors highlight between externally imposed expectations and teachers' convictions about the purpose of education. **Teachers' beliefs about teaching: see also Extract 34.**

Key words & phrases

Advancing achievement, child-centredness, creative learning, guiding principles, imaginative modification, incorporated, interconnected, market-orientated, personal involvement, political consciousness, politics, progressivism, rhetoric, self-renewal, stagnate, standards of education

---

Extract

"In recent years, child-centredness, 'Plowdenism', 'progressivism', group teaching, creativity, even the notion of 'relevance' have taken a hammering in the government's drive for their limited version of raising standards of education. Teachers have struggled with the degree of prescription and constant overload. Coping is an issue in itself, teachers' creativity being diverted into how to manage. For those who go along with the managerialist, market-orientated, performativist cast of the reforms, there is no problem. But what about those who believe in Montessori, Froebel, Dewey, Vygotsky, Bruner and others to do? Coombes provides one notable approach to a solution, one that salvages the best features of the reforms and embraces them within their own discourse.

Among the lessons to be learned here, we would argue, is the need for teachers to have a strong political consciousness. Education and politics cannot be separated in the current climate, though government reforms are often presented as educational 'common sense' – part of the rhetoric or 'spin' to win popular support for them. Teachers need to understand the guiding principles behind them and how their own compare. From this kind of testing comes a greater explicitness and firmness about their beliefs, followed by a plan of action to secure their implementation. Coombes teachers were as dismayed as any others by the changes of the late 1980s and early 1990s. But they have worked their way through them to, in the early years of the twenty-first century, a position of some personal strength.

Other prominent features of the Coombes approach include the highly imaginative and intensive use of the school grounds, and the way it is incorporated into the curriculum and enhances all aspects of teaching . . . There is tremendous resource and goodwill available beyond the school gates and the staff are constantly alert for how it can be employed in providing uncommon interest, rousing enthusiasm, demonstrating skills, advancing achievement, stimulating thought. Teachers' own education and self-renewal benefit from this activity . . . At the centre of this endeavour is an imaginative modification of the curriculum, which evades its domination by the prescriptive programmes. Like everything else at Coombes, this is an ongoing project, discussed every week. Nothing is allowed to stagnate. Within this organisation the school both meets the demands made on it and accomplishes a great deal of its own projects. Curriculum organisation at Coombes might seem complicated but, once [it is] grasped, one can appreciate the interconnected levels of learning that are involved.

Teaching itself is creative, never formulaic. The aim is 'creative learning', with children coming to their own knowledge and skills, being enthused and changed by the process, and having some control of the learning process, but under teacher guidance. Personal involvement and exciting events not only stimulate children but [also] give them something to remember in later life."

Summary

A point that comes across strongly in the above account is the need for teachers and other workers to be actively engaged in reviewing and modifying the curriculum to offset any danger of stagnation. Jeffrey and Woods conclude by describing the school as part of a learning community, characterised by visionary leadership, creativity through teamwork and a supportive community culture as three key ingredients in the successful implementation of a contemporary child-centred philosophy. Thus: 'Coombes creates an authentic learning experience that recognises children's active dynamism and combines it with an openness to the way learners make experiences meaningful' (p. 120).

Questions to consider

1. To what extent has teacher 'overload' been reduced through workload reforms, notably the deployment of large numbers of teaching assistants? What benefits have accrued?
2. What sorts of factors do school leaders and staffs have to take into account when seeking to moderate the influence of externally imposed prescriptive programmes as a means of facilitating a more imaginative curriculum?
3. What are the advantages and disadvantages of striving to ensure that nothing stagnates?

Investigations

Child-centred education. Canvass views from colleagues about their understanding of 'child-centredness'/'student-centredness'.

Community involvement. In the light of the fact that schools are obliged to involve the local community, interview headteachers and/or governors to ascertain the practicalities, benefits and challenges attached to closer partnership.

Formulaic teaching. Interview a number of experienced teachers to find out what sort of lesson structure they tend to use and the reasons for the choice. Try to ascertain the extent to which the choice is pragmatic ('it works for me') or philosophical ('it accords with my educational priorities') or coercive ('I am expected to teach this way') or instinctive ('I just do it this way').

Think deeper

Smith (2009) suggests that American philosopher and educationist John Dewey's significance for educators is fourfold: (1) the view that education must engage with and enlarge experience; (2) the significance of thinking and reflection; (3) the view that interaction and environments for learning provide a continuing framework for practice; and (4) the centrality of educational democracy. Child-centred teachers create an environment that will motivate the children to discover new skills and knowledge for themselves. Teachers do not transfer facts to passive pupils but rather facilitate the discovery of knowledge that is interesting to the children. Advocates claim that children working in this type of environment show greater social competency and more creativity than other children. Opponents point out that children need to be taught basic skills before they can employ them creatively and consider child-centred methods to be an unreliable philosophy. See Central Advisory Council for Education (1967) for an historic perspective on these issues and their implications for primary schools. **John Dewey: see also Extracts 39 and 42 under 'Think deeper', 52 and 53.**

Central Advisory Council for Education (1967) *Children and Their Primary Schools* ('The Plowden Report'), London: HMSO.

Smith, M.K. for Infed (2009) 'John Dewey', online at www.infed.org/thinkers/et-dewey.htm.

Think wider

Creative Partnerships (CP) in England focuses on the most deprived communities in England by nurturing the creativity of learners and educators and developing creative approaches to teaching all aspects of the curriculum. It is claimed that creative partnerships enable headteachers to realise their personal vision for a school and frees them up to innovate and succeed. A creative partnership encourages an approach designed around the needs of the individual school with learning tailored to the needs and aspirations of each child. CP also enables schools to work with creative practitioners to develop a broad, balanced and relevant curriculum by supporting a range of creative practitioners to work in partnership with schools, based on the CP website (www. creativepartnerships.com) and used by Jones and Thomson (2008) in their article about policy rhetoric. These authors conclude that CP 'tends both to run with the hare of teacher autonomy and resurgent progressivism, and to hunt with the hounds of management-driven change'. See also Cropley and Cropley (2008), who attempt to resolve a number of paradoxes associated with creativity by dividing the process into seven phases that depend upon different cognitive processes, each consisting of a 'Phase' and an 'Action'. Thus, (1) *preparation*: general and specific knowledge accumulated; (2) *activation*: problem awareness based on knowledge develops; (3) *cogitation*: information is processed in the person's head; (4) *illumination*: the person sees a possible answer (product); (5) *verification*: the product is checked out and found to be appropriate; (6) *communication*: the product is revealed to knowledgeable others; and (7) *validation*: knowledgeable others confirm that the product is novel, relevant and effective.

Cropley, A. and Cropley, D. (2008) 'Resolving the paradoxes of creativity: an extended phase model', *Cambridge Journal of Education*, 38 (3), 355–73.

Jones, K. and Thomson, P. (2008) 'Policy rhetoric and the renovation of English schooling: the case of Creative Partnerships', *Journal of Education Policy*, 23 (6), 715–27.

Extract 10

Source

Fisher, R. (2004) 'What is creativity?', in Fisher, R. and Williams, M. (eds) *Unlocking Creativity: A teacher's guide to creativity across the curriculum*, London: David Fulton; see pp. 14–16.

Introduction

This extract is taken from a book edited by Robert Fisher and Mary Williams. Fisher opens the chapter by quoting from Einstein that 'imagination is more important than knowledge, for knowledge is limited while imagination embraces the whole world'. After grappling with ways to define creativity, Fisher refers to 'processes of creative evolution', specifically generating ideas, variation of output and originality. Notably, he claims that a creative act is of value if it generates something novel, original or unique (p. 9).

Key words & phrases

Acts of creativity, collaboration, creative capital, creative partnerships, creativity, curiosity, encouragement, fertile ground, foster natural impulses, gestation, inspiration, motivation, rich tasks, significant others, time

---

Extract

"Creativity has its roots in everyday activities. The processes of creativity are not solely expressed through the arts. When we edit a sentence to make it sound more interesting, posit a hypothesis or add something new to a recipe, we are being creative. Without small acts of creativity, great acts of creativity would not be possible . . . Good schools foster natural impulses to creativity by building creative capital . . . It is made up of what enables people to focus creatively on the task in hand and supports them in that task . . . Creative capital is the sum of resources needed to tackle a task, including:

■ the creative self – the skills, commitment and talent brought to the task;
■ the creative environment – the creative resources needed; and
■ the creative partnerships – learning partners that support one another . . .

The key to creativity is *motivation* – not having to but wanting to, and having a purpose to do so. Motivation is what we need to add value to creative effort. 'Passion' is a word often used to describe the way creative scientists and artists feel about their work. We need to know that what we do is worthwhile . . . Creativity needs the encouragement of others . . .

Another key to creativity is *inspiration*. It means being inspired by oneself or by others. Creativity thrives on curiosity, fresh input and rich domains of knowledge . . . Curiosity is contagious, and there is no more important job a teacher, parents or friend can do than to instil a sense of wonder about the world and human experience. A creative climate must be created where models of creativity are shared and celebrated . . .

The best kind of inspiration comes from involvement. We must involve people in creative activities. Creative people look on life as a series of creative projects. They seek out whatever inspires them – or they seek to inspire others by exposing them to the most creative experiences they can find . . . We therefore need to find the people and create the environments that inspire us.

A third key to creativity is *gestation*, that is, allowing time for creative ideas to emerge. Insight and intuition are often associated with creativity and these take time to emerge. Creative insight often results from processes that are unconscious and lie below the level of awareness . . .

A fourth key to creativity is *collaboration*, through the support of learning partners or a community. We are more creative when we have others to support us. In adults, creativity has too often been suppressed through education, but it is still there and can be reawakened. Often, all that's needed to be creative is to have a commitment to creativity and to take the time for it . . . But creative success depends on having a fertile ground where new ideas and activities can take root, an environment in which ideas can be created, tossed around, shared and tried out. For this you need creative partners who you know can multiply what you know and can do."

Summary

Fisher argues that creativity is not something that you possess or do not possess; instead, it can be fostered and nurtured through motivation, inspiration, gestation and collaboration. Teachers can develop a creative classroom by first adopting a more positive stance towards creativity and then modifying the way that they teach and interact with pupils, such that creativity is given opportunity to flourish.

Questions to consider

1. What strategies can teachers use to foster motivation in learners?
2. If the best kind of inspiration comes from involvement, what are the implications for pedagogy?
3. What time issues are significant in developing a more creative learning environment?

Investigations

Analysing creative capital. Use Fisher's framework as the basis for an 'inventory' of the creative capital that currently exists in your institution. Discuss with colleagues your findings, and strategies for building more capital.

Impact of longer thinking times. Incorporate longer 'thinking times' into your sessions and note the impact on pupils' responses.

Enhancing collaboration. Modify your teaching approach for part of, or all of, several sessions to enhance the collaborative element and keep a record of the changes that occur with regard to (1) behaviour; (2) pupil enthusiasm; (3) organisation; and (4) managing the session.

Think deeper

There has been a lot of debate about whether creativity is an innate ability that is possessed or not possessed, or a skill that can be developed, caught, taught or wrought. Two key issues underpin a search for answers: first, whether a creative child behaves non-creatively in particular situations and creatively in others; and second, whether an apparently non-creative child can discover a reservoir of creativity that no one (including the child) realised existed until that moment. In answer, Robinson (2001) claims that everyone has the potential to be creative because creativity is possible in any activity in which human intelligence is actively engaged. Merely being given opportunity to experiment with ideas without possessing basic skills and devoid of adult intervention has the potential to lead to chaos: too little adult guidance can result in aimlessness; too little opportunity to experiment will almost certainly lead to pupil frustration. However, the position is even more complicated, as too much intervention can reduce self-sufficiency, whereas too much freedom may give children the impression that learning is a random process.

Evidence from a small-scale study of children aged nine to eleven years of age by Tunnard and Sharp (2009) indicated that while the children viewed collaboration as a valuable learning strategy, they were divided in their views over its structure and organisation. One of the strongest themes to emerge was the importance to children of good peer relationships for successful collaborative learning and the significance of working together for the establishment and maintenance of friendships.

Robinson, K. (2001) *Out of Our Minds: Learning to be creative*, Oxford: Capstone.
Tunnard, S. and Sharp, J. (2009) 'Children's views of collaborative learning', *Education 3–13*, 37 (2), 159–64.

Think wider

Simister (2004) studied the effects of teaching a twenty-five-lesson 'thinking skills' syllabus to a group of ten-year-old pupils and suggested that pupils' curiosity, inventiveness, discussion skills, ability to think laterally about given situations and understanding of the decision-making process can all be enhanced through specific skills teaching. Simister proposed a two-pronged approach in which thinking skills are taught initially in a child-friendly, test-free context and then integrated throughout the curriculum.

Colcott *et al.* (2009) created a 'toolbox' to equip pupils in an Australian junior school to help them to make their thinking more visible. The idea was to develop strategies that enable pupils to develop ownership of their learning; to think for themselves; to reflect on what they had learned; and to be individually inspired to further their own learning. The toolbox consists of a collection of skills and tools printed on cards and kept in a plastic folder to be used by children, categorised under 'values', 'academic' and 'thinking tools'. Pupils keep their own individual toolboxes and add tools and skills when introduced to them, retrieving them on a daily basis when they are needed. The authors insist that when one is working with younger children these tools need to be visual, tactile, simple, descriptive symbols that children respond to; reflected on every day as part of class discussions; easily accessible; and valued by each child.

Colcott, D., Russell, B. and Skouteris, H. (2009) 'Thinking about thinking: innovative pedagogy designed to foster thinking skills in junior primary classroom', *Teacher Development*, 13 (1), 17–27.
Simister, J. (2004) 'To think or not to think' *Improving Schools*, 7 (3), 243–54.

Wider learning experiences

Source

Humphries, S. and Rowe, S. (1994) 'The biggest classroom', in Blatchford, P. and Sharp, S. (eds) *Breaktime and School: Understanding and changing playground behaviour*, London: Routledge; see pp. 108–9, 113, 116.

Introduction

Humphries and Rowe write from the perspective of practising teachers who have discovered the benefits of using the outdoor environment as a resource. The book was written a few years after the introduction of a national curriculum in England, Wales and Northern Ireland at a time when there was curriculum overload and a surge in teacher accountability. The use of the outdoors as a resource would decline further over the next decade before a renewed wave of interest around the turn of the century through initiatives such as 'forest schools' and a recognition that creative learning opportunities beyond the classroom door were being neglected.

Key words & phrases

Aesthetic, children's responses, curriculum resource, diverse landscape, environment, expectations and behaviour, formal and informal teaching, happy memories, imaginative teacher, outdoor surroundings, social place, teaching and learning space

---

Extract

"The view that children have of their environment is in large part determined by the way in which the adults responsible for the children view and use the same environment. If the adults who foster the children ignore the outdoor surroundings, then the potential of the environment is not realisable for either group. Children tend to take their cues from the adults with whom they have regular contact. We wanted the children to react positively and constructively with the school site, and we had to be the ones to offer the positive models . . .

Each learning experience that took place out of doors, from studies of minibeasts to kite-flying, from clowns performing to tree-planting, imbued the area where the experience had taken place with happy memories. The children could describe in detail why they had drawn a particular landscape feature, and could recall what had happened there even after some months. In the short term, parts of the playground became landmarks, as the tide of interest generated in the topic or event associated with that part remained dynamic and meaningful to the children.

Guidance for our planning came from the children's drawings and from discussions with them about these. From their drawings, we see how important it is to give apparently simple things to the children, and how we as adults tend to overlook the obvious . . . We have used the children's responses to our investigations to guide our work outside, and it seemed to us that as we embarked on work out of doors we should canvass the children, listen to them and interpret regularly and with care what they said.

The opportunities for teaching in the playground are endless and the imaginative teacher is never short of a curriculum resource outside. We have found that what the children do formally in lesson times outside tends to be adapted into their free play and augments it. If the outside areas are planned and set so that they contain challenging regions which can be used for formal and informal teaching, there can be a more thorough use of the environment . . . Somehow the playground becomes a more social place because it has so many purposes: it also becomes a place of intellectual challenge and adventure . . .

We believe that children at work and play in a lively, changing and diverse landscape will react imaginatively and build up high expectations and happy recollections of school life . . . The gains may well be more than curricular or aesthetic: it is possible to add features and events to the landscape which will nurture the social, emotional and spiritual development of every human being in it."

Summary

It is clear that the authors have a passionate belief that outdoor education not only enhances children's learning but also is indispensable for a fully rounded education. A feature of the above extract is the way in which Humphries and Rowe insist that children's perspectives and ideas should be incorporated into planning the outdoor environment. The authors' willingness to relinquish some of their traditional teacher authority for the benefit of children's learning is particularly striking.

Questions to consider

1. How can the work with primary-aged children in the above extract be translated into practice appropriate for pupils in secondary education?
2. To what extent do you accept Humphries and Rowe's contention that the imaginative teacher is never short of a curriculum resource outside?
3. Assess the following statement from the extract: 'It is possible to add features and events to the landscape which will nurture the social, emotional and spiritual development of every human being in it.'

Investigations

Learning opportunities. Take time to evaluate the learning opportunities available in the school grounds in conjunction with a group of sensible pupils.

Free play. Observe pupils in a free play situation outside the classroom and note patterns of friendship and interaction.

Environment and educative values. Survey ways in which a range of schools have adapted their surroundings to facilitate learning, and the educative values underpinning the decisions.

Think deeper

Cramp (2008) insists that learning outdoors has many benefits, including behaviour modification, self-esteem, teamwork development, challenge and self-knowledge. However, he describes how the greatest benefit is learners' personal development, as pupils cultivate 'multidimensional views' of teachers, views that lead to 'warmer personal relationships, a challenge to labelling and the potential for risk-taking back in the classroom' (p. 180). **Pupil behaviour: see also Extracts 1, 48, 49 and 51.**

Environmental studies are normally embedded in the science field of study, and educational visits to local sites of interest – including the school grounds – and remote sites such as a woodland area or farm form an important element of the learning schedule. Some schools broaden the remit to incorporate history, geography and even religious education (often referred to jointly as 'the humanities') into the programme. Where the work is science orientated, children focus on aspects such as investigating pond life, looking at very small creatures in their habitats and tree studies (for example, de Boo 2004). Pupils are also encouraged to find answers to their own questions through scientific investigation of the objects, events or a particular part of the environment being studied, either in the field or in the classroom (Elstgeest and Harlen 1990).

Cramp, A. (2008) 'Knowing me, knowing you: building valuable relationships outside the classroom', *Education 3–13*, 36 (2), 171–82.

De Boo, M. (2004) *Nature Detectives: Environmental science for primary children*, Association for Science Education/Woodland Trust.

Elstgeest, J. and Harlen, W. (1990) *Environmental Science in the Primary Curriculum*, London: Paul Chapman.

Think wider

Mygind (2007), writing from a Danish perspective, measured students' activity levels during outdoor learning days in the forest and compared them with a traditional school day on the one hand, and a traditional school day including two physical education lessons, on the other. Results suggested that from a health perspective the two contexts seem to complement each other. The study indicated that the increased physical activity level found during outdoor learning is comparable to the total activity level of a normal school day, including two PE lessons, and is of great importance if linked to physical health and cognitive benefits. Mygind concluded that the outdoor environment should be complementary to the traditional classroom setting and not attempt to replace it, as both learning contexts are important to children's needs.

Mygind, E. (2007) 'A comparison between children's physical activity levels at school and learning in an outdoor environment', *Journal of Adventure Education and Outdoor Learning*, 7 (2), 161–76.

Extract 12

Source

Casey, B., Casey, N., Calvert, B., French, L. and Lewis, J. (2002) *Television Studies: The key concepts*, London: Routledge; see pp. 20–3, 76–7.

Introduction

The extracts that follow are taken from two of the sections in Casey *et al.*'s book about television studies, namely 'Children and television' and 'Educational television'. Casey and co-workers emphasise the importance of collecting reliable research data rather than relying on hearsay or instinct. Adults who influence children's habits, attitude and learning should examine their own beliefs about childhood, teaching and learning.

Key words & phrases

Acquiring knowledge, actively engage, childhood, communications technology, effects, influences, information, media studies, non-literate modes of teaching, one-way flow, passive activity, pre-existing attitudes, print literacy, social relationships, television, television tuition, visual literacy

Extract

"Issues surrounding television and children are contentious ones framed by a range of interrelated concerns. A good deal of the research in this area has taken place outside of television and media studies – it seems that where children are concerned, everyone (priests, politicians, journalists, parents, teachers, psychologists, sociologists) has something to say. With recent developments in communications technology giving rise to a whole new range of entertainment media within the home (satellite, cable and digital channels, computer games, the internet and video), anxieties concerning the effects of these new media on children have increased, lending a new urgency to contemporary research and debate . . .

Television as a medium of communication cannot be isolated from other influences in children's lives. Television (and media influence in general) is embedded in, and is part of, the matrix of social relationships which combine to make up the experience of childhood. Children do not completely identify with any single source or influence but are influenced by their families, peers, the school and so on. Television, then, is just one component, one source of identification among many. What is apparent is that television is more likely to reinforce pre-existing attitudes and experiences in children than radically to modify or alter behaviour. If this is the case, then the importance of teaching children media literacy, and the responsibility of parents and teachers in influencing children's attitudes, is paramount in shaping the perceptions and beliefs children bring to their experiences of watching television . . .

The idea that television can 'educate' has been contested and subject to considerable debate and scrutiny. First, television, it is argued, cannot 'teach' because it is widely perceived as being a recreational medium, used primarily for entertainment and relaxation. Second – and this criticism is closely related to the above point – television viewing has often been thought of as a passive activity, whereas the acquisition of skills and knowledge is believed to be an active pursuit. Third, television presents a one-way flow of information whereby the viewer (learner) has little or no control over the pace and delivery of information. In other words, the learner is not given the opportunity to actively engage with the material presented in the same way that s/he would be able to in a classroom situation. For example, if a student has a problem comprehending information in the classroom, the teacher can be asked to further explain, reiterate or expand upon the material being taught. Fourth, television relies heavily upon what are traditionally thought of as being non-literate modes of teaching, which are characteristically oral and visual. Television tuition is often seen as a degraded form of learning in comparison to print literacy, which as a means of acquiring knowledge is still privileged over and above other forms of learning. For example, the assertion that 'children shouldn't spend so much time watching television and should instead do something more constructive like reading a book' illustrates the extent to which this privileging of print literacy over visual literacy informs our commonly held ideas."

Summary

At the heart of the authors' argument is an understanding of how children learn and the effectiveness of different teaching approaches. In an age where multi-media touch almost every aspect of human life, the role of the teacher needs continual reappraisal. If television and other media play such a pivotal role in learning, teachers have to determine how such elements can be accommodated into the curriculum and teaching programme to bring about the greatest benefit for learners. In particular, the authors assert that the development of 'media literacy' is of prime importance in the process.

Questions to consider

1. Why does the use of television as a learning medium elicit such strongly held and contrasting opinions?
2. To what extent should television be seen as (a) a teacher; (b) an educator; (c) a teaching aid; (d) an aspect of media studies?
3. What is the validity of the claim that privileging of print literacy over visual literacy informs our commonly held ideas about the significance of television?

Investigations

Conflicting views. Carry out a literature review and list the key points raised by proponents and opponents of the use of television as an educational tool.

Children's views. Interview a group of children (perhaps of different ages) to gain insights into their attitude towards different media, notably television.

Adults' views. Interview a group of (a) parents and (b) teachers concerning their views about the educational value of television.

Think deeper

Fisch (2004) argues that at its best, educational television can provide children with enormous opportunities and serve as a window to new experiences, enrich academic knowledge, enhance attitudes and motivation, and nurture social skills. Van Evra (2004) explores how and to what extent television and other media affect children, and what role other variables may play in mediating their impact to maximise technology's potential for enriching children's cognitive, social and emotional development, while minimising negative influences. Pecora et al. (2006) draw on fifty years of research about children and television conducted by social scientists and cultural studies scholars, including studies of content, effects and policy. They consider the content of programming, children's responses to television, regulation concerning children's television policies, issues of advertising, and concerns about sex and race stereotyping. **Race and equality: see also Extract 56.**

Fisch, S.M. (2004) *Children's Learning from Educational Television: Sesame Street and Beyond*, Mahwah, NJ: Lawrence Erlbaum.

Pecora, N., Murray, J.P. and Wartella, E.M. (2006) *Children and Television: Fifty years of research*, Abingdon: Routledge.

Van Evra, J. (2004) *Television and Child Development*, London: Routledge.

Think wider

In a study of nine- and ten-year old German children by Heins *et al.* (2007), 28 per cent reported going to bed after 9 p.m. on week nights; 16 per cent reported watching television more than three hours daily; and 11 per cent played computer or video games more than three hours daily. Assuming that primary schoolchildren need to be awake at 7 a.m. on weekdays, only one in four of the children had a full ten hours' sleep on weekdays. Such lifestyle factors were considered to be negative influences on their present development and future habits. Heins and colleagues concluded that the need for children to enjoy sufficient sleep necessitates less television viewing and computer leisure time.

Edgar and Edgar (2008) discuss in detail the major changes in children's lives related to media and technology, family and social values. They call for a re-evaluation of the way we think about children, their needs and future development. They suggest a new, more integrated approach to children's policy, one that restores a sense of community-wide responsibility for the development of children.

Edgar, D. and Edgar, P. (2008) *The New Child: In search of smarter grown-ups*, Melbourne: Wilkinson Publishing.

Heins, E., Seitz, C., Schüz, J., Toschke, A.M., Harth, K., Letzel, S. and Böhler, E. (2007) 'Bedtime, television and computer habits of primary children in Germany', *Gesundheitswesen*, 69 (3), 151–7.

Pupil perspectives and well-being

General welfare

Extract 13

Source

Smidt, S. (2006) *The Developing Child in the 21st Century: A global perspective on child development*, Abingdon: Routledge; see pp. 129–31.

Introduction

In her book, Smidt examines what is meant by child development and stresses the importance of history and culture in fostering understanding. She looks at childhood as a concept and develops a workable image of the child in the twenty-first century, as well as touching on the notion of good parenting. The extract below is set within a more general critique of the impact of brain research and 'attempts to coerce parents and teachers to change aspects of the ways in which they interact with or teach children' (p. 120).

Key words & phrases

At risk, child development, cultural influences, dependence to adulthood, economic impact, economic realities and divides, educated, family, incompetent children, non-traditional family, normal development, passive and voiceless, presumptions about childhood, rational thinking, separate from adults, skilled workforce

---

Extract

"The first presumption is that childhood is a universal process, and this is based on much of the work of traditional child development theorists, who saw children as progressing from dependence to adulthood, either through stages or phases, but in an ordered and predictable and rule-governed way – rather like other natural phenomena in the physical world. This allowed theorists to describe some things they saw as 'normal' development and, by implication, other things as 'not normal' development. Add to this the fact that some theorists often ignore the sociocultural and economic impact of facts like family structure, cultural influences, power, status, economic levels of the family, and group and status on the development of the child. We have seen some examples of this even in the developed world, where children in non-traditional family structures – for example, single-parent families – are sometimes described negatively and perceived as being in some ways 'at risk' . . .

The second presumption is that adulthood has normative status, which means that children are seen as 'not there yet' – as being incomplete in some way, as they strive to achieve maturity, rationality, competence, awareness of society and their place in it on this journey towards adulthood . . . The model here is of the incompetent child (or the not-yet-competent child) and this has been powerfully used as a 'scientific' justification for exporting Western models. The intention here seems to be to protect children from access to or participation in the adult world. In this model the incompetent children depend largely on the competent adults, who are the ones to describe, interpret, explain and analyse the development of children. The real actors in the drama of their learning and development – the children – are passive and voiceless. Adults are presumed as knowing and right, and children as ignorant and wrong . . .

The third presumption is that the goals of child development are universal and that these relate primarily to teaching levels of personal, intellectual, social and political autonomy, becoming independent and self-sufficient. Rational thinking in models like Piaget's is the ultimate goal. Yet we know that this is not the case in many cultures where such things as interdependence, collaboration and integration are highly prized. In most developed countries it is the adults who work and there is the need for an educated, skilled, creative, communicative, flexible and independent workforce. So children remain in schools rather than as part of the workforce and they therefore assume and are accorded less responsibility and a high level of dependence. But even in the richer countries, as we have seen, the childhoods of children cannot be seen as homogeneous and in these countries, as in the developing world, there are children who are involved in paid work, children relieve their mothers of some of the burdens of domestic tasks . . .

The fourth assumption is that children should be passive players. This presumption ignores the possibility of children being players or social agents in their own development and keeps children (and hence childhood) as separate from adults, rather than seeing the extent to which children can and do influence adult behaviours and perceptions and can inform decision making and be heard.

The final presumption is, perhaps, the most far-reaching in its consequences on the world's children. This is that those who do not conform are in some ways at risk. This view, which pathologises children from 'other' cultures or minority groups, offers the rich West the opportunity to 'rescue' these children. The dominant view here is that schooling is good and work is bad, and whilst we might prefer all children to be able to go to school and not to have to work, until the economic realities and divides are addressed, the majority of children in the world do work and they need to be viewed not as risk but as part of the world."

Summary

The author describes how a Western model of childhood makes certain assumptions about child development that are contestable, especially when viewed from the perspective of children that live in the developing world. Smidt also challenges four presumptions about child development: (1) that childhood is a universal process; (2) that adulthood is normal and children are 'incomplete'; (3) that the goals of childhood are the same everywhere; and (4) that children are passive players.

Questions to consider

1. What are the implications of Smidt's critique for young people in their teens?
2. To what extent do teachers accept and adopt the deficit model of children into the way that they organise learning?
3. What strategies might teachers use to offset the tendency to treat pupils as passive players?

Investigations

Teachers' views of development. Use the four 'presumptions' as the basis for a survey of teachers' views about development.

Parental perspectives. Discuss with parents from a variety of ethnic and cultural backgrounds their views of what constitutes childhood.

Pupil perspectives. Ask groups of pupils about their views of what being an adult means and the way they think that adults view them in school and at home.

Think deeper

Jean Piaget (1896–1980) suggested that children think differently from adults and proposed a stage theory of cognitive development. He was the first to note that children play an active role in gaining knowledge of the world and considered the most critical factor in a child's cognitive development to be interaction with peers. Piaget's approach is central to the school of cognitive theory known as 'cognitive constructivism'. Piaget particularly stressed the role of maturation (growing up) in children's increasing capacity to understand their world and proposed that children's thinking does not develop smoothly but rather that there are certain points at which it moves into completely new areas and capabilities. Broadly:

- Birth to eighteen months or two years is called the *sensorimotor* stage.
- Two years to seven years is called the *pre-operational* stage.
- Seven years to eleven years is called the *concrete operational* stage.
- Eleven years and older is called the *formal operational* stage.

The theory has been interpreted to mean that before children reach these ages they are not capable of understanding things in certain ways; it has been used as the basis for organising the school curriculum. Wood (1998) argues that the impact of lessons taught by parents or teachers also varies as a function of a child's developmental stage. Thus, 'a major implication of the theory is that the effects and effectiveness of teaching are fundamentally constrained by the structure of the child's intelligence' (p. 38). However, evidence suggests that Piaget's scheme is too rigidly structured because (notably) many children manage concrete operations earlier than the Piagetian model predicts. Some people never function at the level of formal operations or are not called upon to use them.

Garnett (2005) asserts that studies strongly suggest that one side of every person's brain is normally dominant. If the left side of the brain dominates, a person is likely to be analytical, whereas if the right side dominates, a person is more holistic or global. A left-brain-orientated pupil prefers to learn in a step-by-step sequential way, initially concentrating on the fine details and working towards a broad understanding; such an approach can be described as *inductive* – evidence gathered from lots of detail to create a general principle. By contrast, dominance of the right side of the brain means that the pupil prefers to learn by starting with the general principle and then working out the specific details; such an approach can be described as *deductive* – knowledge in different contexts is 'deduced' from the key principle. A person with a right-sided inclination tends to be more random, intuitive and subjective than the left-sided person, and prefers to look at the whole picture rather than the individual parts. In any group or class of children there will be evidence of a variety of learning characteristics as pupils develop and cultivate ways of responding to their experiences and the information presented to them. **Pupils' learning preferences: see Extract 7 under 'Think deeper'.**

Garnett, S. (2005) *Using Brainpower in the Classroom: Five steps to accelerate learning*, Abingdon: Routledge.

Wood, D. (1998) *How Children Think and Learn: The social contexts of cognitive development*, second edition, Oxford: Blackwell.

Think wider

Lancaster and Broadbent (2003) note that the importance of listening to children is increasingly being recognised and recent developments across children's services in education, health and social welfare have reinforced the value that government and service providers place on this basic human right. From their study of pre-school children, Corriveau *et al.* (2009) concluded that children as young as age three and four are able to hold opinions and recognise and trust a consensus. Clark *et al.* (2005) explore how adults listen to young children, the view of the child that different approaches to listening presume and the risks that listening might entail for young children. From a case study of 'looked-after children', Leeson (2007) warns about feelings of helplessness, low self-esteem and poor confidence that follow a lack of opportunities made available to them to make decisions about their own lives. See also Walker-Gleaves and Walker (2008), who introduced a curriculum programme to acquaint student teachers with the educational and wider pastoral experiences of children and young people who are being or have been 'looked after'.

Clark, A., Kjorholt, A.T. and Moss, P. (2005) *Beyond Listening: Children's perspectives on early childhood services*, Bristol: Policy Press.
Corriveau, K.H., Fusaro, M. and Harris, P.L. (2009) 'Going with the flow: preschoolers prefer nondissenters as informants', *Psychological Science*, 20 (3), 372–7.
Lancaster, Y.P. and Broadbent, V. (2003) *Listening to Young Children*, Maidenhead: Open University Press.
Leeson, C. (2007) 'My life in care: experiences of non-participation in decision making processes', *Child and Family Social Work*, 12 (3), 268–77.
Walker-Gleaves, A. and Walker, C. (2008) 'Imagining a different life in school: educating student teachers about "looked after" children and young people', *Teachers and Teaching*, 14 (5/6), 465–79.

Extract 14

Source

Parton, C. and Manby, M. (2009) 'The contribution of group work programmes to early intervention and improving children's emotional well-being', *Pastoral Care in Education*, 27 (1), 5–19.

Introduction

Recent government policy has emphasised links between the acquisition of social skills by children and young people and their educational attainment. Parton and Manby's study focused on the contribution of school-based group work programmes to developing children's social skills. National Society for the Prevention of Cruelty to Children (NSPCC) Children's Services Practitioners ran four groups for a total of thirty-eight Year 7 children from mixed ethnic backgrounds in two high schools in the north of England between 2004 and 2007 in a programme designed to improve children's self-esteem, social skills and behaviour. Parents were involved in identifying objectives and evaluating outcomes. (Based on article abstract)

Key words & phrases

Anti-bullying strategies, attention spans, behaviour improvement, behavioural problems, Children's Plan, children's welfare, clear boundaries and structures, group leaders, liaison, parents, personal health and social education, project workers, social skills, substantial commitment, unrealistic expectations

Extract

"Selection of children for these programmes proved to be an inexact science, particularly when children were chosen shortly after their transfer to secondary school. The seriousness of some boys' behavioural problems only became apparent once the groups were under way. Project workers' experience was that confronting behavioural problems with the whole group achieved the best results, and feedback from children was that they welcomed clear boundaries and structures. Children's attention spans were generally short; Group Leaders responded by ensuring that sessions included a range of clearly defined activities, requiring both practical and cognitive skills, and later on by shortening the sessions.

Group Leaders, school staff and the evaluator spent much time explaining the purpose of the programmes to parents and involving them in assessing children's progress. Parents from all four programmes welcomed this level of involvement, although a small minority, including some non-English-speaking British Asian parents, struggled to understand programme objectives, indicating the need for particular care to be taken with this group at the point parents are approached to obtain their informed consent. Parents newly arrived in the country welcomed the opportunity for children to be involved in a programme that would assist their integration into the school community. Parents generally perceived the acquisition of social skills as an important element in their children's education.

Almost all of the parents involved in the evaluation demonstrated a positive regard for their children's welfare and provided valuable insights about their development and the kind of help they needed. Parents' assessments of their children's needs were astute and they were keen to learn about their progress in the groups. Most parents were realistic about their children's attainments, behaviour problems and emotional needs. Some parents needed additional support themselves at crisis points, and where this was available from the school, for example from the Community Manager in School B, they welcomed it . . .

Evaluations of the three programmes in School B demonstrated the substantial commitment required from the senior school staff representative responsible for overall liaison with the project. This role involved liaison with teachers, pupils and parents; responsibility for organising accommodation; and recruiting and supporting non-qualified teaching staff to help run the groups – all of which placed unrealistic expectations on existing school resources . . .

Group Work Programmes such as those described in this article aim to fill gaps in the development of children's emotional literacy that are now being prioritised by the Government, particularly at the point of transition to secondary schools. Results for the programmes evaluated in this study may prove to be comparable with those of the current UK Resilience Programmes. They can supplement the personal, health and social education curriculum and contribute to behaviour improvement and anti-bullying strategies. The programmes should be seen as one important element in the repertoire of support services required for children with more complex problems. These children and their families are likely to need the kind of longer-term individual support involving a range of professionals and coordinated by personal tutors, described in the Children's Plan . . .

The evaluation concluded that the programmes had been effective for shyer, quieter and more vulnerable boys, and also further improved girls' social skills. Louder, more impulsive boys taking part had developed cognitive skills and awareness of the impact of their behaviour on others, although some of them continued to cause the school concern through unwanted classroom behaviour."

Summary

The study by Parton and Manby demonstrates that links between educational attainment and social skills are far from easy to establish and require a considerable amount of hard work to maintain. The authors found that the process of enhancing pupils' self-esteem, social skills and behaviour was hindered by inattentiveness and behavioural problems. Pressure on senior staff to facilitate liaison between the different bodies was considerable, despite a high level of parental support.

Questions to consider

1. What is your understanding of the phrase 'social skills'? What impact might their acquisition or absence have on learning?
2. What are the practical implications for close parental involvement of this kind? What emotional and psychological pressures have to be taken into consideration?
3. Why were behavioural issues such a central feature of the study?

Investigations

Defining social skills. Conduct a survey among colleagues about what they understand by 'social skills'. Discuss with a focus group the implications of your findings for classroom practice.

The impact of poor social skills. Discuss with a group of colleagues the teaching and learning issues arising from pupils' weak social skills and ways in which the expertise of social work professionals can best be employed to assist.

Social worker perspectives. Interview 'skilled social work professionals' about the sorts of approaches that classroom practitioners might wish to consider in fostering children's self-esteem, social skills and behaviour.

Think deeper

Raymond (1985) argues that social skills are behaviours that are situation specific, have a particular purpose, are under the control of the individual and to a large extent determine the outcome of interactions between people. She goes on to describe social skills as consisting of small component parts under the umbrella terms of verbal and non-verbal communication, suggesting that these parts can together influence the way in which a pupil copes with the more complex skills such as making and maintaining relationships, dealing with criticism, coping with conflict, giving an account of oneself, controlling negative emotions (self-control) and asking for help (see p. 106).

The national Social and Emotional Aspects of Learning (SEAL) programme was introduced to improve children's behaviour and attendance in schools in England. SEAL uses small group work to boost pupils' personal development and develop their relationships with others by improving their self-awareness and motivation. It provides a comprehensive, whole-school approach to promoting the social and emotional skills that are said to underpin effective learning, positive behaviour, regular attendance and emotional well-being (DfES 2005) and is currently used in more than 80 per cent of primary schools across England (Humphrey *et al.* 2008).

As the result of an extensive study of the impact of SEAL in school, Hallam (2009) claimed that the programme had increased staff understanding of the social and emotional aspects of learning and helped staff to better understand their pupils. In turn, these insights had helped to change the behaviour of staff, enhanced their confidence when interacting with pupils and led them to adopt a more thoughtful approach to incidents of inappropriate behaviour, notably playground bullying. A large majority of teachers agreed that the programme promoted the emotional well-being of children and increased pupils' ability to control emotions such as anger. **Emotional well-being: see also Extract 55.**

DfES (2005) *Excellence and Enjoyment: Social and emotional aspects of learning (guidance)*, Nottingham: DfES Publications.

Hallam, S. (2009) 'An evaluation of the Social and Emotional Aspects of Learning (SEAL) programme: promoting positive behaviour, effective learning and well-being in primary school children', *Oxford Review of Education*, 35 (3), 313–30.

Humphrey, N., Kalambouka, A., Bolton, J., Lendrum, A., Wigelsworth, M., Lennie, C. and Farrell, P. (2008) *Primary Social and Emotional Aspects of Learning (SEAL): Evaluation of small group work*, Research Report DCSF-RR064, London: Department for Children, Schools and Families.

Raymond, J. (1985) *Implementing Pastoral Care in Schools*, London: Croom Helm.

Think wider

Stott (2009) suggests that by definition – and in parallel with improving behaviour – well-developed social skills should allow the pupil to:

- live and work as part of a community (school, classroom, home);
- value friendships and relationships with others in that community;
- work well in a group and be able to cooperate to achieve a joint and amicable outcome;
- be able to resolve conflicts;
- solve problems by thinking of all the options, identify the pros and cons, and finally evaluate the outcome.

Stott insists that pupils should understand how communication forms the basis of socialisation, which means that teachers give consideration to the need to become confident speakers and effective listeners when planning lessons. He therefore argues that the following issues should all be given regular attention:

- appropriate eye contact;
- appropriate use of humour;
- turn taking;
- active listening;
- risk assessment.

Deuchar (2009) studied a diverse sample of Scottish primary schools to show how older pupils are encouraged to participate in decision-making processes and engage in the discussion of contemporary social issues of their own interest both in the classroom and during pupil council meetings. Primary pupils appeared to have a say in the type of groups they worked in and were encouraged to make decisions about the current issues they would like to discuss. Evidence suggests that they felt supported, enjoyed debating challenging issues and were either directly or indirectly involved in discussing controversial issues. On transfer to secondary school at age twelve, however, pupils tended to revisit issues that they had already explored in primary school and were given less responsibility to become active in working towards change. The pupils often seemed unaware of and unimpressed by the work of the school council and felt that they had fewer opportunities for contributing towards agendas than existed when they were in primary school. In the secondary classroom, pupils were given fewer opportunities to make decisions about the work of the council or to make decisions about how they would like to learn. **Decision-making: see also Extract 46 under 'Think wider'.**

Barratt *et al.* (2000) offer a series of resources to assist teachers, teaching assistants and therapists to develop and improve the social skills of their younger pupils through verbal and non-verbal games and activities to encourage social interaction.

Barratt, P., Border, J., Joy, H., Parkinson, A., Potter, M. and Thomas, G. (2000) *Developing Pupils' Social Communication Skills*, London: David Fulton.

Deuchar, R. (2009) 'Seen and heard, and then not heard: Scottish pupils' experience of democratic educational practice during the transition from primary to secondary school', *Oxford Review of Education*, 35 (1), 23–40.

Stott, D. (2009) 'Developing pupils' social skills to improve behaviour', *Behaviour Matters*, online via www.teachingexpertise.com.

Happiness and self-esteem

Extract 15

Source

Cullingford, C. (2008) 'A fleeting history of happiness: children's perspectives', *Education 3–13*, 36 (2), 153–60.

Introduction

Cullingford addresses an area of school life that is rather taken for granted, namely that happiness ('well-being') is an important factor in motivating pupils to learn. However, he contrasts the government's 'instrumental' approach that happiness can be manipulated with a more philosophical approach. In particular, Cullingford addresses the importance of insight and contentment. Thus: 'Of all the things that young children most prize, it is the gift of insight' and 'The first important notion concerning happiness is that it essentially means contentment' (p. 155).

Key words & phrases

Accountability, educational experience, feel better, happiness, imposition, manipulate, mantra of the political world, perform better, personality, philosophical, pragmatic age, praise, satisfaction, trust, well-being, wisdom

Extract

"The notion of happiness, as a contrast with sadness, is a philosophical one. One state of mind is a shadow of the other. This ancient notion has been joined with a more modern one. This is that happiness depends not only on personal circumstances but on contrasts to others. Whereas in the past only a few were allowed to be happy, the democratisation of the concept has meant that all can be happy, but only if others are less so.

In all the experimental work on people's satisfactions, it is clear that money itself does not bring happiness but relative wealth does . . . When people think about their own status they always do so in relation to others . . .

Given such pragmatism, one can see that happiness is no longer a philosophical concept, but a manipulative possibility. The notions of whether happiness consists of feeling good or doing good are replaced by the possibility of affecting one's own mood. Personality is seen by children to be significant. Certain people possess a disposition to be happy, a propensity to cheerfulness. The displays of temperament are very clear and those who demonstrate optimistic outlooks are envied . . .

When three groups of students, all learning English, coming from different parts of Europe, were asked to produce a pamphlet explaining their cultural differences, they were divided into three groups. At the two extremes, one group was presented with a very clear target that they had to achieve. If the pamphlets they produced were not of the highest standards, they would be punished; if good enough, they were to be rewarded. At the other extreme, a group of students were asked to talk to each other about cultural differences for a day, enjoy themselves as much as possible and, if they felt like it, produce a pamphlet that they could then share with others. This last group produced by far the highest standards.

The question is, in this pragmatic age, whether it is possible to induce happiness . . . The kind of pragmatism that children express is of a more old-fashioned kind. They link happiness not with lifestyle techniques but with the more palpable rewards of behaving well . . . There are, however, many findings that show that even if we understand notions of well-being and believe in the gross national product of happiness, the age-old contradictions remain. We know, for example, that performance related pay does not have the effect that is intended, and yet the Government persists with the notion. We know that setting targets and blaming people for not meeting them does nothing to raise standards, and yet this policy is pursued. We know that the notion of accountability, which takes away trust and responsibility, does not work. And yet it remains the mantra of the political world. The very Government that wants to promote well-being is involved in destroying it . . .

We learn from the experience of children that the imposition of inflexible demands and controls has the opposite effect to those intended. Even imposing 'well-being' on them, as an extra part of the curriculum, would not address the real issues of their discontents . . .

At least the notion of well-being, even of fulfilment, as opposed to skills, appears to be something to be considered. Putting happiness (with its connections to motivation, conduct, understanding and engagement) on the agenda could have the effect of people helping take their educational experience more seriously."

Summary

Cullingford has carried out a lot of research about pupil perceptions of their education experiences, as a result of which he claims that children are less concerned with greater happiness than with greater understanding of their priorities and feelings. He suggests that adults (parents as well as teachers and assistants) may *think* that they know which children are struggling with low self-esteem, but in fact they are frequently mistaken. Pupils' perceptions of happiness and well-being are deep and profound and should not be dismissed. (See Porter (2010) for perspectives on ways to access the views of all pupils, including those with a disability and those who are less articulate.)

Porter, J. (2010) 'Missing out? Challenges to hearing the views of all children on the barriers and supports to learning', *Education 3–13*, 37 (4), 349–60.

Questions to consider

1. Is it possible to 'induce happiness'? To what extent should happiness and well-being be formally 'taught' and to what extent 'caught'?
2. What strategies can teachers use to promote a relaxed but purposeful learning environment?
3. How can teachers and school leaders exude a positive attitude while insisting on high standards?

Investigations

Pupil self-esteem. Ask a teacher to rank pupils into high, medium and low self-esteem groups. After discussing self-esteem issues with them, ask each pupil to rank him- or herself and write a brief comment. Compare the results.

Happiness and contentment. Ask pupils to either (1) write or (2) draw or paint a picture or (3) both write and draw to describe or show when they are happiest.

The impact of praise and encouragement. Ask a number of colleagues to make a special effort for (say) one week to be especially positive towards pupils. At the end of the time ask them (and the teaching assistant if appropriate) to comment on any discernible changes in pupils' self-confidence.

Think deeper

Seldon (2008) suggests that it is possible for a school to 'teach happiness' by developing the following priorities (amended):

■ School should be a place children love to be; they should feel deeply loyal to their school, their fellow pupils and its teachers.

■ School should develop all aspects of children's personalities and aptitudes, not just their intellect; they should learn who they are and what they want to do with their lives, both at work and at play.

■ They should know how to look after themselves, taking responsibility for their bodies, their emotions and their minds.

■ Parents should be fully involved in the whole experience of learning, as should the wider community.

■ The teachers at the school should be valued and respected, with the pupils treating them with civility and gratitude.

Pupil happiness: see also Extract 55.

Seldon, A. (2008) 'Teaching happiness', *Ethos*, online at www.ethosjournal.com/article-archive/item/107-teaching-happiness.

Think wider

MacConville (2008) piloted what she termed 'the happiness curriculum' in west London schools during the autumn of 2007 with classes of ten- to thirteen-year-old pupils to help them to negotiate the transition from primary to secondary school. The programme was designed to build resilience, increase optimism, promote adaptive coping skills and teach children effective problem-solving skills. Children were given strategies to help them demur from negative and unhelpful thinking and experience positive emotions. In all the activities there was an emphasis on developing thinking and participatory skills. Among other things, children were encouraged to 'stop the gossip in your head' by focusing on the present situation and not being deflected from learning by concerns about the past or future; to be thankful; to have specific and attainable goals of personal significance (i.e. not school 'targets'); to think good, feel good; to accept setbacks; and to take control of their lives to make themselves and school a happier place.

MacConville, R. (2008) *Teaching Happiness: A ten-step curriculum for creating positive classrooms*, Milton Keynes: Speechmark Publishing.

Extract 16

Source

Jepson, M., Walsh, B. and Turner, T. (2009) 'Adolescence, health and well-being', in Capel, S., Leask, M. and Turner, T. (eds) *Learning to Teach in the Secondary School*, Abingdon: Routledge; see pp. 173–85.

Introduction

The chapter by Jepson *et al*. addresses issues associated with pupils' health and well-being by outlining characteristics of adolescence and explaining how they impinge upon a young person's attitude to learning, peers and adults. The authors are targeting trainee and new teachers but their descriptions act as a timely reminder to all adults working with secondary pupils about the pressures and challenges associated with 'growing up'.

Key words & phrases

Adolescence, behaviours, challenges, changes, confidence, conforming, development, differences, differentiate, feeling, normal, peer group, personal appearance, personal autonomy, personalised learning, pressure, relationships, success

Extract

"Most pupils want to be normal, to conform to what they see in others of their peer group. The idea of 'fitting in' is extremely important to them at this stage. You can begin to see the friction that can occur when pressure from their peers contradicts expectations of parents and teachers. Conforming, in part, concerns appearance: personal appearance becomes a highly sensitive issue during adolescence—because of the notion of normality, shape, size, etc. but also sexuality and emerging relationships. In these respects the place of a balanced diet is important; school has an important part to play in countering obesity and anorexia, both aspects of self-image as well as areas of concern nationally . . .

Adolescence is full of changes and full of challenges . . . adolescents can be excited one minute and depressed the next. It is a time when pupils are searching for a personal identity that often gives them a feeling of insecurity . . . School may be, for some, the only place where they find consistent messages and a place where their personal autonomy can grow. Schools are crowded places and require a strong discipline for all; these conditions are not necessarily compatible with those for the emergence of the autonomous individual . . .

As well as obvious gender differences between pupils in a coeducational context, the differences between individuals within a group of boys, or a group of girls, can be quite large and obvious . . . it can happen that some pupils who have developed physically earlier than their peers may dominate activity in a class, causing a number of pupils to reduce their involvement for fear of being ridiculed by more 'grown-up' members of the class . . .

Adolescence can begin at age 10 for some, for others much later, and may finish around the age of 19 . . . this means that a 12-year-old girl may be in a pre-pubertal, mid-pubertal or post-pubertal state. A 14-year-old boy is similarly placed. Thus it is not sensible to talk to a 14-year-old cohort of pupils as though they are a homogeneous group . . .

The variation in physical development of pupils shown, for example, in any year cohort, has implications for your management of classes. These differences are particularly apparent in Years 7–9 [eleven to fourteen years of age] and may stand out in activities which prosper on physical maturity or physical control. Boys in early adolescence who develop late often cannot compete with their peers in games; and girls who mature earlier than their friends can also be advantaged in physical activity and games but, at the same time, feel embarrassed . . .

When pupils feel good about themselves, they feel confident and ready to experience new things, but the opposite feeling often means that they take every small setback as destroying their confidence. It is important for you to differentiate your tasks so every pupil achieves some success; personalised learning helps give them belief in their own abilities and the confidence to take on more challenging tasks."

See also Child, D. (2007) *Psychology and the Teacher*, London: Continuum.

Summary

The authors emphasise the important role that teachers play in providing a relevant and 'personalised' curriculum, with a particular emphasis on personal, social and health education (PSHE) and citizenship. They argue that adolescence is a period of time when emotional, physical and psychological changes take place. Pupils are more likely to enjoy higher self-esteem and motivation for learning and make sensible choices when they are well informed, comfortable with themselves and able to resist damaging forms of peer pressure.

Questions to consider

1. How might teachers provide a learning environment that offers adolescents an increased amount of independence without sacrificing too much authority?
2. What sort of class management issues do teachers have to address in taking account of pupils' differing physical development?
3. Some student (trainee) teachers are not much older than some of the pupils they teach. What are the implications for relating to pupils, discipline and classroom practice?

Investigations

Adult memories of adolescence. Invite colleagues to share some memories of their adolescence, with special reference to the sorts of issues raised in the extract above.

Peer group pressures. Through lesson observations, note the ways in which selected pupils respond to their classmates' behaviour. Evaluate the ways in which teachers adjust their teaching in response to these behaviours.

Teachers' views about differentiation. Discuss with colleagues the claim that 'it is not sensible to talk to a 14-year-old cohort of pupils as though they are a homogeneous group'.

Think deeper

Vitto (2003) argues that positive teacher–student relationships are an important factor in increasing student achievement and motivation as well as decreasing a student's risk of dropping out or engaging in substance abuse, bullying and violence. Vitto claims that these positive relationships are more influential than more highly publicised factors such as classroom size, teacher training or school policy in protecting adolescents from destructive behaviours. Teachers can raise student achievement by fostering social-emotional learning, thereby creating a more positive classroom environment and helping in the prevention of future risk, notably with students who exhibit more challenging behaviour.

Bond *et al.* (2007) state that young people's experiences of early secondary school and their relationships with others may continue to affect their moods and their substance use in later years, together with the likelihood that they will complete secondary school. Having both good school connectedness and good social connectedness is associated with the best outcomes. The authors contend that the main challenge is how best to promote both school and social connectedness to achieve positive health and learning outcomes.

Kellough and Kellough (2007) have written a comprehensive book about methods, guidelines and resources for teaching students aged from about twelve to sixteen years. They provide education models and guidelines to help teachers decide the most appropriate approach to use at a given time. The book also includes exercises for active learning to help teachers develop particular skills that relate to specific teaching approaches. Both the Vitto and the Kellough and Kellough books are written from a North American perspective. **Equal opportunities: see also Extracts 26 and 56.**

Bond, L., Butler, H., Thomas, L., Carlin, J., Glover, S., Bowes, G. and Patton, G. (2007) 'Social and school connectedness in early secondary school as predictors of late teenage substance use, mental health and academic outcomes', *Journal of Adolescent Health*, 40 (4), 357.e9–18 (electronic publication).

Kellough, R.D. and Kellough, N.G. (2007) *Teaching Young Adolescents: A guide to methods and resources for middle school teaching*, Upper Saddle River, NJ: Prentice Hall.

Vitto, J.M. (2003) *Relationship-Driven Classroom Management*, Thousand Oaks, CA: Corwin/Sage.

Think wider

Hartley (2009) presents personalisation as an emerging 'movement' within education whose roots can be traced to marketing theory rather than educational theory. He claims that the concept of personalisation causes a lot of confusion, as it can either refer to a new mode of governance for the public services or qualify the noun 'learning', as in 'personalised learning'. Hartley further argues that the semantic similarity between child-centred education and personalisation may appeal especially to the generation of older teachers whose professional ideology was formed and secured during the early 1970s, despite the fact that connections between a child-centred ideology and the centralising reforms of education are tenuous. However, Hartley insists that relabelling these reforms as 'personalisation' may give the impression that something of the so-called progressive era is being resurrected. He concludes that although the government has firmly distanced itself from child-centred education – and therefore the 'permissive' description that some attach to it – personalisation continues to prompt an association with it.

Rowe *et al.* (2007) found that health-promoting schools have the potential to build school connectedness through inclusive processes: first, those that involve the diversity of members that constitutes a community, the active participation of community members and equal power relationships or equal partnerships among community members; and second, supportive structures such as school policies, the way the school is organised and its physical environment that reflect the values of participation, democracy and inclusiveness and/or that promote processes based on these values.

A comprehensive text by Kay (2004) aims to help educators of all kinds to enhance motivation for achievement through establishing better understanding both from a student perspective and from their own perspective, and thereby to provide the basis for strategies to foster motivation at all levels of student performance – from those deemed academically at risk through to the high-achievers. Kay suggests that in doing so, teachers have two key roles in the classroom: (1) establishing a classroom structure and instruction that provide an environment for optimal motivation, engagement and learning; and (2) helping students to develop the attributes that will enable them to be self-regulated learners.

Hartley, D. (2009) 'Personalisation: the nostalgic revival of child-centred education?' *Journal of Educational Policy*, 24 (4), 423–34.

Kay, M. (2004) *Motivation for Achievement: Possibilities for teaching and learning*, Mahwah, NJ: Lawrence Erlbaum.

Rowe, F., Stewart, D. and Patterson, C. (2007) 'Promoting school connectedness through whole school approaches', *Health Education*, 107 (6), 524–42.

Bullying

Extract 17

Source

Varnava, G. (2002) *How to Stop Bullying: Towards a non-violent school*, London: David Fulton; see pp. 60–2, 63.

Introduction

The part of Varnava's book from which this extract is taken is headed 'Permeating non-violent attitudes through the curriculum' and explores one aspect of they way in which schools can take action in tackling violence. The book is primarily intended as 'a practical support for schools seeking to create a non-bullying culture, a culture in which the welfare of all members is protected and where everyone feels secure' (p. 1).

Key words & phrases

Anti-racism, attitudes, behaviour, bilingualism, bullying, cross-curricular activities, degree of autonomy, educational priority, equal opportunities, formulate strategic development, interpersonal conflict, negotiation, personal commitment, problem solving, relationships, review existing provision, sharing, specific skill, study skills, violence

---

Extract

"Cross-curricular activities aimed at implanting a specific skill or concept have been widely practised, often in response to a perceived educational priority or the supposed absence of a fundamental aspects of learning. Study skills, anti-racism, bilingualism and equal opportunities, for example, have been prominent in this respect. Permeating the whole curriculum, however, with a culture of non-violence is a different process, requiring the exploration of feelings, attitudes and relationships, the focus being more on the person than on the subject area of the curriculum. There is no definitive model for the process of permeation, since each school will choose its own priorities and its preferred methods. A school may, for example, select generic principles that have a particular bearing on the prevention of bullying or other violence. These can be presented in a matrix and linked to sections of the curriculum to show the contact points where teachers can introduce each of the principles. Teachers have control of the process, retaining the freedom to develop ideas with the students where and when suitable opportunities arise . . .

Effective communication is a basic skill for any part of the curriculum to which these principles may apply. Situations requiring negotiation arise constantly. Problem solving is a prominent feature of maths, science, design/technology and information/communications technology (ICT). Much of religious teaching in the world's many faiths is built on these and similar principles. Elsewhere in the school curriculum, links may seem more tenuous but can be productive, nevertheless. Arithmetical division and team games are about sharing; designing and using a computer are processes in which making choices is an essential first step; in English, languages, history and PE, students learn to empathise with one another and self-esteem is built through literary self-portraiture, pride in bilingualism, creativity and physical ability. There is fertile ground throughout the curriculum for teachers to develop a culture that excludes all forms of inter-personal conflict.

In practice, schools do have a degree of autonomy in constructing a whole curriculum, building on the national curriculum with what is considered to be most relevant to their particular needs. Where student behaviour is of concern because it inhibits learning, the curriculum can be honed as an effective tool to shape pro-social behaviour. Although new reforms often seem prescriptive, the requirement to innovate is an opportunity to review existing provision and formulate strategic development. In spite of occasional government assurances on a relaxation of school reform – even offering a promise of a five-year moratorium – schools cannot stand still. Curriculum does, after all, mean 'a racing chariot' . . .

There is a sensitive balance between the dependence upon intellectual criteria for evaluation and the importance of personal relationships as the foundation of effective learning. Young people's attitudes towards one another, their corresponding behaviour and their personal commitment to learning are fundamental to their success or failure and how they are judged. A 'democratic society' is one in which we treat one another equally and well."

Summary

Varnava is adamant that schools and individual teachers play a vital role in combating bullying and creating a peaceful learning environment. He argues that there are ways of approaching learning through the formal curriculum (notably through problem-solving) that help to strengthen interpersonal relationships. Despite the imposition of external impositions, Varnava encourages schools to be innovative and develop the curriculum in such a way that young people's attitudes towards one another are enhanced.

Questions to consider

1. What are the opportunities and challenges in promoting 'feelings, attitudes and relationships' to promote non-violence?
2. To what extent do you agree with the author when he claims that 'the curriculum can be honed as an effective tool to shape pro-social behaviour'?
3. What other analogies to describe the curriculum may be employed other than 'racing chariot'?

Investigations

Cross-curricular activities. Explore with colleagues the opportunities that cross-curricular activities might provide to promote a culture of non-violence.

Problem solving as a strategy. Review the use of problem solving, team activities and investigations as teaching strategies across your institution. Consider the implications for achieving a more collaborative and harmonious environment.

Pupil and teacher perspectives. Discuss with learners and teachers or support staff their responses to Varnava's claim that 'Young people's attitudes towards one another, their corresponding behaviour and their personal commitment to learning are fundamental to their success or failure and how they are judged.'

Think deeper

As teachers become aware of the power of friendships and the fears, frustrations and joys of complex child–child relationships, they discover that it is essential to pay attention to its consequences. Children do not attend school solely to develop friendships, but attention to the implications arising from the quality of relationships is important in the quest for a good teaching and learning environment (Mosley and Sonnet 2006; Hewitt 2007).

Hewitt, S. (2007) *Bullying*, London: Franklin Watts.
Mosley, J. and Sonnet, H. (2006) *Helping Children Deal with Bullying*, Cambridge: LDA.

Think wider

A new psychodynamic approach to bullying in schools under the acronym CAPSLE (Creating a Peaceful School Learning Environment) was trialled by UCL (University

College London) and US researchers (Fonagy 2009). The research involved more than 1,300 eight- to eleven-year-olds in nine US elementary schools over a period of three years and concluded that encouraging all pupils to reflect on incidents at the end of the day was a more effective way to resolve conflicts. Thus, rather than targeting aggressive children, educationalists developed a programme to develop skills in pupils and staff aimed at preventing a regression into the roles of victim, victimiser and bully. In practice, teachers were discouraged from disciplining the aggressor unless absolutely necessary, and fifteen minutes at the end of the day was taken to reflect on the day's activities. It was found that pupils were far tougher on themselves than teachers would have been under similar circumstances. The research did not make any attempt to give bullies or victims special treatment, and over time the study found bullies came to be disempowered. The CAPSLE approach was compared with what was found in schools that receive no intervention for bullying; although the study found that bullying increased across all the schools being monitored, the percentage of children victimised was substantially less in CAPSLE schools. See also an online summary at www.ucl.ac.uk/media/library/bullying.

Fonagy, P. (2009) 'A cluster-randomised controlled trial of child-focused psychiatric consultation and a school systems-focused intervention to reduce aggression', *Journal of Child Psychology and Psychiatry*, 32, 159–73.

Extract 18

Source

Lee, C., Buckthorpe, S. Craighead, T. and McCormack, G. (2008) 'The relationship between the level of bullying in primary schools and children's views of their teachers' attitudes to pupil behaviour', *Pastoral Care in Education*, 26 (3), 171–80.

Introduction

It is known that the incidence of bullying reported by primary school children varies greatly between schools. The study by Lee *et al.* examines the children's views about the level of care and attention that the teachers pay to issues relating to behaviour and the social organisation of their school. It is shown that the children's views are a good indicator of the frequency of bullying that will be found in that school. (Based on article abstract)

Key words & phrases

Behaviour, being different, bullying, children's perceptions, children's views, degree of care and attention, differences between schools, feel cared for, formulating actions, frequency of bullying, gender differences, physical contact, primary, school grounds, social organisation

---

Extract

"During the summer and autumn terms of 2006 a Department for Education and Skills (DfES) [now the Department for Education] questionnaire on bullying was completed by primary school children in Years 3–6 in an area of the North West of England. The purpose of the survey was to establish a local picture of children's perceptions of bullying in primary schools and to assist in formulating actions to address the issue . . .

Bullying usually took place outside the school buildings, in the school grounds. Only 9% took place in classrooms, and 3% occurred in toilets or cloakrooms. Eighty per cent of the bullying reported was classified as 'mild': pushing or calling names. Seventeen per cent was classified as 'moderate': scrapping or punching. Only 3% was 'severe', involving physical injury or serious verbal abuse. None was judged to be 'very severe', for which the criteria had been fixed as bullying which was prolonged and serious or bullying which resulted in pupils self-harming or leaving a school. Half of the reported bullying involved physical contact, and verbal abuse accounted for almost all of the rest. Theft or abuse of personal property, social exclusion and children being made to do things against their will made up only 6% of reported bullying in total.

The reasons that were given for children being picked on mostly related to their being different in some way: younger (or older) children (37%), physically different children (20%), racially different children (11%), quiet children (7%), disabled children (4%). There were no significant gender differences in those being bullied, with the proportion of boys reporting having been bullied in the previous two weeks at 21% and the proportion of girls at 20%. Similarly, there were no noticeable ethnicity differences, with 20% of white children, 21% of Asian children and 18% of black children reporting having been bullied . . .

The amount and nature of bullying have been related to the children's, rather than anyone else's, views of how much they feel cared for by their school and how well issues of behaviour and bullying are addressed by their teachers. Again, there is a potential weakness in this approach. It may be that children are more likely to answer positively questions such as 'Adults in this school are good at making sure that children are kind to each other and treat one another with respect' if they are in a school in which there is little bullying, regardless of the actual skills which the adults demonstrate in this respect. If that is the case then bullying behaviours which are being imported from outside the school, and which may vary from one school to another because of the environments which they are in, may be affecting both the frequency of bullying and the measure of perceived care simultaneously. There is, however, some evidence within the data that this factor on its own could not explain the effect that has been observed . . .

The general level of bullying reported in this study is relatively modest, with a number of schools having only minor occurrences, the great majority of the bullying reported being classified as 'mild', and no problems having been identified with respect to gender or ethnicity. However, this study does provide evidence that there were significant differences between schools in the frequency of bullying reported by children. It was also found that children reported significantly higher levels of the more severe types of bullying in schools in which bullying was more frequent. Further, it was shown that the frequency of bullying is strongly correlated with the children's views of the degree of care and attention that their teachers pay to issues relating to behaviour and the social organisation of their school."

Summary

In many ways the above research findings are quite reassuring in that the extent of bullying (as perceived by children) is limited; and serious bullying is very rare. It is noteworthy that most bullying takes place in the playground, raising the prospect that adult supervision may be inadequate during these periods of time. One of the more challenging claims is that the frequency of bullying is strongly correlated with the children's views of the level of teachers' care and attention.

Questions to consider

1. How do the results of the study by Lee *et al.* compare with your perceptions of the situation in your school?
2. How do we distinguish between bullying and 'rough-and-tumble'?
3. What are the issues attached to referring to a pupil responsible for bullying as 'a bully' and the one who is bullied as 'a victim'?

Investigations

Note the extreme sensitivity of conducting research in this area.

Pupils' perceptions of bullying. Discuss their experiences in school with a group or class of pupils, with particular emphasis on friendship, quarrelling and 'critical incidents'. (Avoid reference to bullying unless it is raised by pupils.)

Teachers' perceptions of bullying. Interview colleagues about their views of what constitutes bullying and strategies for improving the situation.

Pupils' relationship with adults. Conduct a survey among older primary pupils by employing a few questions, such as: 'How do you know that an adult in school likes you?' and 'When does a teacher show that s/he cares about you?' Or with secondary pupils: 'How does the attitude of adults affect behaviour in school?' and 'What can adults do to improve the school's learning environment?' (Prohibit the naming of individual adults.)

Think deeper

Rigby (2001) argues that it is important to deal with bullying because it has three potential adverse effects. First, it lowers mental health. Second, it induces social maladjustment. Third, it creates physical illness. Sanders (2004) offers the following observation: 'Most definitions of bullying categorize it as a subset of aggressive behaviour that involves an intention to hurt another person . . . Not only can it be displayed physically but it can also be subtle and elusive' (p. 4). Sanders goes on to warn that emotional harassment is much more difficult to identify and prove but should still be included under the definition of bullying. Barton (2006) is more expansive in her definition of bullying as 'any behaviour that results in physical or emotional injury to a person or animal, or one that leads to property damage or destruction. It can be verbal or physical' (p. 6). Garner (2009) notes that bullying can also include mobile text messaging; initiatives to control bullying have to take cognisance of the fact that pupils must develop their understanding of social and emotional aspects of learning – not least those pupils who exhibit challenging behaviour.

Barton, E.A. (2006) *Bully Prevention*, London: Corwin Press.

Garner, P. (2009) 'Behaviour for learning', in Capel, S., Leask, M. and Turner, T. (eds) *Learning to Teach in the Secondary School*, Abingdon: Routledge.

Rigby, K. (2001) *Stop the Bullying*, London: Jessica Kingsley.

Sanders, C.E. (2004) 'What is bullying?' in Sanders, C.E. and Phye, G.D. *Bullying: Implications for the classroom*, Amsterdam: Elsevier.

Think wider

A study of 663 children from state primary schools in north London and Hertfordshire by Wolke *et al.* (2009) found that girls are tormented by playground bullies for longer than boys; thus, half the number of girls who are bullied between the ages of six and nine are still being bullied when they are aged ten or eleven compared with 30 per cent of boys enduring the same miserable experience. However, boys generally appear more likely to be the victims of bullies, as one in four admitted to being kicked, hit or teased at least once a week, compared with 20 per cent of girls. Girl bullies are more likely to spread rumours about their classmates and deliberately ostracise them, while boy bullies tend to use violence or make verbal threats. Wolke *et al.* also found that children use less physical bullying and more psychological bullying between the ages of eight and eleven. As evidence of this trend, the study discovered that whereas about 10 per cent of the children aged between six and nine claimed that rumours had been spread about them or that they had been deliberately excluded from social groups, the number had risen to 25 per cent by the time they were ten or eleven years old.

Wolke, D., Woods, S. and Samara, M. (2009) 'Who escapes or remains a victim of bullying in primary school?' *British Journal of Developmental Psychology*, online at dx.doi.org/10.1348/026151008X383003.

Relationships with adults

Extract 19

Source

Carrington, B., Francis, B., Hutchings, M., Skelton, C., Read, B. and Hall, I. (2007) 'Does the gender of the teacher really matter? Seven- to eight-year-olds' accounts of their interactions with their teachers', *Educational Studies*, 33 (4), 397–413.

Introduction

In this paper the authors draw on children's replies to a number of questions to elicit information about (1) their levels of academic engagement; (2) their motivation; and (3) their rapport with their teacher. The research was conducted in fifty-one Year 3 classes (ages seven to eight years) drawn from a convenience sample of primary schools in England, utilising data from interviews with more than 300 seven- to eight-year-olds attending primary schools in the north-east and south-east of England. The questions were as follows:

- Does your teacher make you want to work hard?
- Does your teacher encourage you?
- Does your teacher treat everyone in the class fairly?
- How does your teacher let you know if you have broken the class rules or not worked as hard as you could?

> **Key words & phrases**
>
> Educational needs, feminised, gender, gender matching, gendered response, male recruitment, needs of boys, pedagogic and interpersonal skills, role models, significant others, teacher recruitment

Extract

"As Mills *et al.* (2004, p. 355) have pointed out, underpinning the drive to bolster the recruitment of men teachers is an unexamined assumption that the teaching profession has become increasingly 'feminised' and thus the education of boys has suffered because of the resultant lack of male role models. Such policies tend to be predicated upon a number of taken-for-granted beliefs about the impact of the teacher's gender on children's levels of academic engagement and achievement. For example, it is commonly assumed that children identify more readily with teachers of the same gender and, as a consequence, boys fare better in school when taught by men teachers and vice versa . . . policy-makers have also tended to make unwarranted generalisations about the respective educational needs of boys and girls . . .

One working day was spent in each of the 51 classes observing pupil–teacher relationships and interactions. The observations were followed up with one-to-one, semi-structured interviews with the teachers. The interviews sought to explore their opinions about, among others, current policies to bolster male recruitment to the teaching profession, teachers as 'role models' and the perceived impact of gender differences on classroom interaction . . .

The interviews revealed that the teacher's gender had little apparent bearing on the children's level of academic engagement or the perceived quality of their classroom experiences. The majority of children, irrespective of gender, felt that their teachers – whether men or women – encouraged them and wanted them to work hard. Similarly, the majority believed that their teachers acted in a consistent, fair and even-handed manner . . . from the children's standpoint, the gender of the teacher was largely immaterial. Although the findings may have pointed to higher levels of disaffection and recalcitrance among the boys, there is no evidence to suggest that this gendered response to schooling was less marked in classes taught by men . . .

Although teacher recruitment policies tend to emphasise the importance of providing boys with male 'role models' in schools, little is known about the extent to which children show any greater affinity for teachers of the same gender, or indeed identify with their teachers *per se*. During the course of our investigation, we attempted to ascertain the children's 'significant others' by asking them whether there was anyone that they would 'like to be like' when they were grown up . . . The children tended to select same-gender 'role models', nominating family members or friends (44% boys, 47% girls), well-known singers or actors (13% boys, 24% girls), sporting celebrities (31% boys, 2% girls), fictional characters (28% boys, 25% girls) and teachers (13% boys, 33% girls). Although relatively few boys appeared to regard their teachers as a 'role model', those who did were just as likely to nominate a female member of staff as a male . . .

Our study indicates that simplistic and unsupported claims about the benefits of gender matching should have no place in driving either education policy or practice . . . it is the teacher's pedagogic and interpersonal skills that are vital in engaging them as learners, regardless of their gender."

Mills, M., Martino, W. and Lingard, B. (2004) 'Attracting, recruiting and retaining male teachers: policy issues in the male teacher debate', *British Journal of Sociology of Education* 25 (3), 355–69.

Summary

Carrington *et al.* engaged with assumptions that underpin contemporary policies to increase male recruitment to the teaching profession, especially to the primary or elementary sector. They concluded from interviews with children that there is little or no evidence to support the view that the female-dominated character of the teaching profession and associated shortage of male role models in schools has an adverse effect on boys' levels of academic motivation and engagement.

Questions to consider

1. Does it matter if schools have an all-female staff?
2. Would it matter if all the teachers in a primary school were male?
3. Does gender make any difference to the school's ambience, the nature of 'out-of-class' activities, parental attitudes or behaviour?

Investigations

Pupil attitudes to teacher gender. Conduct a straightforward survey of pupils about teacher gender by asking whether, given a choice, they would prefer to be taught by a male or a female teacher. Conduct follow-up discussions about the subject, strictly avoiding any specific reference to individual teachers in the school.

Teacher attitudes to gender. Interview a range of teachers – ideally, equal numbers of male and female – about the specific qualities they believe men and women bring to the job. Invite respondents to expand upon their thinking.

Parental attitudes to gender. Interview a range of parents – ideally, equal numbers of male and female – inviting them to disclose their views about teacher gender.

Think deeper

A survey of 600 eight- to eleven-year-olds by YouGov for the Training and Development Agency (TDA) in 2008 suggested that many boys would welcome more men in schools. The survey found that 39 per cent of boys did not have any men teaching them and one in twelve had never been taught by a man; 48 per cent of boys believe male teachers set good examples for them; and 28 per cent said men understood them better. More than half (51 per cent) of the boys said the presence of a male teacher made them behave better; a good proportion of the boys said men helped them enjoy school more (44 per cent) and feel more confident about themselves (37 per cent).

Hutchings *et al.* (2008) asked 307 seven- and eight-year-old children in England (half taught by male and half by female teachers) three questions: (1) What did they like about their teachers? (2) In what ways would they like to be like them? (3) Who, if anyone, would they like to be like? Results showed that a higher percentage of the girls identified being nice, kind, generous and helpful as important characteristics. The boys more often liked their teachers because of the work they were asked to do and more often wanted to be like their teachers because of their authority, knowledge and intelligence. Boys generally spoke about male and female teachers in much the same way, except that only male teachers were referred to as 'fun' or 'funny'. The girls focused more on relationships and appearance in talking about women teachers but said they would like to be like their male teachers in terms of their skills and humour. Men were more often seen as making jokes, shouting and having skills in music or sport, while women were described as being kind, not shouting and giving rewards. The authors found that both boys and girls tended to refer to teachers of the same sex as themselves as 'nice' and wanted to emulate their behaviour, while 'other-sex' teachers were described as being good teachers; children wanted to be like them in terms of their knowledge and authority, or simply in being a teacher.

Hutchings, M., Carrington, B., Skelton, C., Read, B. and Hall, I. (2008) 'Nice and kind, smart and funny: what children like and want to emulate in their teachers', *Oxford Review of Education*, 34 (2), 135–57.

Think wider

Gannerud (2001) conducted interviews with twenty experienced women teachers in Sweden and identified a number of themes that were significant in their daily work. First, the teachers saw their professional role as gender neutral but also felt that being female affected their daily work. Second, experiences of motherhood and of teaching as work and the meaning of a professional attitude were linked. Third, there was a need to balance the demands of private life and work life, in which both spheres are characterised by gender-specific responsibilities and an ethics of care. Fourth, the emotional demands were exhausting and time-consuming but also very important for work satisfaction and personal motivation. Fifth, informal collegial ('non-hierarchical') interaction provided a source of emotional support as well as development of professional knowledge. Finally, a perception of teaching as a low-status profession is linked in people's minds with the job being a suitable one for women.

In their exploration of four-year-old children's perspectives of teachers' roles, Harris and Barnes (2009) noted that a difference between girls' and boys' responses was in the perception of a teacher as someone who teaches, in that sixteen girls and ten boys identified the male teacher as someone who teaches, whereas eleven girls and fifteen boys identified the female teacher as someone who teaches. From their analysis of pupil responses, it appeared that the gender of the teacher does not significantly affect children's perceptions of what their teachers are able to do. However, the presence of a male teacher in early childhood settings may impact positively on children's understanding of gender roles in society and on the development of non-sexist attitudes and beliefs. The authors claim that this finding raises questions as to how young children view their male and female teachers' roles, bearing in mind that owing to the tiny percentage of men in the early childhood profession, children rarely have the opportunity to experience a male–female teaching team. See also *Early Child Development and Care*, vol. 178, issue 7/8 (2008) for a range of articles about the male role.

Thornton and Bricheno (2000) argue that reasons for limited career development for many women are multifaceted, but include the disproportionate promotion of men, traditional gender differences in work–home orientation, and expectations about the role of women in school. A study by Riddell *et al.* (2005) in Scotland about gender balance in the teaching workforce found that women students were significantly more likely than men to regard teaching as a good job for people with family responsibilities. A higher proportion of women than men thought primary teaching more attractive than secondary teaching. **Teacher gender: see also Extracts 59 and 60.**

Gannerud, E. (2001) 'A gender perspective on the work and lives of women primary school teachers', *Scandinavian Journal of Educational Research*, 45 (1), 55–70.

Harris, K. and Barnes, S. (2009) 'Male teacher, female teacher: exploring children's perspectives of teachers' roles in kindergartens', *Early Child Development and Care*, 179 (2), 167–81.

Riddell, S., Tett, L., Burns, C., Ducklin, A., Ferrie, J., Stafford, A. and Winterton, M. (2005) *Gender Balance of the Teaching Workforce in Publicly Funded Schools*, The Moray House School of Education, University of Edinburgh.

Thornton, M. and Bricheno, P. (2000) 'Primary school teachers' careers in England and Wales: the relationship between gender, role, position and promotion aspirations', *Pedagogy, Culture and Society*, 8 (2), 187–206.

Extract 20

Source

Meeus, W. and Mahieu, P. (2009) 'You can see the funny side, can't you? Pupil humour with the teacher as target', *Educational Studies*, 35 (3), 553–60.

Introduction

The authors asked a variety of students on a teacher education degree course at two universities in Flanders (Belgium) to write a brief account of a humorous situation that they remembered from their time in secondary education. Two conditions were imposed on the accounts: (1) the student concerned (or his or her classmates) had to be the originators of the humour; and (2) the teacher had to be the target of the humour.

Key words & phrases

Atmosphere–maker, classroom atmosphere, classroom discipline, dissipates tension, fun, funny side, humour, innocent intention, intention, pedagogical practice, provokes tension, rebellion, relationships

Extract

"The teacher uses humour, *inter alia*, in order to grab pupils' attention, to provide mnemonics, to jazz up dull material and to curb misbehaviour by pupils. There is no mention made [in the literature] . . . of pupils as users of humour, despite the fact that it is unlikely that only teachers use humour . . . it is frequently said that the use of humour by the teacher fosters a positive classroom atmosphere, which in turn raises the question as to whether the same does not also apply to pupils' humour. It may be that pupils' humour tends to be seen as disruptive and would need to be sought not with the keyword 'humour', but rather under 'misbehaviour' or 'baiting' . . .

Humour is often recommended as a powerful weapon, although sometimes a word of caution needs to be sounded: there is appropriate and inappropriate humour. There is humour which dissipates tension and humour which provokes tension. There is humour that works and humour that doesn't work. In other words, humour is not automatically either positive or negative . . . Humour used with a negative intention is humour intended to be wounding. Humour used with a positive intention is humour which is meant to contribute to creating a good classroom atmosphere. Our hypothesis is that pupils also use this latter category of humour and are therefore not only out to make life difficult for the teacher . . .

Pupils' humour is used as a form of boundary-seeking and boundary-crossing behaviour. Every teacher remembers being tested out by his or her pupils as a novice . . . Some, however, are excessively strict and pupils pay them back in a way that is at least humorous, while others continue to have a discipline problem and end up suffering the consequences. It is, incidentally, very doubtful that these teachers see the pranks played on them by pupils as humour. The fact that humour is used more as a form of rebellion than as misbehaviour is not an indication of the number of strict or weak teachers. It is more likely that pupils would be inclined to think twice before playing a prank with strict teachers.

However, the clear winner is pupils' humour as atmosphere-maker. A significant feature of this category is that the pupils do not use jokes or pranks as a reaction to an unpleasant situation or as a reaction to excessive or lax classroom discipline. These pupils use humour to make things more fun. Of course, the teacher is still the object of that humour, but it is not the pupils' intention to tease or hurt the teacher. The humour is consistent with a pleasant classroom atmosphere and a good relationship between pupils and teachers, although sometimes there is a difference between the innocent intention of the pupil and the effect on the teacher, for example if he or she doesn't (initially) see the funny side. However, in such cases this is simply an error of judgement on the part of the pupils."

Summary

Meeus and Mahieu's central argument is that pupils' use of humour has an important function as an indicator of classroom control, so advocate that teachers adopt a positive approach to pupils' humour. The authors conclude that pupils' humour directed at teachers makes a predominantly positive contribution to the relationship between pupil and teacher and to pedagogical practice.

Questions to consider

1. Why do teachers generally assume that pupil humour is a form of misbehaviour?
2. What factors help teachers to distinguish between humour that dissipates tension and humour that provokes tension? What strategies might a teacher use to deal with negative forms of pupil humour?
3. To what extent do you agree with the authors' assertion that humour also has an important function as an indicator of class control?

Investigations

Literature search. Enter 'humour' and 'education' as part of a word search into journal publications and summarise the key ideas and concepts presented by authors.

Understanding pupil humour. Share key points from the above extract with a mixed group of colleagues and invite their responses. In doing so, try to ascertain the extent to which gender, teaching experience or personality of the group's members appears to influence their viewpoints.

Adults reflecting on humour. Ask colleagues to write or relate a brief account of a humorous situation from their own time in secondary education. Ask them to reflect and comment on the implications of their experiences.

Think deeper

Woods (1990, chapter 7) describes the various purposes served by humour among older pupils and describes how pupils' humour is closely associated with their personal identity and the social formation of the group to which they belong (e.g. the 'gang'). Sharing a joke can be a joint enterprise in mutual interest, such as offsetting boredom or 'playing up' a teacher to elicit a reaction. Woods also explains ways in which shared humour between pupils and adult can enhance the relationship and serve to 'oil the wheels' of learning. Quinn (1997) argues that during deep episodes of interaction between adults and pupils through speaking and listening, 'all can instantly be captivated by a great laugh together' (p. 115). Furthermore, genuinely laughing together not only relieves tension but also brings about increased emotional intimacy between the teacher and learners.

Loomans and Kolberg (2002) insist that laughter distinguishes a boring classroom from a learning classroom and teachers should therefore navigate away from what they refer to as a 'limiting' teaching style to a 'laughing' style that inspires creativity and helps pupils learn faster and better. Loomans and Kolberg's main premise is that teachers and parents should make learning fun while instilling self-esteem, solid work habits and the joy of learning in children. Suggested activities for younger children include using silly songs; special dressing-up days; vocabulary building; enhancing observation skills; different forms of communication; interactive social skills; and opportunities for self-expression.

Berk (2002) orientates the content of his book towards teachers and tutors of older pupils and students. He argues that the two principal reasons for using humour in the classroom are (1) that it helps to build the teacher–student connection; and (2) that it instantaneously engages students in the learning process. He refers to the process of engagement as 'the hook' and describes it as an 'instructional defibrillator', a term that mimics the name of the machine that dispenses a therapeutic dose of electrical energy to resuscitate a person who has had a cardiac arrest. Finally, an in-depth and rigorously academic text that deals with the psychology of humour by Martin (2007) is available.

Berk, R.A. (2002) *Humour as an Instructional Defibrillator: Evidence-based techniques in teaching and assessment*, Sterling, VA: Stylus Publishing.

Loomans, D. and Kolberg, K. (2002) *The Laughing Classroom: Everyone's guide to teaching with humor and play*, Tiburon, CA: H.J. Kramer.

Martin, R.A. (2007) *The Psychology of Humour*, London: Elsevier Academic Press.

Quinn, V. (1997) *Critical Thinking in Young Minds*, London: David Fulton.

Woods, P. (1990) *The Happiest Days? How Pupils Cope with School*, London: Routledge.

Think wider

Hobday-Kusch and McVittie (2002) note that adults and older children use humour as a negotiating tool to determine where power resides in the classroom. They claim on the basis of observations and interviews that most pupils and adults new to the school soon realise that certain forms of spoken language and discourse are appropriate and others are proscribed. However, a minority of pupils 'feed' off humour with reference to their peers' reactions and, after a time, their expectations. Certain pupils who find much of what they do at school to be irrelevant and tedious use humour as a means of relieving tension and getting through the day, despite the irritation and sanctions that their actions might incur.

Hobday-Kusch, J. and McVittie, J. (2002) 'Just clowning around: classroom perspectives on children's humour', *Canadian Journal of Education*, 27 (2/3), 195–210.

Pupil–adult interactions

Extract 21

Source

Hart, S. (2000) *Thinking Through Teaching: A framework for enhancing participation and learning*, London: David Fulton; see pp. 19–20.

Introduction

Hart's innovative thinking framework offers a tool that teachers can employ for reflecting on and learning from experience, and for generating soundly based ideas to guide the development of practice. In doing so, the author uses 'five questioning moves' (see p. 18):

1. *making connections* . . . which takes into account the immediate and wider learning environment;
2. *contradicting* . . . which takes into account our own expectations and assumptions;
3. *taking a child's-eye view* . . . which takes into account the child's meanings and agendas;
4. *noting the impact of feelings*. . .which takes into account how our feelings shape our interpretations;
5. *postponing judgement* . . . which takes into account the limits of what we know.

Key words & phrases

Adjustments, behaviour, defence mechanisms, different understanding, dynamics of teaching and learning, implications, innovative thinking, interpreting, judgements, monitor, open mind, reaction, reading of a situation, responses

---

Extract

"Trying to 'make connections' . . . is something that we constantly do during the course of ordinary teaching, as we continuously monitor what is going on in our classrooms and make whatever adjustments we judge to be needed . . . We make a judgement based on our prior knowledge of the class and reading of the current situation, adjust accordingly and then use the children's responses as further feedback, and if necessary begin the process again.

It is also our expertise, as teachers, to be able to counter one reading of a situation with one or more others as a way of deciding how best to respond ('contradicting'). Our first reaction to a child who grins, looks nonchalant or answers back when told off may be to think that the child does not care and is untouched by our disapproval. Yet we also know from experience that such reactions are very often defence mechanisms and provide evidence that the child *is* touched by our words and *does* care. Recognising this, we can change our own behaviour and avoid action that might lead to confrontation.

Trying to think ourselves into the child's shoes and view the situation from that perspective is a familiar strategy for many teachers . . . We also try to remain open to the possibility that what at first glance appears to be a misunderstanding or a wrong answer may turn out to be an ingenious but *different* understanding from the one that we were expecting . . .

Behaviour that prompts friendly banter on Monday morning may seem like a serious challenge to our authority on a wet Friday afternoon. Pupils' failure to co-operate with a request will tend to prompt a different response on our part depending upon whether the perpetrator is an individual or class with whom we usually get on well or not. We recognise that such differences of perception are partly a product of our own states of mind, and try to correct imbalances that we are aware of in our treatment and perception of pupils.

Even postponing judgement, because we recognise that we lack adequate information or resources, is a strategy that will be familiar to teachers . . . Teachers are very aware of the dangers of the 'self-fulfilling prophecy' and are conscious of the need to keep an open mind about individuals, particularly on first meeting . . .

All experienced teachers have extensive knowledge about the dynamics of teaching and learning, and about what makes a difference to how children behave and to how well they learn in school. We draw on this knowledge constantly, both consciously and intuitively, in planning lessons, in interpreting what is happening minute-by-minute in classrooms and especially in reviewing what happened in order to plan future lessons . . .

The five questioning moves (see the introduction, above) that support the process of innovative thinking are the means by which we marshal this knowledge and use it flexibly and imaginatively to support us in the vital process of reviewing our judgements and practices and drawing out the implications for future work."

Summary

Hart treads a careful line between acknowledging the tough choices and decisions that teachers need to make during every lesson, and the importance of taking time to review and reconsider interpretations made in the midst of practice, particularly when these have led to judgements that reflect negatively on a child's behaviour or learning.

Questions to consider

1. What sort of adult assumptions and decisions about pupil behaviour can lead to a more harmonious and to a less harmonious classroom?
2. What are the characteristics of reflection that takes place after the session (reflection on action) and during the session (reflection in action)?
3. How do teachers balance postponing judgements with decisive action?

Investigations

Types of teacher decision. Observe three teachers teaching a full session. Note the occasions when they make decisions. Discuss your findings with each teacher concerned and register their perceptions.

Links between teachers' emotions and actions. Ask a few teachers to keep a diary of their emotional states over a period of (say) two weeks, using broad headings such as (1) times I felt good; (2) times I felt low; and (3) times I felt indifferent. Subsequently, discuss with the teachers their perceptions of the impact of emotions on their teaching.

Variations in teacher and pupil perceptions. Compare teachers' and pupils' perceptions of specific lessons by interviewing each teacher and conducting group interviews with children.

Think deeper

Coultas (2007) claims that judging the usefulness of pupils' responses depends partly on the adult's instinct and experience (i.e. exercising an ability to see beyond a child's words) and partly on the learning objectives (i.e. the extent to which the response is located within the parameters of the lesson purpose). Pupil passivity does not create a climate for deep learning unless accompanied by opportunities for children to grapple with issues and concepts in subsequent tasks and activities. In similar vein, Dean (2009) suggests that one element of effective teaching is teachers spending time talking to pupils individually about their work, as this approach always has a positive effect on progress. Such teachers create a high level of industry within their classrooms and organise so there is always plenty for the pupils to do (see p. 68). In addition, a teacher's ability to observe and interpret behaviour is crucial, particularly at the early stages of education when children are more dependent on the teacher and may be more limited in their ability to express their needs (see p. 89).

Coultas, V. (2007) *Constructive Talking in Challenging Classrooms*, Abingdon: Routledge.
Dean, J. (2009) *Organising Learning in the Primary School Classroom*, Abingdon: Routledge.

Think wider

Cullingford (2006) describes how primary children usually respond to questions thoughtfully and on more than one level; for instance, he explains how they have the ability to understand the concepts of truth and falsehood at an earlier age than some child development educators have formerly claimed possible. The same author also claims that children want to learn and 'listen to experts, enthusiasts, specialists, anyone who is not put into a position of authority. From their point of view the best teachers are the best people, not the best managerial performers' (p. 220). **Pupil questions: see Extract 8 under 'Think deeper'.**

Capel and Gervis (2009) encourage the use of an 'autonomy-support' learning environment in which teachers offer pupils an increasing level of responsibility in making choices and selecting options to engage and motivate. These authors provide a theoretical model to illustrate the link between teachers' actions in creating a motivational learning climate and pupils' responses. The seven theories in the model are as follows:

1. *theory 'x' and theory 'y'*, based respectively on assumptions that workers are lazy ('x') or motivated ('y');
2. *achievement motivation*: individuals set their own standards of achievement;
3. *achievement goal theory*: individuals choose to focus on enhancing their skills and expertise – or judge their success with reference to that of others.
4. *attribution theory*: individuals attribute their success or failure to ability, effort, difficulty of task or luck;
5. *expectancy theory*: a range of cues is used by one person to form expectations of another person;
6. *hierarchy of needs theory*: based on work by Maslow from 1970, beginning with basic creature-needs: safety; love and belonging; self-esteem; and, lastly, fulfilling one's potential.
7. *behavioural learning theories*: an activity or behaviour is reinforced by a pleasurable outcome and thereby is likely to be repeated.

See pp. 128–9 for full details.

Capel, S. and Gervis, M. (2009) 'Motivating pupils', in Capel, S., Leask, M. and Turner, T. (eds) *Learning to Teach in the Secondary School*, Abingdon: Routledge.
Cullingford, C. (2006) 'Children's own vision of schooling', *Education 3–13*, 34 (3), 211–21.

Extract 22

Source

Rex, L.A. and Schiller, L. (2009) *Using Discourse Analysis to Improve Classroom Interaction*, Abingdon: Routledge; see pp. 19–21.

Introduction

Rex and Schiller base their book on analyses of teacher and student classroom talk to illustrate how learning is built interactively. Thus: 'Group dynamics shape individual choices about what can be said, when, and to whom' (Preface). Furthermore, social stability depends on mutual recognition of worth and identity. The extract included here is based on Chapter 3, titled 'Interacting and positioning'.

Key words & phrases

Adolescent literacy, capability, choices, comprehension, different contexts, discourse analysis, disengagement, identity, importance, learning community, mutual recognition of worth, participate, perceive, productive, relationships, students' perceptions, understanding our students

---

Extract

"Discourse analysis methods offer three concepts related to identity that are particularly helpful when working with learners, whether children or adults. The first is the concept of identities and relationships. The second is the concept of recognising identities, your own and others. The third discourse analysis concept related to identities is how positioning affects identity. Understanding these three concepts is essential to successful teaching and learning . . .

Think of yourself as a teacher in a classroom. Where are you physically? How do you sound? What are you saying? Now think of yourself as a colleague in a staff meeting. Do you sound the same? Do you speak with the same tone of voice? Where are you physically? The point is, you speak and act one way in the classroom where you are the teacher. You speak and act in a different way when you are a colleague. The relationships we have with people in different contexts influence the identities we present.

. . . How do your colleagues perceive you and vice versa? What about your students? What do they think of you? Think of a challenging student. How do you perceive that student? When you're in a staff meeting, can you predict which teacher will usually disagree with the majority? In your classroom is there a class clown? . . . The student who jokes repeatedly during class becomes known as the class clown. It takes repeated displays for others to recognise someone's identity.

The same is true for your students' perceptions of you. They recognise you as a particular kind of person by the ways you interact with them over time. The concepts of identities and relationships and identities and recognition are easy to understand if we apply them to a media celebrity . . . In less public contexts, teachers and students construct recognisable identities for each other, even if it's as 'the silent one' or 'the voracious reader'. These identities may evolve within a single school setting or differ across settings. They can even change within the same classroom when the discourse patterns change or a member leaves or enters.

Choices of what to say and when are related to who we are and how we want to be perceived. Every person needs to feel a sense of [his or her] own importance and capability and will gravitate towards others who signal, in the ways they talk to them, a recognition of their importance and worth . . .

People do not want to participate in conditions where they feel devalued and powerless. And we don't want to train our students to be passive towards powerful authority. We see disengagement when students resist classroom activity and when teachers decline to participate in professional learning communities. For learning to go forward, the mutual recognition of worth and identity must be present. Who one wants to appear to be, and whether or not that identity is recognised as productive for the work in hand, determines whether individuals will participate in building and sustaining a learning community."

Summary

In the above passage, Rex and Schiller emphasise the importance of understanding and recognising the perceptions that teachers and students have of one another. The authors argue that individuals can and will deliberately alter the way in which they act and speak, depending upon the context and their feelings of their self-worth. Similarly, the manner in which people address one another is influenced by the way in which they perceive the other person. The best learning environment is created where teacher and learner have mutual respect for each other's identity. **Professional identity: see also Extracts 34–36.**

Questions to consider

1. What sorts of identities might a teacher (a) deliberately promote, and (b) unintentionally portray to students? What impact might these identities have on teacher–pupil relationships and learning?

2. What sorts of identities might a teacher (a) deliberately promote, and (b) unintentionally portray to colleagues? How might these identities affect their perceptions of the teacher as a person and as a professional?

3. What kinds of signals indicate that (a) adults recognise a student's importance and worth; (b) students recognise one another's importance and worth; and (c) students recognise an adult's importance and worth?

Investigations

Adult identities. Discuss with colleagues the issues raised in the extract about the shaping of identities with reference to context.

Student identities. Discuss with groups of students the issues raised in the extract with a view to finding out whether they deliberately choose to portray a particular identity in class.

Analysing discourse. Record a group discussion involving at least one adult and a group of learners. Analyse the content with special reference to the shaping of identities as described in the extract.

Think deeper

Hood (2008) set out to discover what a group of young learners might understand by an *identity as learner* under the abbreviation PPIL, standing for pupils' perceptions of their identities as learners, thereby moving from pupils as sources of data to pupils as agents of change. The eight- and nine-year-old mixed ability group of children demonstrated that they were

> very capable of talking and writing about their perceptions of a variety of aspects of being a learner, that they respond well to probes which ask for simple opinions or decisions about their lives in the classroom and are willing then to think more deeply in response to supplementary questions which may demand greater reflection.
>
> (p. 149)

Hobday-Kusch and McVittie (2002) insist that adults have an obligation to socialise pupils into school culture and thereby marshal the discourse, decide who will speak and when and what about, as well as communicating acceptable forms of behaviour. Contrarily, the prevailing school culture and even the physical environment ('learning context') can also constrain the way that the teacher speaks, acts and behaves; for instance, the headteacher may insist that classrooms are quiet and calm places, which a naturally extrovert teacher is likely to find difficult to maintain. Pupils also have to submit to adult expectations about speech and use of language, such that if the pupils fail to understand or conform, they may be labelled as troublesome and rebuked. In practice, there is a negotiation of power between pupils and other pupils, and between teachers and pupils. If the teacher intervenes too much, the flow of conversation becomes fragmented; if intervention is minimal, the talk may stray too far from the intended topic or dissolve into a series of trivial comments (Black 2004).

Black, L. (2004) 'Teacher–pupil talk in whole-class discussions and processes of social positioning within the primary school classroom', *Language and Education*, 18 (5), 347–60.

Hobday-Kusch, J. and McVittie (2002) 'Just clowning around: classroom perspectives on children's humour', *Canadian Journal of Education*, 27 (2/3), 195–210.

Hood, P. (2008) 'What do we teachers need to know to enhance our creativity?', *Education 3–13*, 36 (2), 139–51.

Think wider

Since the establishment of the Criminal Records Bureau in 2002, more than a third of British adults have had to get a certificate to say they are safe to be near children, and the numbers are increasing. Furedi and Bristow (2008) argue that the growth of police vetting has created a sense of mistrust between grown-ups and young people because adults are afraid to interact with any child not their own. The result of the mistrust is that generations are becoming distant, as adults suspect each other and children are taught to suspect adults. The authors claim that vetting encourages risk aversion, such that it is better to ignore young people rather than risk accusations of improper conduct. Furedi and Bristow argue for a more common-sense approach, based on the assumption that the vast majority of adults can be relied on to help and support children and enrich their lives.

Furedi, F. and Bristow, J. (2008) *Licensed to Hug*, London: Civitas Institute for the Study of Civil Society.

Teachers teaching

Pedagogy

Extract 23

Source

Taubman, D. (1999) 'Critical pedagogy and the professional development of the NQT', in Cole, M. (ed.) *Professional Issues for Teachers and Student Teachers*, London: David Fulton; see pp. 61–3.

Introduction

'Pedagogy' is a term used regularly by two groups of people: (1) student teachers and their lecturers; and (2) qualified teachers studying for a higher qualification. It is not, however, a word in common usage by teachers in school. Taubman argues that serious attention should be paid to pedagogy as it is the 'DNA of teaching'. In this extract the author explores pedagogy from a variety of different perspectives and emphasises the teacher's responsibility to provide effective and relevant teaching.

Key words & phrases

Aims of education, coherent model, effective learning, effective pedagogy, effective teacher, engaging and relevant, learning encounter, liberal education, optimal pedagogy, pedagogic bases, purposes and execution, science of teaching, subject and object of teaching, teacher–pupil relationship, teacher's perceptions

---

Extract

"Pedagogy is from the Greek word *paidagogos*, meaning 'to lead a child'. In modern usage it is generally accepted as a technical term for the 'science of teaching' (perhaps the term should more properly be 'pedagology'). However, it can be argued that pedagogy should include not only the component of technique but also central moral and political components. Pedagogy is determined by the teacher's perception of the aims of education, which in turn determine the nature (or sub-text) of the teacher–pupil/student relationship (or 'dialogue').

Pedagogy as the science of teaching is holistic, in the sense that it must address the whole subject and object of teaching, giving a coherent model of the component parts . . . Pedagogy is the DNA of teaching, the deep structure informing, guiding and constituting in all its parts the purposes and execution of teaching . . .

There is no secret winning formula for optimal pedagogy. Rather, it is a process which is infinite and varied, unique to every teacher and fine-tuned to each class and individual at each learning encounter. The teacher must be sensitive to the needs of the moment and situation, and modify the 'pedagogic frequency' (but not the fundamental 'wavelength') as appropriate. For example, a science lesson in which the teacher adopts a pedagogy stance of co-investigator with the students might get out of hand with a lively Year 9 class [fourteen-year-olds] in the last lesson on a Friday afternoon, so the teacher might take a firmer tone or apply sanctions, but this should not involve the total abandonment of her or his co-investigative pedagogy. While it is good practice to use a variety of teaching and learning strategies with any given class over time, switching pedagogic bases (e.g. from 'enthusiastic co-investigator' to 'didactic authoritarian' within a lesson) can unsettle pupils or students. It can show weakness (inconsistency and fundamental uncertainty) in the teacher and is likely to detract from effective learning.

In teaching, effective pedagogy is that which enables teaching and learning to develop without undue tension between competing educational objectives. It harmonises 'liberal education' (the pursuit of altruistic personal development) and 'exam' objectives, for instance. In developing your own pedagogic stance it should be remembered that, at root, to be an effective teacher one must have 'something to teach'. We should be clear about why we want to teach our subject and about how pupils can benefit from learning it, and we should be able to transmit that purpose to the pupils.

Effective pedagogy also consists in keeping up to date with developments in one's teaching subject, as well as in the teaching of it, helping to keep both teacher and pupils fresh and engaged, and helping to keep the subject itself fresh, engaging and relevant (i.e. bringing it to life)."

Summary

Taubman argues that successful pedagogy requires continuous attention because the 'science of teaching' is, paradoxically, an art that can only be improved by in-service work and reflection on the nature of teaching, both during and after sessions. At the heart of Taubman's argument is a belief that there must be interplay between the teacher's subject knowledge and teaching skills. Stale pedagogy is almost certain to create a depressed learning environment, and pupil disengagement with the lesson content.

Questions to consider

1. In what ways can 'central moral and political components' be incorporated into pedagogy?
2. How might 'switching pedagogic bases' in mid-lesson prove (a) harmful; (b) beneficial?
3. What pedagogical strategies can teachers use to transmit to pupils that learning is worthwhile?

Investigations

Pedagogy and educational aims. Investigate the validity of Taubman's claim that pedagogy is 'determined by the teacher's perception of the aims of education' by interviewing some teachers about their educational beliefs and priorities and the way this impacts upon the way they teach.

Changing pedagogy mid-lesson. Discuss with colleagues or teachers occasions when they have felt it necessary or would feel it necessary to modify their teaching approach during the lesson.

Bringing the subject to life. Discuss with colleagues or teachers ways in which they seek to keep themselves up to date and use the knowledge to enthuse pupils.

Think deeper

The Effective Pedagogy in the Early Years (EPEY) study (Siraj-Blatchford *et al.* 2002) was developed to identify the most effective pedagogical strategies applied in the Foundation Stage to support the development of young children's skills, knowledge and attitudes, and to ensure they make a good start at school. The authors define the term 'pedagogy' as referring to the instructional techniques and strategies that enable learning to take place. Pedagogy also refers to the interactive process between teacher and learner, and it is also applied to include the provision of some aspects of the learning environment. The study paid special attention to four areas of impact to identify how practitioners supported the children in making developmental progress: (1) adult–child verbal interactions; (2) differentiation and formative assessment; (3) parental partnership and the home education environment; and (4) discipline and adult support in talking through conflicts. Among numerous other findings, Siraj-Blatchford *et al.* concluded that effective pedagogy in the early years involves a balance of (1) a teacher-directed, programmed learning approach, and (2) an open framework approach where children are provided with 'free' access to a range of instructive learning environments in which adults support children's learning.

Alexander (2004) raises some significant issues about pedagogy, creativity and curriculum. He describes pedagogy as

> the act of teaching, together with its attendant discourse. It is what one needs to know, and the skills one needs to command, in order to make and justify the many different kinds of decisions, of which teaching is constituted. Curriculum is just one of its domains, albeit a central one.
>
> (p. 11)

Teacher decisions: see also Extract 57.

Alexander, R. (2004) 'Still no pedagogy? Principle, pragmatism and compliance in primary education', *Cambridge Journal of Education*, 34 (1), 7–33.

Siraj-Blatchford, I., Sylva, K., Muttock, S., Gilden, R. and Bell, D. (2002) *Researching Effective Pedagogy in the Early Years*, Research Report RR356 for the DfES, Norwich: Queen's Printers.

Think wider

In her study of twenty-five teachers, Ollin (2008) suggests that many different types of silence may be used productively in pedagogical practice. She provides examples of questions that might be asked when observing teachers' uses of silence rather than talk and concludes that teachers make conscious decisions to abstain from intervention based on their continuous reading of what is happening in the classroom. Smedley (2006) raises an important issue about whether pedagogical practices differ between male and female teachers and particularly the adjustment that some men (as a minority group in primary schools) have to make in teaching younger children. **Male teachers: see also Extract 19.**

Ollin, R. (2008) 'Silent pedagogy and rethinking classroom practice: structuring teaching through silence rather than talk', *Cambridge Journal of Education*, 38 (2), 265–80.

Smedley, S. (2006) 'Listening to men student primary school teachers and some thoughts on pedagogy', *Changing English*, 13 (1), 125–35.

Extract 24

Source

Kyriacou, C. (2009) 'The five dimensions of social pedagogy within schools', *Pastoral Care in Education*, 27 (2), 101–8.

Introduction

Kyriacou notes that in continental Europe the term 'social pedagogy' is widely used to refer to the theory and practice underpinning the work of professionals involved in supporting and fostering children's personal development, social education and overall welfare. In some countries there are professionals known as 'social pedagogues' in settings such as residential care, nurseries, schools and youth clubs. He further describes that in the United Kingdom there has been a growing interest in social pedagogy within schools, stimulated by the need to review the organisation of agencies and the professional roles of those individuals involved in the care, welfare and education of children, triggered by *Every Child Matters*. The author argues that the needs of the whole child are best expressed in terms of five key dimensions: care and welfare, inclusion, socialisation, academic support and social education.

Key words & phrases

Academic support, all pupils, care and welfare, collaborative working, inclusion, inclusive practices, mediator, pastoral curriculum, pupils with problems, social education, social pedagogues, socialisation

---

Extract

"In recent years some job adverts have begun to appear in the United Kingdom for 'social pedagogues'. Such job descriptions tend to focus on the role of a social pedagogue as someone who acts as a mediator working on behalf of children. For example, they may be involved in mediating between children and their families when relationships have become problematic; or between children and their schools in relation to the threat of exclusion; or between children and the police when children have become involved in gang crime. This mediating role can be seen as acting as an advocate for the child's interests. However, it is important to recognise here that the notion of social pedagogy includes *all* pupils, not just (or even primarily) those pupils having 'problems' or identified by the school as giving a cause for concern. Inevitably, however, a disproportionate amount of time and attention by teachers operating within the context of social pedagogy will involve supporting pupils with problems . . .

It appears that social pedagogy within the context of schools is best thought of as involving five discernible but to some extent overlapping dimensions:

Care and welfare

This dimension refers to the health and social care of the child and their physical and mental well-being. [It] includes meeting children's health needs and ensuring they live in a safe and secure environment, and, in general terms, that children are adequately cared for.

Inclusion

This dimension refers to ensuring that all children feel themselves to be fully involved in, rather than marginalised from, the 'mainstream' of society and mainstream school life. Whilst inclusion was initially used to refer to how pupils with special educational needs can fully participate in mainstream school life through the use of inclusive practices (namely, practices that cater for pupils with widely differing needs), inclusion is now widely used to refer to pupils who are in danger of feeling marginalised from mainstream school life for a wide variety of reasons, such as race, gender, social class, disabilities, disaffection, low ability, lack of parental support and being bullied.

Socialisation

This dimension refers to enabling children to behave in accordance with what society as a whole has deemed to be desirable social norms and expectations regarding attitudes, values and behaviour. In particular, it includes helping pupils to develop an understanding of how to act in socially appropriate ways in a range of social settings. This will also involve helping pupils to resist peer pressure to engage in undesirable and anti-social behaviour, such as bullying, truancy, drug abuse and criminality. As such, the socialisation advocated within social pedagogy may sometimes be in tension with certain social norms and expectations that are evident in pupils' immediate family and social setting.

Academic support

This dimension refers to offering support concerning the knowledge, understanding and skills content of the academic curriculum to children who are at risk of failing to attain the minimal levels of competence in literacy and numeracy needed to participate adequately in adult life, and/or who – because of the challenging personal and social circumstances they face (e.g. ill health, living in care, victims of child abuse, involvement in criminal activity) – are under-achieving.

Social education

This dimension refers to the progress of children concerning the knowledge, understanding and skills content of the pastoral curriculum. The pastoral curriculum is concerned with the child's personal and social development and well-being, and covers such aspects as how to behave towards others, moral education, sex education, citizenship, career planning and health education."

Summary

Kyriacou argues that if social pedagogy does become adopted within schools, one of the first tasks will be to develop a clearer understanding of the relationship between the five dimensions noted above, and the extent to which they can form a basis to guide practice concerning *all* pupils. The author adds that collaborative working between teachers and other professionals will need to work from the perspective of the pupils' needs, rather than from a narrow notion of their own professional roles.

Questions to consider

1. In what ways is the teacher's role changing?
2. Which of the five dimensions of social pedagogy are likely to be most significant for (a) teachers, and (b) support staff?
3. What arguments might be advanced for and against the view that teachers are gradually becoming 'glorified social workers'?

Investigations

Teachers' perceptions of social pedagogy. Discuss the five dimensions of social pedagogy with teachers to ascertain their views about the nature of their role.

Parents' views of social pedagogy. Discuss the five dimensions of social pedagogy with parents to ascertain their views about the nature of their role.

The SENCO's views. Discuss the issues raised in the article with the school special educational needs coordinator.

Think deeper

According to Smith (2009), the expression 'social pedagogy' has been used to describe a range of work straddling social work and education. Often more holistic and group-orientated than dominant forms of social work and schooling, social pedagogy (*Sozialpädagogik*) has its roots in German progressive education and is sometimes translated as 'community education' or 'education for sociality'. Etymologically, pedagogy is derived from the Greek *paidagōgeō*, meaning, literally, 'to lead the child'. Stephens (2009, p. 347) defines social pedagogy as the study and practice of deliberative care, education and upbringing, viewed holistically rather than as separate entities, with an emphasis on finding pedagogical ways of nurturing and supporting positive social development. He argues that social pedagogy is an academic discipline that can be applied in 'hands-on settings'. Furthermore, the way that social pedagogy is understood lies in the semantic meanings attached to the words 'social' and 'pedagogy', and in the values of the person who proposes how social pedagogy should be practised; however, Stephens underlines the fact that the care aspect must be planned rather than left to chance.

Smith, M.K. (2009) 'Social pedagogy', in *The Encyclopaedia of Informal Education*, online at www.infed.org/biblio/b-socped.htm.

Stephens, P. (2009) 'The nature of social pedagogy: an excursion in Norwegian territory', *Child and Family Social Work*, 14, 343–51.

Think wider

Jackson (2009) refers to the importance for understanding social pedagogy of the philosopher Jean-Jacques Rousseau, who stressed the importance of the natural environment and that learning will take place if the provision for a learning experience is planned and acted upon, not merely left to chance. Jackson posits that while social pedagogy has been a key organising idea in many European countries, it has only recently become a focus for exploration in English-speaking countries. She goes on to say that social pedagogy is often used to embrace the activities of youth workers, residential or day-care workers (with children or adults) and occupational therapists. Social pedagogy can also be used to describe those concerned with community learning and overlaps considerably with the notion of informal education. Jackson states that as a practice, social pedagogy tends looks to group work, association, relationship and community, and to holistic educational processes, depending heavily on the character and integrity of the educator and his or her ability to reflect-in-action and reflect-on-action.

Jackson, V. (2009) 'Social pedagogy: the impact of Rousseau', *Children Webmag*, November 2009, online at www.childrenwebmag.com/articles.

Professional expertise

Source

Cullingford, C. (2009) *The Art of Teaching: Experiences of schools*, Abingdon: Routledge; see pp. 70–3.

Introduction

Cullingford's book is aptly named the *art* of teaching, as opposed to the science or craft of teaching. He regrets that teaching has become associated with the control and command of children – with discipline and authority – rather than satisfying the deep-seated human desire to learn. The chapter from which the extract that follows is taken is concerned with teachers as they see themselves and as others see them.

Key words & phrases

Best practice, body of knowledge, clients, commitment to a subject, control of the system, deliverers, difficult to define, inspection, interference, measurement of outcomes, needs of the people, profession, shifts of emphasis, significance, social workers, status, statutory commands, teachers in society, unique skills

---

Extract

"Teachers are like social workers. They are in the anomalous position of being employed by the state, but rather than carrying the authority of the state, they see themselves as representing their clients. There was a time when, like teachers, social workers embodied all the significance of 'the man from the ministry', like the district nurse telling people what to do and having the confidence that she would be accepted . . .

Like social workers, who fight for their clients against the very people who are their employers, teachers are caught between the demands of the state in all its statutory commands and inspection, and the needs of the people . . . Their role is interpreted as 'deliverers' of the curriculum, as carrying out the orders that are seen as the best examples of collective enterprise. And yet, teachers also prize their autonomy and the sense that they are professionals who know what they are doing. It is an international conclusion from research that the more independence schools and teachers have, and the less interference from outside, the better they do. But this is not how it is seen by those who are in control of the system . . .

The concept of a 'profession' is complex and changing. In its original form it is based on professing a commitment to a subject, as in the idea of a professor. It implies the mastery of the subject, its defence, the protection of a body of knowledge. This is the heart of the problem. The established professions like law or medicine protect their knowledge from outsiders as keenly as their status. In this sense knowledge is power. The position of knowledge creates a small body of people who use it and only give it away for profit. Anyone entering into the field is vetted, not just for promise but for the belief in retaining this body of knowledge. And yet teachers are supposed to give away knowledge freely. They are not supposed to have arcane mysterious secrets that only they possess. They neither guard their knowledge nor rely on its possession for status . . .

Teachers rightly feel that they have unique skills but that these are not fully recognised. There is little more complicated and demanding than dealing with a large cohort of individual learners. The amount of human insight and instinctive understanding is impressive. The question remains: to what extent is intelligent performance a 'body of knowledge'? Is there a well-developed theory being applied? Does it take the study of subjects or the central subjects of human behaviour to demonstrate mastery? The problem for teachers in this sense is that their best practice is tacit, instinctive and immediate, not looked up first in a textbook nor properly justified by a complex language . . .

Those who have the privilege to observe teachers realise how subtle and intelligent is their art, but it remains difficult to define and can never be judged by a simple checklist or by the measurement of outcomes, which depend on so many factors."

Summary

Cullingford describes a number of paradoxes that exists in the teacher's role: first, being representatives of the state yet in a sense guarding pupils against state imposition that they perceive as injurious to learning; second, having knowledge and insights, which, because teachers act as professionals, ought to be 'protected', yet freely sharing them for the benefit of learners; and third, possessing sophisticated skills on which their competence is judged yet being unable to present them in a directly measurable form. Cullingford concludes the chapter by restating his central premise that 'the art of teaching is subtle because it is individual and it rests on the recognition of the power and importance of learning' (p. 80).

Questions to consider

1. What unique skills do teachers possess? How can their effectiveness be demonstrated other than through pupils' performance in formal tests?
2. What are the implications for teacher professionalism with respect to (a) status; (b) remuneration; (c) job satisfaction; (d) professional standards; and (e) societal expectations?
3. If teachers cannot and should not be judged by a simple checklist or the measurement of outcomes, how *should* they be judged?

Investigations

Defining profession and professionalism. Survey as many colleagues as possible, asking them to answer three questions: (1) In what ways can teaching be described as a profession? (2) What are the characteristics of a professional teacher? (3) On what basis should classroom teachers be judged – and should the same criteria be applied to teachers regardless of the ages of pupils they teach? If possible, arrange for a group discussion with respondents about the issues raised through their answers.

Exploring perspectives on teacher professionalism. Use Cullingford's own questions as the basis for a literature search about teacher professionalism; thus: 'To what extent is intelligent performance a "body of knowledge"? Is there a well-developed theory being applied? Does it take the study of subjects or the central subjects of human behaviour to demonstrate mastery?'

Teachers of very young children. Interview a selection of early years teachers concerning the specialist knowledge and unique skills teachers possess that qualifies them for the designation 'professional'.

Think deeper

Findings about teachers' child-centred orientation reflect research carried out (for instance) among aspiring primary teachers in England by Hayes (2004) and secondary students in Australia (Manuel and Hughes 2006), which confirmed that *altruism* and a *desire to care for children and young people* provided the most powerful incentives for a large majority of trainees to pursue teaching as a career. Manuel and Hughes conclude that many prospective teachers enter teaching 'with a sense of mission to transform the lives of young people and open opportunities for growth through learning and connecting' (p. 21).

Scott and Dinham (2008) suggest that teaching expertise is something of a mystery even to those who practise it, because teachers are particularly likely to learn their craft behind closed doors through a combination of trial and error, augmented by memories of how they were taught and attempts to emulate experienced colleagues. Scott and Dinham further claim that learning on the job is based on the notion that teachers are born and not made, thereby implying that teacher education is unnecessary. One of their conclusions is that the ways that teaching is learned and the context – both cultural and subcultural – in which it is learned predispose teachers to experience and explain their own and others' expertise and talent for teaching as 'inborn'. Scott and Dinham argue that teachers need opportunity, incentives, structures, standards, knowledge and experience to change their thinking and practice; perceiving effective teachers as being 'born and not made' militates against this process.

Cullingford (2006) describes how children usually respond to questions thoughtfully and on more than one level; for instance, he explains how they have the ability to understand the concepts of truth and falsehood at an earlier age than some child development educators have formerly claimed possible. The same author also claims that children want to learn and 'listen to experts, enthusiasts, specialists, anyone who is not put into a position of authority. From their point of view the best teachers are the best people, not the best managerial performers' (p. 220). **Pupil perspectives: see also Extracts 50 and 51.**

Connell (2009) explains why we need to think about the question of what constitutes a good teacher and suggests that we do not need a picture of 'the good teacher' in the singular but pictures of good teachers in the plural and good teaching in the collective sense. Connell also claims that the new practice of accrediting teacher education programmes in terms of point-by-point compliance with a list of teacher competencies is an extremely questionable way of controlling teacher quality. The author advocates models of teacher education that will support creative, diverse and just teaching practices in what is certain to be a different sort of educational future.

Connell, R. (2009) 'Good teachers on dangerous ground: towards a new view of teacher quality and professionalism', *Critical Studies in Education*, 50 (3), 213–29.
Cullingford, C. (2006) 'Children's own vision of schooling', *Education 3–13*, 34 (3), 211–21.
Hayes, D. (2004) 'Recruitment and retention: insights into the motivation of primary trainee teachers in England', *Research in Education*, 71, 37–49.
Manuel, J. and Hughes, J. (2006) 'It has always been my dream: exploring pre-service teachers' motivations for choosing to teach', *Teacher Development*, 10 (1), 5–24.
Scott, C. and Dinham, S. (2008) 'Born not made: the nativist myth and teachers' thinking', *Teacher Development*, 12 (2), 115–24.

Think wider

Doherty-Sneddon and Phelps (2007) investigated whether teachers detected children's gaze behaviours and, if so, how they interpreted them. The researchers found that teachers were aware of children averting their eyes ('gaze aversion', GA) but took it to mean different things. GA is a potentially useful cue during teaching and learning interactions. It can indicate that a child is finding it difficult to find an answer or that a child is concentrating on thinking of an answer. If teachers think GA only signals that the child is finding it difficult to think of an answer, they are more likely to interrupt the child's thinking time by offering help. If they see GA as a sign of active engagement with difficult material, they are more likely to wait for the child to respond. Links with assessment for learning approaches are evident in that the time teachers allow children to think silently before giving an answer (wait time) is critical for effective learning. The ability to distinguish between the different possible reasons for children averting their gaze may assist teachers in deciding what sort of help to give children. **Body language: see also Extract 41 under 'Think wider'.**

Doherty-Sneddon, G. and Phelps, F.G. (2007) 'Teachers' responses to children's eye gaze', *Educational Psychology*, 27 (1), 93–109.

Extract 26

Source

Hayes, D. (2009) *Primary Teaching Today*, Abingdon: Routledge; see pp. 16–17.

Introduction

In the book Hayes explores the realities of teaching for new teachers and explains how the existing practices and 'taken-for-granted' procedures have to be learned and absorbed by the newcomer before progress in teaching can occur. He goes on to compare and contrast two teaching approaches: both of the teachers help pupils to learn but only one wins their hearts as well as minds.

Key words & phrases

Conventions, decisions, instinctive, learning experiences, lived experience, newcomer, passion for learning, policy implementation, positive strategies, principles, processes, pupil learning, traditions, well-educated routines

---

Extract

"Schools have many routines and processes embedded in their daily practice that are not evident to the outsider but quickly become apparent when someone begins to work there. There are traditions, conventions, professional disputes, personality tensions, bureaucratic procedures, implicit and explicit pedagogies and a tangle of well-considered and instinctive responses to situations to which the newcomer is gradually exposed. The world of teaching requires determination and the ability to think 'on your feet', as you respond to an endless flow of children's questions and make decisions with knowledge, care and wisdom . . .

You will gather that teaching is not the smooth, seamless robe that official documents present as normal and achievable. Pupil learning is often messy, unpredictable and difficult to assess formally. Despite the fact that shelves are groaning with the weight of numerous publications allegedly helping us to understand the educative process, the truth is that the teachers mainly rely on a 'sixth sense' to guide their actions, honed through months and years of direct experience with children.

Teachers also use a bank of positive strategies to reinforce behaviour and shape class discipline, supported by rewards, sanctions and punishments agreed by the staff and written into a policy document. However, a policy is only a guideline and not a blueprint for action; over and above the formal requirements, you have to be the final arbiter of what is appropriate in any given situation. It is in the minutiae of the moment-by-moment 'lived experience' as a teacher that principles of teaching and learning are worked out. It is the way that each teacher *exercises* her or his judgement to implement the requirements that distinguishes the effective practitioner from the merely efficient one.

The best example of the truth that it is teachers rather than systems that make the essential difference to pupil learning is seen when a class is shared between two teachers. The first teacher is abrupt, unsmiling and regularly finds things to moan about. Pupils are compliant and subdued. They complete the tasks and work feverishly, ever conscious of the teacher's steely glare and uncompromising stance. Lunchtime comes as a welcome relief.

The second teacher arrives a little later, full of smiles, chatting to the children, greedily absorbing their news and brimming with life. She is aware of the children's carefully coded criticisms of the morning teacher but studiously avoids being drawn into a discussion. The children work enthusiastically for her, if a little noisily, and strive to achieve their best. They are sometimes mischievous but think too highly of their teacher too much to take unreasonable advantage. Anyway, they know that she can be fiercely uncompromising if pushed too far. When school ends, the children skip from the classroom, their minds full of the learning experiences they have recently enjoyed; they cannot wait to tell their friends, siblings and people at home about what they have been doing.

The first teacher is full of jargon and endlessly quotes from government circulars to her colleagues. The second teacher makes sure that bureaucracy serves the children, and not the other way around. The first teacher is largely concerned with policy implementation; the second teacher wants principles to precede practice. The first teacher is admired and gets results in measurable ways; the second teacher is loved and gets results in measurable *and* immeasurable ways, such as fostering determination, perseverance, support for others, an encouraging attitude and a willingness to accept temporary failure to achieve lasting success. Which teacher do you think is more likely to assist the children to develop their thinking, creativity, passion for learning and thirst for knowledge? Which teacher will produce well-educated pupils? Yes, I think so, too!"

Summary

A key question is whether pupils need to like and admire their teachers in order to make optimal progress. The extract also raises the issue about whether particular personalities are best suited to teach and, if so, whether a 'suitable' personality with (say) early years is also appropriate with (say) teenagers, and vice versa. The extract ends by drawing a distinction between effective, measurable pupil progress and the sorts of skills and attitudes that characterise a good education.

Questions to consider

1. In what ways do teachers have to think on their feet? What place does instinctive behaviour have in a highly regulated system?
2. How much is personality a factor in motivating learners?
3. How much should teachers be concerned with non-measurable outcomes?

Investigations

Pupil perspectives. Ask a large sample of pupils to list ten characteristics of 'the teacher I most admire'. If possible, ask pupils of different ages and compare the results.

Popularity. Initiate a discussion among a group of colleagues around the proposition that 'the best teachers are always the most popular'.

Memorable teachers. Interview a random group of adults about their memories of their 'best' teachers.

Think deeper

Haydn (2007) claims that teachers place a high premium on 'getting on' with their pupils, which

> was felt to derive in part from their skills of interaction with pupils but also the degree to which they developed an understanding of the pupils they were teaching in terms of their attitude to being in the classroom, learning a school subject and to the enterprise of education.
>
> (p. 107)

Teachers can never say that every pupil likes them equally but they have a duty to try to ensure that personality issues do not stop those in their care from receiving the best possible standard of education.

Kitching *et al.*'s (2009) study of everyday events ('the little things') that motivate or discourage early-career teachers in Ireland found that the level of student engagement and achievement were major factors in triggering regular positive feelings; by contrast, students' behaviour and perceived difficulties around home influences were a major source of teachers' ongoing dissatisfaction. The study underlined the importance of intrinsic motivation, as the new teachers seemed to draw sustenance from their *ordinary work*. One of the authors' conclusions was that teachers felt good not so much because pupils were learning but because they were engaged with the subject matter. While many were happy to receive affirmation, extrinsic recognition and reward did not seem to figure particularly highly. In addition, it appears that positive routine events do more to enhance a commitment to teaching than negative events impede such commitment. **Motivation factors: see also Extracts 35, 59 and 60.**

Haydn, T. (2007) *Managing Pupil Behaviour: Key issues in teaching and learning*, Abingdon: Routledge.

Kitching, K., Morgans, M. and O'Leary, M. (2009) 'It's the little things: exploring the importance of commonplace events for early-career teachers' motivation', *Teachers and Teaching*, 15 (1), 43–58.

Think wider

Teaching methods (as opposed to approaches or styles) are concerned with the principles of instruction in educating or activities that impart knowledge or skill, implying that there is a specific and systematic way of doing something in an orderly logical arrangement. A teaching method is unlikely to favour learning by 'doing' (discovery learning) and places more emphasis on visual means (use of pictures, diagrams, etc.) and auditory means (learning by listening). Teachers tend to follow the textbook and curriculum closely and avoid prompting discussion by asking questions. In Bloom's taxonomy (Bloom 1976) the teaching method is based on the premise that learners receive individualised instruction as appropriate, so they all master the course material stage by stage. The model presents three domains of learning: cognitive, affective and psycho-motor, each of which is organised as a series of levels or prerequisites. It is suggested that one cannot effectively address higher levels until those below them have been covered. Bloom's taxonomy suggests a way of categorising levels of learning in terms of the expected 'ceiling of attainment' for a given programme.

Bloom, B. (1976) *Human Characteristics and School Learning*, New York: McGraw-Hill.

Learning how to teach

Facilitating pupil learning

Source

James, M., McCormick, R., Black, P., Carmichael, P., Drummond, M.J., Fox, A., MacBeath, J., Marshall, B., Pedder, J., Procter, R., Swaffield, S., Swann, J. and Wiliam, D. (2007) *Improving Learning How to Learn: Tools for schools*, Abingdon: Routledge; see pp. 217–19.

Introduction

This book is ostensibly about learning rather than teaching but, of course, the two elements are inextricably linked. In this extract the authors emphasise the key role of the teacher in providing the kind of working environment that allows pupils to be an active part of the process rather than spectators. In the extract, note the emphasis placed on assessment for learning (AFL); the tension between taking principled (thoughtful) and spontaneous (instinctive) action; and the importance of collaboration among teachers. **Teacher collaboration: see also Extract 36.**

Key words & phrases

Assessment for learning, collaboratively, creating space, high stakes testing, involve pupils, performing teaching, reconceptualise, reflective, regulating activity, responsibility, role in pupils' learning, supporting learning, think and reflect

---

Extract

"If learning how to learn is about pupils taking responsibility for their own learning, then teachers need to provide learners with opportunities to exercise responsibility. This does not mean abandoning them to their own devices but it does mean planning activities with this in mind and developing the 'flow' of lessons to maximise these opportunities . . . This presents a considerable challenge because it asks teachers to reconceptualise their roles and the familiar division of labour in the classroom and move away from 'performing teaching' to 'supporting learning'.

Refocusing on the regulation of the learning process – being watchful, reflective and strategic so that teachers can help pupils to be watchful, reflective and strategic in their own learning – does not imply that the 'process' is all and that what is being learned is of no account . . . There is a sense in which teachers' thinking and regulating activity in the classroom needs to operate on at least two levels at the same time: moving between the learning itself and learning how to learn . . .

The practices associated with assessment for learning [AFL] are helpful tools in this respect because they are ways of making space for explicit dialogue about learning and for sharing and transferring the responsibility for learning to the learners themselves. However, as our evidence illustrates, they can unwittingly be used (or even misappropriated) for other purposes if teachers are not clear about the principles that underpin them. This implies that even if novice teachers are encouraged to try out the practices first before they fully understand their rationale, they will benefit from thinking more about their underpinnings as soon as they have developed some confidence in using them. They will then find ways of adapting them to new contexts or using the principle to create new practices. The AFL practice of increasing 'wait time' between the teacher asking a question and taking an answer is an example . . .

Moreover, as teachers become aware of the principles underpinning AFL, they blend such practices into the stream of lesson activity. They no longer feel the need, for instance, to write lesson objectives on the board but can internalise them and refer to them at any appropriate moment in classroom dialogue. Further, they involve pupils in discussion about objectives and how they relate to pupils' personal objectives and learning. This avoids the danger of such practices becoming ritualised and ultimately ineffective . . .

Our interviews with teachers provided much evidence of the pressures they experience from the demands of central initiatives and a high stakes testing regime. Yet a minority were able to rise above this and, instead of blaming circumstance beyond their control, they reflected critically on their own role in pupils' learning and how they might improve things . . . Opportunities to work collaboratively, in an atmosphere of trust and mutual respect, will help build the social capital needed for teachers to share, reflect upon and develop their ideas and practices. These constitute the intellectual capital of schools."

Summary

Teachers need to root their classroom practice in principled action that views both learning and teaching as a collaborative rather than individualised process. Trust and mutual respect are essential ingredients for success.

Questions to consider

1. In what ways might new and very experienced teachers differ with regard to their priorities, extent of principled actions and willingness to work collaboratively?
2. What factors may facilitate and hinder a teacher's desire for pupils to have more thinking time and a higher degree of participation during lessons?
3. What sorts of dilemmas and tensions might be eased or resolved through teachers sharing and reflecting on their work with colleagues?

Investigations

Different teacher roles. Interview a number of teachers about the different roles they perform across an academic year. Compare and contrast differences and similarities between new and experienced teachers, and between teachers with different responsibilities.

Novice teachers. Observe lessons taught by (say) three novice teachers. Discuss with them after the lesson occasions when their actions and decisions were guided by principles, occasions when their responses were spontaneous and times when they did what they thought would please the evaluator.

Your own educational priorities. Write an account of your own beliefs and priorities about education, including areas in which you do not possess a fully matured view. Discuss your ideas with trusted colleagues.

Think deeper

Black *et al.* (2003) claim that the purposes of assessment can be categorised in one of three ways: (1) assessment for accountability; (2) assessment to provide certification (exams); and (3) assessment for learning. Notably, they define assessments that fall into the third category – assessments for learning – as those for which the priority is to promote student learning. That is, information from the assessment can be used in constructive feedback to students, which in turn leads to a modification of the teaching and learning process. The authors identify 'formative assessment' as when evidence from the assessment is used by the teacher to modify the teaching approach to meet students' learning needs. **Assessment and learning: see also Extracts 5 and 6.**

David (2008) argues that a growing body of evidence suggests that when teachers collaborate to pose and answer questions informed by data from their own pupils, their knowledge grows and their practice changes. She also insists that teacher collaboration does not occur naturally; it runs against prevailing norms of teacher isolation and individualistic approaches to teaching. Without specific training, teachers often lack the necessary collaboration skills as well as skills in collecting data, making sense of the information and figuring out its implications for action. Harris and Muijs (2004) insist that teachers are uniquely placed to influence the quality of teaching and learning and they are important gatekeepers to development and change. Thus, 'where teachers work together in meaningful partnerships, much can be achieved for the benefit of schools and the young people who learn there' (p. 140).

Black, P., Harrison, C., Lee, C., Marshall, B. and Wiliam, D. (2003) *Assessment for Learning: Putting it into practice*, Maidenhead: Open University Press.

David, J.L. (2008) 'What research says about collaborative inquiry', *Educational Leadership*, 66 (4), 87–8.

Harris, A. and Muijs, D. (2004) *Improving Schools through Teacher Leadership*, Maidenhead: Open University Press.

Think wider

Teachers not only persevere to improve their competence through self-evaluation at the end of a lesson or series of lessons (reflection *on* action) but also are constantly evaluating their practice during their teaching (reflection *in* action). Newly qualified primary teachers tend to use the teaching approach that they developed during training or modelled on an experienced teacher whom they admired but change occurs during their careers as they gain promotion and encounter new challenges. Teachers gradually extend the reaches of their intellect, focus their energies more efficiently and, for the most part, become more caring, wise and sanguine. Neil and Morgan (2003) and Bubb (2004) provide overviews of issues attached to professional progression across a career.

Attard (2008) systematically maintained a reflective journal as a record of his own observations and reflections over a thirty-month period in which he discovered that (1) uncertainty is ever-present; (2) reflection helps in revealing the complexity and uncertainty of teaching; and (3) a tolerance of uncertainty promotes ongoing enquiry. His main argument revolves around a claim that far from being a disadvantage, uncertainty for the reflective practitioner can be a sign of constant growth, development and learning. Attard concludes by asserting that the reflective practitioner should learn to live with what he describes as a suspended state of not knowing because we need to engage in a never-ending process of reflection where the possibility of various solutions is analysed – the final objective being the need for continuous change with the aim of constant improvement. **Evaluating competence by levels of reflection: see Extract 39.**

Attard, K. (2008) 'Uncertainty for the reflective practitioner: a blessing in disguise', *Reflective Practice*, 9 (3), 307–17.

Bubb, S. (2004) *The Insider's Guide to Early Professional Development*, London: RoutledgeFalmer.

Neil, P. and Morgan, C. (2003) *Continuing Professional Development for Teachers*, London: Kogan Page.

Extract 28

Source

Hayes, D. (2008) *Foundations of Primary Teaching*, London: David Fulton; see pp. 56–9.

Introduction

The extract is taken from the second chapter of the book, which focuses on the work and person of the teacher and the challenges and opportunities facing every teacher, especially an inexperienced one. There is a progression in securing a relationship between the teacher and pupils that has to be negotiated if learning and teaching are to be successfully managed.

Key words & phrases

Adjustment, boundary walls, bridge-building, courtship, enhancement in learning, even-handed, fair, fulfilment, guest, interaction, mutual respect, partnership, perseverance, preliminaries, rapport, relationship, social mix

---

Extract

"Establishing a working relationship with a class of children requires patient per-severance . . . It is helpful to think of the route to a working relationship in terms of three stages: preliminaries, courtship and partnership.

Preliminaries

It is rightly claimed that first impressions count for a lot. It is also true that appearances can be deceiving . . . Preliminary encounters with children are often very demanding owing to the need to strike a balance between establishing a rapport and ensuring that you are not overwhelmed . . .

The preliminary stage demands a lot of bridge-building between adult and pupils, who must learn to relax together as trust is slowly gained through regular interaction, resulting in better understanding through the vagaries of classroom life . . .

Courtship

It is not possible to get to know all the pupils straight away. Some children prefer to weigh teachers up and others almost jump into their laps! Some children remain aloof because they are shy or suspicious of teachers or because they are contented with life as it is and do not want to be influenced too much by the presence of another adult. Children's coolness towards new teachers is not an indication that they hold something against them; similarly, effusive children do not necessarily like teachers. Sometimes you will find that the relationships with children that take longer to establish prove to be the most fruitful in the longer term. You must try to be even-handed with the children and give them the opportunity to speak when they want to express something and remain silent when they prefer to listen or reflect. Children do not mind a firm teacher, but they despise a gullible, domineering or weak-willed one.

As the courtship continues, boundaries between acceptable and unacceptable behaviour can be clarified. Children will test the limits to see how far they stretch. If teachers are too lenient, they may find that the boundary walls are made of elastic! On the other hand, rigidity may lead to resentment. It is important for you to explain to your pupils why things are permitted and refused, but done as matters of fact, not as issues for negotiation. Children may not always approve of a teacher's methods but providing they are seen as fair, relationships will gradually settle and consolidate. As a guest in the classroom with a limited time in which to make an impression and learn from your experiences, it is sensible to adopt the class teacher's approach as closely as possible until you feel more confident . . .

Partnership

The ideal teaching and learning situation is one in which teachers and pupils are at ease with one another and respond easily and naturally, so that learning is purposeful, children are motivated and discourse is more of a conversation between adult and child than a monologue dominated by the adult . . . In such an environment, children will have confidence to ask questions and express an opinion without being dismissed before they have had chance to finish speaking. Rules will be adhered to sensibly, though there will be opportunity to discuss their application. The work will be meaningful, and though there may be spells when the children find the work tedious, they will persevere in the sure knowledge that more exciting moments are never far away. The most striking characteristics of the partnership environment will be the sense of mutual respect, good eye contact and natural use of the voice. Both the teacher and the children will find fulfilment in their work."

Summary

The 'rite of passage' with a new class inevitably involves a degree of adjustment as adult and pupils become better acquainted and familiar with one another's personalities, hopes and expectations. Even more experienced teachers have to negotiate this tricky period of time and accommodate the needs and understandings of the new class.

Questions to consider

1. How many types of relationships are specifically or overtly referred to in the extract?
2. What is the key role of the teacher, mentor or tutor in helping to secure a 'partnership' as described above?
3. What sort of questions should teachers be asking themselves as they reflect on their practice to enable progress to be made and confidence to increase?

Investigations

Interview inexperienced teachers. Use the extract as the basis for interviews with inexperienced or trainee (student) teachers.

Interview experienced teachers. Use the extract as the basis for interviews with more experienced teachers.

Interview mentors. Use the extract as the basis for interviews with mentors who regularly supervise trainee (student) teachers.

Think deeper

Dean (2009) stresses the importance of finding out about the academic achievements and the social and emotional disposition of new pupils as a guide to planning and differentiating lessons. However, she warns against drawing too many premature conclusions and establishing unreasonable expectations based on records and another teacher's opinions, and the danger of labelling pupils too soon, as initial impressions may be inaccurate. Dean stresses the importance of careful observation about aspects such as the way pupils settle to their work, their comments and responses to questions, and the quality of their written work. An additional factor for new entrants (the reception class) is information from and liaison with parents being of prime importance in negotiating the 'rite of passage' from home or nursery to school (see chapter 2).

Whitebread (2009) emphasises the need to ensure that classes are well organised, not least in the case of new children. In particular, classrooms that 'support children's growing confidence as learners are first and foremost characterised by emotional warmth, mutual respect and trust between adults and children' (p. 27). Whitebread insists that three other additional factors are relevant: (1) children need to feel in control of their environment and their learning; (2) children have achievable challenges and sufficient support from adults so they can meet them; and (3) children need to learn to talk about and represent their learning and thinking (see pp. 28–30).

Dean, J. (2009) *Organising Learning in the Primary School Classroom*, Abingdon: Routledge.
Whitebread, D. (2009) 'Organising the early years classroom to encourage independent learning', in Whitebread, D. and Coltman, P. (eds) *Teaching and Learning in the Early Years*, Abingdon: Routledge.

Think wider

Learning to cope with the vagaries of children's behaviour is helped when teachers admit that unacceptable behaviour is sometimes due to an uncertainty in children's minds about where the boundaries lie. Thus, McPhillimy (1996) issues a warning about the need for teachers to examine the *cause* of problems rather than their symptoms: 'Misbehaviour in itself is therefore mainly a symptom of a problem rather than the problem itself. If the underlying problems are dealt with, then the symptom is likely to disappear' (p. 61). **Behaviour issues: see also Extracts 48 and 49.**

McPhillimy, B. (1996) *Controlling Your Class*, Chichester: John Wiley.

School placement

Extract 29

Source

Hobson, A.J., Malderez, A., Tracey, L., Giannakaki, M., Pell, G. and Tomlinson, P.D. (2008) 'Student teachers' experiences of initial teacher preparation in England: core themes and variation', *Research Papers in Education*, 23 (4), 407–33.

Introduction

The findings reported in this article derived from a major research project using survey method and in-depth face-to-face interviews carried out with a representative sample of student ('trainee') teachers (in England) from each of the main initial teacher preparation (ITP) routes. The research team recruited trainees from a total of seventy-four ITP providers, with nineteen of these also participating in the face-to-face interviews. Sampling ensured that a representative cohort of interviewees participated – male and female, different age and ethnic groups, and (for secondary trainees) student teachers following a range of subject specialisms.

Key words & phrases

Belonging, choices, degree of autonomy, desire for fun, desire for success, emotional responses, experiences, freedoms, identity, individualised, personalised, preparation, productive recruitment, psychological needs, relationships, retention, security, student teachers, success, trainees, unique characteristics

Extract

"What our findings suggest is that student teachers' experiences of ITP are the result of a complex interplay of factors including the nature of the ITP route and the specific programme they are following, and what individual trainees 'bring' to those courses in terms of both their prior conceptions and their personal characteristics such as age, gender and ethnicity. One implication of these findings must be that 'one size' of ITP does not 'fit all', and that those people responsible for the preparation (education, training and development) of student teachers need, as far as is practically possible, to be sensitive to the variety of issues highlighted here and to seek to facilitate 'personalised' (National College for School Leadership, NCSL 2005) or 'individualised' learning, that which is responsive to the unique characteristics of the individual trainee . . .

However . . . our data also reveal that there are a number of core features of the experience of ITP which appear to be common to all or most student teachers, and which policy-makers, ITP providers and individual teachers of teachers might take account of and be responsive to. A review of the literature on initial and early professional learning shows that each of what we have termed 'core themes' of student teachers' experiences – identity, relationships, relevance and emotion – have been identified, some more explicitly than others, in reports of earlier research . . .

One way in which all four themes identified as central to student teachers' experiences of ITP might be drawn together is by seeing trainees' experiences as attempts to meet their basic psychological needs as human beings, with their emotional responses relating to their perceived success or frustration in meeting those needs. Using Glasser's (1998) typology, humans' basic needs are for: (1) a sense of security; (2) belonging; (3) success; (4) freedoms; and (5) fun.

In relation to the first basic need, psychological or emotional *security* appears to be central to a number of findings relating to the identity and relationships themes in particular. Student teachers' desire for a sense of *belonging* is evident, for example, in the salience of the relationships theme and findings revealing their hopes for collegiality and in difficulties encountered in this respect. Third, trainees' need or desire for *success* is reflected in some of the findings relating to the themes of relevance (e.g. trainees' concerns about whether different aspects of ITP course provision will help them to become effective teachers), identity (trainees' concerns about whether others see them as 'proper teachers'), and relationships (e.g. the demoralising effect of negative mentor relationships and comments). Student teachers' need for *freedoms* or 'choices' is illustrated in findings relating both to the identity theme (with the degree of autonomy afforded in their placement schools being one of the major contributors to some trainees' development of their identities as teachers and others looking forward to the freedom to establish their own routines once they had secured their first teaching post) and to the relationships theme (e.g. those trainees who encountered difficulties with mentors they perceived as too prescriptive). Finally, a desire for *fun* may be seen in, for example, the enjoyment procured or hoped for through the development of productive relationships, with pupils, teacher colleagues or mentors.

A final implication of the findings presented and discussed in this article thus concerns the advisability, for reasons relating to student teachers' self-efficacy, and to teacher and student teacher recruitment and retention, amongst others, of paying explicit attention at all levels of decision-making – from policy to local implementation – to student teachers' basic psychological needs."

Glasser, W. (1998) *Choice Theory*, New York: HarperCollins.
National College for School Leadership (NCSL) (2005) *Leading Personalised Learning in Schools*, Nottingham: NCSL.

Summary

Being a student ('trainee') teacher is a demanding personal experience that requires considerable engagement and commitment in the face of built-in challenges and risks, and which engenders, for many, highly charged affective responses. Student teachers are centrally concerned during this time with their changing identities, their relationships with others and the relevance of course provision. In some respects, student teachers' accounts of their experiences are systematically differentiated, especially depending on the initial teacher preparation route being followed, their age and their prior conceptions and expectations of teaching and of learning to teach. (Based on article abstract)

Questions to consider

1. How might student teachers' preconceptions impinge upon their experiences in school?
2. What strategies and approaches might tutors and host teachers employ such that Glasser's five needs are fulfilled?
3. What sort of considerations should tutors and host teachers take into account in determining the scope of a student teacher's freedom during school placement?

Investigations

Student teachers' perceptions. Interview a range of student teachers (1) before they commence school placement, and (2) close to the end of the placement concerning their expectations and aspirations.

Psychological security. Use the Glasser typology as a basis for interview questions to use with host teachers and tutors about the welfare of student teachers.

Critical episodes on placement. Interview a range of student teachers about the most significant events that happened during their school placement.

Think deeper

The age profile of trainee teachers shows that the majority of students pursuing a first degree begin the course in their late teens or early twenties, whereas postgraduate trainees tend to be in their twenties or thirties. However, cohorts include a significant proportion of more mature students, especially in early childhood studies courses (for children aged three to five years) and early years courses (for the lower primary age range). See Duncan (1999) for case studies about mature women entering teaching.

Hagger *et al.* (2008) found that although student teachers (trainees) all learn from classroom experience, the nature and extent of that learning vary considerably. They argue that there are limits to what beginning teachers with little accumulated experience of practice can learn from simply reflecting on their classroom practice. While some trainees were able to develop their knowledge and skills and function as competent classroom practitioners, there was no indication that they had learned how to go on learning. Other trainees regarded experience as important, but viewed it as but one of a range of sources of learning, as they continued to draw on the expertise of their tutors and mentors and on research and scholarship.

Duncan, D. (1999) *Becoming a Primary School Teacher: A study of mature women*, Stoke-on-Trent: Trentham Books.

Hagger, H., Burn, K., Mutton, T. and Brindley, S. (2008) 'Practice makes perfect? Learning to teach as a teacher', *Oxford Review of Education*, 34 (2), 159–78.

Think wider

Barnes (2008) explored the perceptions and experiences of secondary student teachers over the course of the training year. Five important themes emerged:

1. *Future-wishing and magical fantasies.* Future-wishing is a term invented by the author to indicate a feeling of 'fast forward' – waiting for the next event to happen, while still involved in current experiences, as if student teachers wish to be catapulted forward in time rather than focusing on the present.
2. *Time and workload.* Excessive workload and exhaustion are factors frequently identified as major concerns for student teachers, particularly at the start of the course, when many of them felt overwhelmed with new ideas, documentation and experiences and the lack of time.
3. *Becoming a 'real' teacher.* Becoming a 'real' teacher is perceived as something almost magical, which might float away unless they are being one in school every day.
4. *Professional decision making.* When fully involved in their main placement, the student teachers appear to reach a decision about teaching as a career; pivotal in these decisions appears to be a need for reassurance about their teaching ability.
5. *Discipline and class management.* Class management issues grow in perceived importance, with a peak at the start of each school placement; discipline and concerns about pupils' behaviour remain uppermost in the minds of some trainees throughout the year and can become a perceived or actual barrier to effective teaching.

Eilam and Poyas (2009) investigated the effect of an intervention course at Haifa University that included video-recorded teaching situations, transcripts of lessons, interviews with teachers and experts, and related tasks, on pre-service teachers' awareness of the complexity of teaching and their ability to construct an initial body of knowledge to facilitate further professional development. They found that in order to construct such holistic knowledge, student teachers needed to be keenly aware of the components of classroom teaching–learning episodes and their interrelations.

Perry *et al.* (2008) emphasise the importance of having emotionally literate teachers (as well as pupils). An emotionally literate teacher is described as someone who is 'aware of and understands their own feelings, listens to children, can use emotive language, understands that children have feelings too and takes these into account, [and] can empathise and provides a secure and comfortable environment for the children to learn in' (p. 35). The authors add that emotionally literate teachers need to have high self-regard, self-knowledge and emotional awareness, though stress that emotional literacy cannot be imposed upon staff and needs to be created through a whole-school approach. White (2009) claims that 'transformative teacher preparation' must engage at intellectual and at emotional levels with particular reference to gaining a better understanding of multicultural approaches when working with pre-service teachers. **Equality: see also Extract 56.**

Barnes, A. (2008) 'Future-wishing, magical fantasies, yet being "real": snapshots of student teachers' perceptions during their initial training', *Teacher Development*, 12 (1), 3–13.

Eilam, B. and Poyas, Y. (2009) 'Learning to teach: enhancing pre-service teachers' awareness of the complexity of teaching–learning processes', *Teachers and Teaching*, 15 (1), 87–107.

Perry, L., Lennie, C. and Humphreys, N. (2008) 'Emotional literacy in the primary classroom: teacher perceptions and practices', *Education 3–13*, 36 (1), 27–37.

White, K.R. (2009) 'Using pre-service teacher emotion to encourage critical engagement with diversity', *Studying Teacher Education*, 5 (1), 5–20.

Extract 30

Source

Davies, I., Mountford, P. and Gannon, A. (2009) '*Every Child Matters*: the perceptions of a sample of initial teacher education trainees in England', *European Journal of Teacher Education*, 32 (4), 383–99.

Introduction

Davies *et al.* discuss the results of their investigation into the understandings of trainee (student) teachers about the UK government's goals for young people in integrated systems of welfare provision as revealed in the policy document *Every Child Matters* (ECM), which resulted in the Children Act 2004. These authors' research was based on data from 197 initial teacher education trainees in three institutions in England drawn from six subject areas, and focused on (1) trainees' reactions to the anticipated outcomes of ECM, and (2) their confidence that they would be able to help implement the initiative in their roles as form tutors (home room teachers) and subject teachers.

Key words & phrases

Common sense, community support, complete overhaul, current teacher roles, ECM outcomes and roles, getting involved, knowledge of pupils, lack of comprehension, personal lives, pupil progress, traditional pastoral roles, trainees, working with others

---

Extract

"The trainees' difficulty in understanding ECM is revealed directly in their comments about the language used to express ECM outcomes and roles . . . We do not get a sense that the respondents had completely failed to understand ECM. We are not wishing to argue that there is a lack of comprehension of basic terms such as 'enjoy and achieve'. However, we are signalling their irritation with the jargon which is used to present ECM and suggesting that they are not clear about the nature of education that is being proposed. What, they seem to be asking, lies beneath the statements with which we, obviously, cannot disagree? . . .

They seem, for example, to judge that their contributions made to assessment for learning will be made principally as subject teachers. This may be true. This sort of response, however, does raise two other possibilities: first, that if there is an ECM vision to break down the barriers between current teacher roles (and we may have strengthened any existing notions of role distinctiveness by asking separately about these roles), then that is not accepted by our respondents; and, second, the trainees may not understand what can be done in order to operate more dynamically . . .

Perhaps there is more engagement with the nature of ECM when trainees expressed uncertainty about their experience and skills. This was, principally, apparent in relation to developing their knowledge of pupils and in working with others. There was uncertainty about the means by which an appropriate communication style could be developed and the ways in which key indicators related to ECM could be recognised. Trainees referred to 'parental resistance' and 'teacher apathy'. They expressed concern about what would be required by 'getting involved in pupils' personal lives' and wanted to 'ensure that my personal approach is appropriate'. They wanted to know how to 'take into consideration the background history of the children which I teach in order to appreciate the implications which may impinge on their behaviour and work produced'. Some worried that 'there are aspects of ECM that are hard to deal with – especially as teachers don't know the full story'. They expressed a lack of knowledge about what was meant by 'community support', suggested they needed to know about specific contexts such as 'pupil inclusion units' and 'partnership organisations' and wanted to know more about how to 'track pupil progress and create a safe and open environment' . . .

Some trainees in their responses to ECM outcomes and roles are asking explicitly what it means to be a teacher. They find it challenging to know whether ECM is a reaffirmation of traditional pastoral roles in schools or an attempt to transform the education system and their role in it. Some felt that ECM is 'really only common sense – most followed by teachers for years but by formalising procedures it adds to workload'. Others, however, suggested that ECM was an opportunity for 'the whole [education] system to have a complete overhaul'.

Summary

The research project revealed that the trainee teachers reacted positively to the concept of ECM but were unclear about its precise meaning and the roles they would need to adopt as teachers. Davies *et al*. conclude that it is unreasonable for governments to expect teacher educators and pre-service teachers to assist with the implementation of policies that lack sharpness of focus and clarity.

Questions to consider

1. What are the principal purposes of the ECM legislation?
2. What significant impact has the introduction of ECM had on the teacher's role and priorities?
3. What validity is attached to the view expressed by some trainee teachers that ECM is 'really only common sense – most followed by teachers for years but by formalising procedures it adds to workload'?

Investigations

Purpose of ECM. Conduct a survey of teachers' opinions as to (1) the principal purpose of ECM, and (2) the subsidiary purposes.

Impact of ECM on work. Interview a group of teachers about the impact that ECM has had upon their working practices and priorities.

Safeguarding children and young people. Interview school or college leaders about policy and practice with regard to safeguarding pupils.

Think deeper

Through accessing the voice of pupils aged seven to eleven years, Hopkins (2008) gained insight into what they believed to be the ideal 'classroom conditions' to enable them to enjoy and achieve at school. Hopkins argues that pupil voice and the active engagement of pupils in shaping their own educational experience are integral to the success of the 'enjoy and achieve' strand of the *Every Child Matters* programme. Data analysis indicated eight classroom conditions that contribute to their enjoyment and achievement in lessons: (1) activities that require participation; (2) an appropriate amount of teacher talk; (3) appropriate social demands made by activities; (4) opportunities for challenge and struggle; (5) a firm, fair, positive and psychologically safe regime; (6) a focus on the learning and achieving of individuals; (7) plenty of variety of activities; and (8) appropriate length of activities.

Cheminais (2009) provides practical suggestions for use by teaching assistants. **Teaching assistants: see also Extracts 43–45.**

Cheminais, R. (2009) *Every Child Matters: A practical guide for teaching assistants*, Abingdon: Routledge.

Hopkins, E.A. (2008) 'Classroom conditions to secure enjoyment and achievement: the pupils' voice: listening to the voice of *Every Child Matters*', *Education 3–13*, 36 (4), 393–401.

Think wider

In an article outlining the challenges involved in implementing ECM, Harris and Allen (2009) conclude by asserting that the idea of what constitutes a school is shifting dramatically. As schools move towards greater partnership, working with other schools, external agencies and other organisations, there will be inevitable challenges and periods of rapid change. The wider involvement of service users in decision making will require careful negotiation about roles and responsibilities. It is inevitable that, with such a major transformation, barriers and blockers exist and stand in the way of progress. Harris and Allen go on to say that schools that are successfully implementing ECM share the following strengths and characteristics:

- ECM is the central priority that drives the school's development agenda.
- Leadership is context attuned and community focused.
- Local authority support and guidance for schools is of the highest standard.
- Funding is used strategically and creatively to support the core priorities and ECM agenda.
- Leadership is distributed in the optimum way for the school and its partners.
- Parents, governors and community groups are involved in decision making.
- Targeted training is provided to staff, students and the community.
- ECM is aligned to workforce remodelling.
- The school has a strong internal locus of control; it is innovative, confident and outward-looking.
- ECM is considered central to raising standards.
- ECM is acknowledged as a student and community entitlement.

Harris and Allen are clear that this sort of transformation of education cannot happen in isolation from wider societal changes and reform of the public sector. They suggest that despite the challenges of implementing ECM, only through schools engaging with it in a significant and sustained way will the aspirations outlined in the Children's Plan and the recommendations made in the Laming Report (2003; see also Laming 2009) be achieved.

Harris, A. and Allen, T. (2009) 'Ensuring every child matters: issues and implications for school leadership', *School Leadership and Management*, 29 (4), 337–52.

Laming, Lord (2003) *The Victoria Climbié Inquiry: Report of an inquiry by Lord Laming*, Cm 5730, London: The Stationery Office.

Laming, Lord (2009) *The Protection of Children in England: A progress report*, HC 330, London: The Stationery Office.

Supervising and mentoring

Extract 31

Source

Hall, K.M., Draper, R.J., Smith, L.K. and Bullough, R.V. (2008) 'More than a place to teach: exploring the perceptions of the roles and responsibilities of mentor teachers', *Mentoring and Tutoring: Partnership in Learning*, 16 (3), 328–45.

Introduction

As the authors had experienced a wide variety of views about the school mentor's role with pre-service trainees, they designed a study in which they asked open-ended questions designed to allow the mentors to describe the ways in which they envisioned their role to 264 teachers serving as mentors. Follow-up telephone interviews were conducted with thirty-four randomly selected mentor teachers to further determine the relative value they placed on different aspects of mentoring.

Key words & phrases

Beginning teacher's learning, cooperating teacher, effective practice, mentoring, mentors' beliefs, pre-service teachers, roles and responsibilities, teacher educators, university educators, views of mentoring

Extract

"Our experience has suggested that universities and public schools likely hold very different conceptions of mentoring. We have often witnessed situations where a mentor is asked to take a pre-service teacher 'under her wing' but is not given any sense of the university's expectations and/or the kind of support that will be available during mentoring. In essence, the mentors have to 'make it up as they go along' and hence they may not understand the critical role they play beyond just providing the pre-service teachers with a place to teach . . .

These findings suggest that not only did the mentors hold views of mentoring that were different from those held by teacher educators, but they held views of mentoring that were different from each other's, based on whether they had encountered difficult and challenging pre-service teachers and whether these teachers had made adequate professional progress . . .

Believing that ways the mentors define effective practice and understand their mentoring roles and responsibilities do influence their practice, we sought to create an instrument that would identify mentors' beliefs concerning their abilities to carry out those roles and responsibilities . . .

Teacher educators generally agree on the conditions that distinguish mentoring as a professional practice from simply serving as a cooperating teacher. Indeed, mentoring should enable pre-service teachers opportunities to learn about teaching beyond what could be learned simply by trying things out in a classroom . . . mentor teachers must model effective practice and provide opportunities for beginning teachers to observe and critique practice, and coach the beginning teacher, including engaging in dialogue focused on practice. Ultimately, the mentor teacher must work to create a context that will facilitate the beginning teacher's learning, engage in discussion, reflection, and criticism of teaching (Loughran 2006). It is only when these conditions are present that a cooperating teacher is functioning as a mentor . . . we noted lack of a shared understanding between university teacher educators and public school teachers about the roles and responsibilities of mentoring, and we noticed a good deal of confusion about the meaning of the terms *mentor* and *mentoring*. The data analysis also revealed that what we initially took to be a normative concept for *mentoring* is, in fact, rarely held by teachers, who often think of mentoring as synonymous with the designation *cooperating teacher* and means nothing more than providing a place for the pre-service teacher to practise teaching and offering a little support.

Therefore, the results of the present research point toward a fundamental need to reconsider not only mentor selection processes but especially the nature of the interaction that takes place among university faculty, experienced mentors, and pre-service teachers. University-based teacher educators must collaborate with school-based teacher educators to conceptualise the work of mentors and to distinguish it from that of cooperating teachers, for whom giving support and offering a place to teach define good practice."

Loughran, J. (2006) *Developing a Pedagogy of Teacher Education: Understanding teaching and learning about teaching*, Abingdon: Routledge.

Summary

Hall *et al.* make an important distinction between the role of the mentor and that of the cooperating teacher. In discussing the characteristics of mentoring, they conclude that teachers who aspire to be true mentors must 'create a context that will facilitate the beginning teacher's learning, engage in discussion, reflection, and criticism of teaching'. Without these features, the host teacher's role is restricted to giving general support and offering a place for the trainee to teach.

Questions to consider

1. What distinguishes the process of mentoring from the process of tutoring? In what ways are the two terms equivalent?
2. Why is the interaction between university faculty members, experienced mentors and pre-service teachers so crucial? How can this be facilitated?
3. What unique role might cooperating ('host') teachers play in mentoring?

Investigations

Defining the mentor's role. Ask a range of people involved in supervising trainee teachers – mentors, tutors and host teachers – about the essentials of effective mentoring.

Mentor training. Conduct a survey among mentors about (1) the type and quality of their initial training; (2) the ways in which they have developed expertise as mentors; and (3) the limitations and constraints attached to their training and development.

Trainees' experiences of mentoring. Interview a range of trainee teachers about the type, quality and helpfulness of mentors and cooperating teachers they have encountered.

Think deeper

Lock *et al.* (2009) examined written lesson appraisals (WLAs) by thirty mentors of pre-service trainee teachers (secondary age phase) from two different mentoring regimes. The authors analysed the WLAs in terms of their length and content using professional knowledge categories derived from perceptions of the content of WLAs, as follows: 'topic-specific pedagogy', 'class management' and 'generic issues'. Considerable variations were found across the appraisals offered to the trainees, both in their length and in the emphasis given to each professional knowledge category. **Trainee teacher development: see also Extract 48.**

A study focusing on the nature and complexity of the role of the initial teacher training (ITT) coordinator/mentor in schools in England conducted by Mutton and Butcher (2007) found that while most time was spent carrying out administrative and organisational tasks, it was the pedagogical work that gave coordinators the most satisfaction and offered opportunity for significant growth and development. Findings identified a wide range of responsibilities for coordinators, which were defined to a great extent by the requirements of the ITT providers with whom the coordinators were working but also determined to a lesser extent by the coordinator's personal interests and initiative. The authors concluded that coordinators are well placed to provide leadership in effecting change and to use their experience and expertise as both teachers and teacher educators to ensure that they are doing more than just managing.

Lock, R., Soares, A. and Foster, J. (2009) 'Mentors' written lesson appraisals: the impact of different mentoring regimes on the content of written lesson appraisals and the match with pre-service teachers' perceptions of content', *Journal of Education for Teaching*, 35 (2), 133–43.

Mutton, T. and Butcher, J. (2007) 'More than managing? The role of the initial teacher training coordinator in schools in England', *Teacher Development*, 11 (3), 245–61.

Think wider

Hardy (2009) argues that time spent by pre-service trainee teachers on school placement should reflect praxis-orientated approaches to learning as well as more technical emphases. He describes praxis-oriented approaches as the desire to promote active and socio-politically informed learning in relation to assessment practices and tutorial discussions. By contrast, more technical emphases seem to override concerns about learning that derives from such practices when trainees are completing mandatory assessment tasks. Hardy suggests that the technical emphases originate, in part, from (1) concerns about accountability and performativity within the university; and (2) the conservative and unreflective ways in which teaching is undertaken by education tutors during formal sessions. He summarises the position by claiming that teaching practices are characterised by complex tensions between, on the one hand, tutor-centred tutorial discussions to fulfil 'accountability and performativity' requirements and, on the other hand, the provision of opportunities for students to actively engage with issues to make meaning out of them for themselves ('praxis'). **Trainee teacher perspectives: see Extracts 33 and 48.**

Hardy, I. (2009) 'Teaching for self or others? Lessons from an educator's log', *Teaching Education*, 20 (2), 163–74.

Extract 32

Source

Laker, A., Laker, J.C. and Lea, S. (2008) 'Sources of support for pre-service teachers during school experience', *Mentoring and Tutoring: Partnership in Learning*, 16 (2), 125–40.

Introduction

The purpose of the study was to report on the changing sources of support structures utilised by pre-service teachers during a series of school experiences (SEs). A sample of pre-service teachers in their last year of a four-year Bachelor of Education degree at a college in southern England were interviewed after their final school experience. The study raises questions about the maturing of pre-service teachers from one contextually located identity into another contextual but professional identity.

Key words & phrases

Assessment parity, college tutor, community of practice, conflict of priorities, constructivist theory, contextually relevant, full professional, learning about teaching, legitimate teacher tutor, peripheral participation, pre-service teachers, school experience, socially constructed

Extract

"When looking at the support structures available to pre-service teachers the situated learning theory of Lave and Wenger (1991) has much to commend it. This theory is based in the constructivist theory of learning and suggests that learning does not occur in isolation; rather, it is a social and active process . . . Becoming a teacher is a social process with pre-service teachers bringing a set of support structures that interact with new structures in the school. In this way their legitimate peripheral participation, i.e. their SE [school experience], partially equips them to become part of the community of practice, i.e. the teaching profession. Legitimate peripheral participation means that active involvement is real or authentic, and begins with novice status before moving towards full membership of the community as participants, developing the characteristics and relationships that signify sub-culture membership. For experience to be real and authentic it must assume some importance to its participants; the SE is certainly important to these pre-service teachers as their future careers depend upon it . . . A number of other issues arising from the data are worthy of further comment.

First, it was seen as important by the sample that higher education institutions provide clinical educational experiences that are contextually relevant and as similar as possible to real situations. In situated learning terms, this is called 'legitimate peripheral participation'. Many commented on the fact that the support that was most valuable was support that was immediate, relevant, collaborative, contextual and non-threatening . . .

A second point of note was an increasing awareness that teaching, and learning about teaching, are essentially social activities. The least threatening of all sources of support and the most easily given and received support was from other pre-service teachers in social situations. Interactions with teacher tutors were also quite social in nature, probably because of their proximity to the pre-service teachers during SE. The least social of all sources of support were the college tutors . . . This may be due to the lack of common social territory; the pre-service teachers were not seeking acceptance into the college tutors' social world, but they were attempting to become part of another community of practice (i.e. the world of teachers) . . .

This naturally leads into a third theme . . . There comes a time when pre-service teachers, rightly or wrongly, consider themselves to be full members of the community of teachers. For some this is earlier than others, and some are reluctant to let go of the safe and familiar environment of the college. By the end of the series of the SEs there was a majority of responses in the data indicating a readiness to be considered a full professional, a part of a bigger community of practice. This evolution is also somewhat evident in the shifting influence from the college tutor to school-based teacher tutor . . .

The final theme that warrants further comment is that of assessment parity and moderation of the whole school experience. It will have been clear from the data that college tutors have ultimate responsibility for assigning the grade for the SE. It will also be clear that the final grade, in good practice, is usually assigned after considerable discussion and consultation with the teacher tutor. While this process is known to the pre-service teachers, there still remains an uncertainty and an anxiety about how the process really works. This is manifested in a doubt about whom the pre-service teacher should try to please most. In extreme cases, the pre-service teacher experiences a conflict of priorities and is uncertain whose requirements should predominate: the remote but influential college tutor or the teacher tutor with whom they work on a daily basis?"

Lave, J. and Wenger, E. (1991) *Situated Learning: Legitimate peripheral participation*, New York: Cambridge University Press.

See also Wenger, E. (1998) *Communities of Practice: Learning, meaning and identity*, Cambridge: Cambridge University Press.

Summary

Evidence suggested that the respondents moved from formal to informal sources of support as they progressed through series of school experiences. They particularly valued immediate professional support and advice from their teacher tutors and the social support of their pre-service and teacher colleagues. Findings suggest that learning to teach is a constructivist activity where novices move from peripheral participation into a full community of practice – the world of teachers – as suggested by situated learning theory. (Based on article abstract)

Questions to consider

1. To what extent do you agree that learning is a social and active process rather than an individual one?

2. What strategies can a trainee teacher employ to begin the transition from peripheral participation towards full membership of the school community?

3. What part does assessment of teaching competence play in facilitating or hindering a trainee's attempts to become a full member of the school community?

Investigations

New teacher rite of passage. Interview existing staff about the things that new teachers need to be aware of and adjust to in order to facilitate their rite of passage into the community of practice.

Trainee teachers' perceptions. Interview trainee and/or newly qualified teachers about the quality and appropriateness of their clinical educational experiences that are contextually relevant ('legitimate peripheral participation') as defined by Laker *et al*.

Assessment of trainee teachers. Ask a teacher tutor and college tutor to observe and evaluate the same lesson independently. Compare and contrast their perceptions. Note: select a highly competent trainee; ensure that he or she is comfortable with the prospect of being closely observed; use the observation formatively rather than an assessment of competence.

Think deeper

Hale and Starratt (1989) interviewed eight student teachers in the United States to determine whether rites of passage are experienced by new teachers in the teaching culture. They reported their findings using three stages in the rite of passage: separation, transition and incorporation. In an associated but more comprehensive study, McNamara *et al*. (2002) explain how classical anthropologists presented transitions in terms of three phases: (1) separation; (2) transition; and (3) reincorporation; these phases are also referred to as (1) preliminal; (2) liminal; and (3) post-liminal. The transition stage was depicted as the liminal stage of a 'rite of passage'. McNamara *et al*. explored student teachers' perceptions of the most recently imposed 'ritual ordeal' (the numeracy skills test in England), and described the process as a 'rite of intensification' used by government to police the boundaries of the teaching profession. McNamara *et al*. present the rite of passage as a complex process of what they refer to as extended and ambiguous 'in-betweenness' involving play, performance and ordeal. They depict pre-service teachers' symbolic acts and undertaking of 'ritual ordeals'. They also report how trainees narrate their passage as a complex game of 'being' and 'becoming'. **Rites of passage: see also Extract 28.**

Lawless (2008) explores links between communities of practice theory and critical action learning and highlights how 'legitimate peripheral participation' can provide an analytical tool for understanding learning by shifting the analytical focus from the learner as an individual to learning as participation in the social world.

Hale, L. and Starratt, R.J. (1989) 'Rites of passage: a case study of teacher preparation', *Journal of Educational Administration*, 27 (3), 24–9.

Lawless, A. (2008) 'Action learning as legitimate peripheral participation', *Action Learning*, 5 (2), 117–29.

McNamara, O., Roberts, L., Basit, T.N. and Brown, T. (2002) 'Rites of passage in initial teacher training', *British Educational Research Journal*, 28 (6), 863–78.

Think wider

As part of a new teacher's development, a fellow staff member is allocated as mentor, officially known as the *induction tutor* or *teacher tutor* (in Northern Ireland). Jonson (2008) emphasises that such a person must possess high-quality mentoring skills, such as demonstration teaching, positive observation and feedback, informal communication, role modelling and providing direct assistance. The induction tutor is likely to be a senior teacher, though in a smaller school it may be the deputy head or, in the case of small primary schools, the headteacher. The tutor encourages the new teacher to contribute to working parties and visit other local schools to enhance his or her experience of education. The tutor is also available to offer advice about diverse aspects of school life, such as time management, handling paperwork, dealing with troublesome children, relating to parents and maintaining a reasonable work–home balance (see Bubb 2007).

Bubb, S. (2007) *Successful Induction for New Teachers*, London: Paul Chapman.

Jonson, K.F. (2008) *Being an Effective Mentor: How to help beginning teachers succeed*, London: Corwin Press.

Extract 33

Source

Hastings, W. (2008) 'I felt so guilty: emotions and subjectivity in school-based teacher education', *Teachers and Teaching*, 14 (5/6), 497–513.

Introduction

Hastings reports her findings from a study that focused on the emotional dimension of the practicum (school experience/school placement/teaching practice) for school-based teacher educators (school mentors/tutors) as they support pre-service teacher colleagues (student/trainee teachers) in New South Wales. The extract deals with a specific situation in which an experienced teacher mentor is emotionally distressed by her encounters with a recalcitrant first-year trainee teacher ('Neil') and her subsequent feelings of powerlessness as matters are taken out of her hands when she seeks support and help.

Key words & phrases

Behaviour, bewilderment, classroom teacher, education student, emotional distress, expectations, guilt, intersecting discourses, isolation, lack of preparedness, make sense, power relations, powerlessness, practicum, pre-conflicting emotions, programme, refusal

Extract

"Therese is a woman of maturity and an experienced classroom teacher who had previously supported pre-service teachers with few problems or tensions. In relation to this study, she worked with a young first year undergraduate primary education student who I have named Neil. Neil was placed at Therese's school for a four-week block practicum, typical of many undergraduate pre-service teacher education programmes . . .

Therese described the circumstances surrounding her time with Neil as 'very difficult' and 'particularly unpleasant' – unlike anything she had known before . . . Therese recalls experiencing guilt, anger, frustration, shame, regret, fear, relief, sadness and a sense of isolation during and after her time working with Neil . . .

She described how he undertook to do everything his own way . . . He appeared disdainful of her support, refusing to acknowledge her skills as a teacher and incorporate Therese's suggestions into his lesson design, even when, according to Therese, it was not appropriate for the students with whom he was to work. When he was given simple directions, such as attending playground duty, he simply ignored her . . . It was behaviours such as these that resulted in Therese's decision to notify the University that Neil was at risk of failing the practicum. The decision to contact the University in relation to Neil's progress resulted in a series of events that caused further emotional distress for Therese . . .

Therese, like many other teachers, experiences an ever-changing range of emotions in her daily work. What is particularly noteworthy in a study such as this is the heightened complexity of relationships and emotions evident when another person comes to work in the classroom. Here we have seen how Therese struggled to make sense of the situation in which she was placed as school-based teacher educator. She attempted to understand the attitudes and behaviours of a young male pre-service teacher for whom she was given responsibility. She had certain expectations of how he should behave and respond, based on her own experiences with previous pre-service teachers. She also had expectations from experiences with her own children in terms of how he should behave with an adult. In addition, she could draw on the experiences of her colleagues. However, those expectations coalesced to form her 'construction' of a pre-service teacher, which did not match Neil's beliefs about how he could or should 'be' as a pre-service teacher . . . Simultaneously, she struggled to make sense of the intersecting discourses in which she found herself positioned – as teacher, colleague, mother, gatekeeper, assessor– and the conflicting emotions which resulted from her attempts to operate within the competing discourses. She felt frustration when she could not make clear to her colleagues the need to balance the role of supporter/nurturer with that of gatekeeper/assessor/task master; she felt a maternal and professional sense of loss when her request for assistance in dealing with Neil resulted in loss of control over the situation; she felt a sense of bewilderment in relation to the difference in behaviour between her own children and the 'child' Neil when she adopted the discourse of carer.

Therese's negative emotional experiences were exaggerated because other critical colleagues did not respond as she had expected. When she needed support, both the principal and university supervisor took control of the situation from Therese, thus rendering her powerless – a response that Therese did not expect . . . Therese's identity in these situations was constituted through power relations rather than some given or fixed element – on one hand she is constructed as caring and nurturing while at the same time firm and controlling, and in another instance, found wanting. Running in tandem with these constructions is the disciplining of her emotional expression – she is shaken by the experience with her student so her principal marginalises her; she fails to 'discipline' her student, so her colleagues marginalise her; and when she fails to 'control' her emotions and exhibits anger she creates further emotions in terms of guilt, i.e. reproducing the emotions."

Summary

It is clear from Hastings' research that support and training for school educators/mentors/tutors must give attention to the self-development associated with negative emotions that arise in situations of conflict. Educators' knowledge of school cultures, power relations and ideology in which emotions are embedded would benefit by allowing them opportunities to explore the nature of school-based pre-service teacher education as a specific 'discursive frame' to better understand causes of the heightened emotions and reduce the impact of negative emotions.

Questions to consider

1. What does Neil's attitude tell us about (a) his preparation prior to the school placement/practicum; (b) his personality; and (c) differing expectations about his behaviour?
2. To what extent can we discern the impact and influence on Neil's behaviour on (a) the school context, and (b) the teacher's attitude?
3. Why did the teacher feel powerless and helpless? What was the impact upon her emotional state? What are the likely implications for her future work with trainee (pre-service) teachers?

Investigations

Mentors' experiences with trainee teachers. Interview mentors or tutors who have been responsible for trainees about the issues that caused them greatest concern and occasions that afforded them greatest satisfaction.

Trainee teachers' experiences of school placement. Interview trainee teachers of newly qualified teachers about the issues that caused them greatest concern during school placement, and occasions that afforded them greatest joy.

Keeping diaries on school placement. Ask several trainee teachers to keep a diary (video, written, spoken) of their emotions just prior to, midway through and following their time on school placement.

Think deeper

Trainee teachers on school placement have to observe protocol, both overt and subtle forms (Hayes 2003, chapter 4). Obvious ways include the structure of the timetable, the extent of specialist teaching and the types of extra-curricular opportunities. Subtle ways include the nature of the relationship between teaching and support staff, the tone of staff room conversations, social divisions and expectations about conformity in teaching. Trainees have to tread a fine line between demonstrating their confidence and aptitude for teaching, and inadvertently coming across as supercilious or overbearing. If trainees are too cautious, they are unlikely to impress the supervising teacher; if they are too brash, they may irritate the existing staff. Boyd and West (2010) insist that beginning teachers should be encouraged to evaluate their progress through the use of self-audit tools at the end of each phase of their training. This process would be linked to portfolio development, which is a feature of most initial teacher education routes.

A study by White (2009) from the perspective of a white, female, middle-class teacher educator in the United States attempted to help pre-service teachers to think beyond their own experiences. White argues that transformative teacher preparation must be engaging on both intellectual and emotional levels. While the implications of the findings support the personal value of self-study, they also contribute to our understanding of multicultural approaches when working with pre-service teachers. White concludes by asserting that emotion can be used as a strategy to encourage predominantly white, middle-class and privileged individuals to listen to multiple perspectives, hear what the different perspectives say and compare the perspectives with their own experiences. This type of emotional engagement must be supported by establishing a learning environment that develops a cohesive classroom community, connects theory to practice and encourages student teachers to take a stand on important issues.

Boyd, P. and West, L. (2010) *Successful Secondary School Placement*, Maidenhead: Open University Press.

Hayes, D. (2003) *A Student Teacher's Guide to Primary School Placement*, London: Routledge.

White, K.R. (2009) 'Using pre-service teacher emotion to encourage critical engagement with diversity', *Studying Teacher Education*, 5 (1), 5–20.

Think wider

Barnett (2008) argues that the nature of successful mentoring relationships brings with it certain risks for participants, including inappropriate sexual behaviour. He insists that issues of boundaries and multiple relationships must be understood and successfully navigated to help ensure that mentors' objectivity and judgement are not impaired and that the people being mentored are not exploited or harmed. Although the study deals with the professional development of psychologists, Barnett provides helpful suggestions about establishing and maintaining appropriate relational boundaries without damaging the essence of the mentor–protégé relationship. He emphasises that a mentor's action is often less important than the intent behind it.

Trout (2008) chronicles the journey she made as a teaching supervisor when she worked with one of her student teachers in a school in the United States. She charts the many issues that arose around ethical care as she tried to engage the student teacher in dialogue about his growth as a beginning educator. Trout portrays her ongoing struggle to allow his needs to guide their relationship while simultaneously responding to the continuing issues that arise from the ongoing assessment of his performance.

Barnett, J.E. (2008) 'Mentoring, boundaries, and multiple relationships: opportunities and challenges', *Mentoring and Tutoring*, 16 (1), 3–16.

Trout, M. (2008) 'The supervision dance: learning to lead and follow a student teacher', *The New Educator*, 4 (3), 383–99.

Teacher development

Professional identity

Source

Nias, J. (1989) *Primary Teachers Talking: A study of teaching as work*, London: Routledge; see pp. 202–5.

Introduction

Jennifer Nias's classic book presents an insider's view of teaching through interviewing primary teachers and using their written accounts to present 'a living picture of what teaching is like for those who practise it' (p. 1). In doing so, the author allows teachers to voice their own thoughts and feelings to reveal, as Nias admits, 'a distorted picture of the messy, uncertain complexity which is teaching' (p. 2).

Key words & phrases

Educational ideas, human nature, intermittent narcissism, kindly older colleagues, occupational competence, person, possessive dependence, potentially dangerous emotions, primary teacher, reference groups, resistance to change, self, self-image, socially constructed, socially regulated selves, substantial self, symbolic interactionism

Extract

"The teacher as a person is held by many within the profession and outside it to be at the centre of not only the classroom but also the educational process. By implication, therefore, it matters to teachers themselves, as well as to their pupils, who and what they are. Their self-image is more important to them as practitioners than is the case in occupations where the person can easily be separated from the craft.

It follows that an understanding of primary teachers must rest upon some conceptualisation of the notion of 'self'. I have accepted the formulation offered by symbolic interactionism, which sees the self as, simultaneously, socially constructed (the 'me') and autonomous (the 'I').

I have argued throughout this book that no account of primary teachers' experience is complete if it does not make room for potentially dangerous emotions such as love, rage and jealousy on the one hand, and intermittent narcissism and outbreaks of possessive dependence on the other. Although much of this book focuses upon teachers' socially regulated 'selves', their own descriptions of their feelings about pupils, and their relationship with them and with their colleagues, reminds us that the regressive, passionate and unruly aspects of human nature are always present in the classroom and may sometimes escape from rational control.

The 'me' is a less slippery concept than the 'I', in part because we create it by self-reflection and are therefore conscious of its existence and nature. In other words, it *develops*, as from childhood we respond to the actions and expectations of 'significant' and 'generalised' others. Because it may alter as we interact with different people in different contexts, we can be said to have multiple 'situational' selves. But part of the 'me' is not susceptible to environmental influences. The 'substantial self', a set of self-defining beliefs, values and attitudes, develops alongside our situational selves and is highly resistant to change. Our most salient beliefs about 'the sort of person I am' are deeply internalised and are not easily altered. In consequence, the core of our self-image is well defined and stable . . .

Although the professional focus of individual teachers altered over time, they were always at pains to protect their substantial selves from change, avoiding the necessity to behave 'in ways I don't believe in' and the company of those who 'think differently from me'. From the start of their careers they developed strategies that protected their 'selves' from situational influences while at the same time allowing them to draw upon the support and companionship of the rest of the staff group (particularly that of kindly older colleagues, whom they cast in the role of 'professional parents') . . . Reference groups which were located within individuals' schools were particularly potent in protecting them from situational influences, but discussion with likeminded people outside the school also had the effect of stiffening their resistance to change within it. In many cases it also helped them make up their minds to leave the profession."

Summary

Nias emphasises the significance of the 'self' and identifies two strands: (1) the 'I' that is shaped and influenced by external factors – the social world we inhabit; and (2) the 'me' that is largely immune to the influences of external social factors and created through core beliefs and convictions, though these necessarily evolve as we reflect on and consider them throughout our lives. Teachers are necessarily constrained by external demands and expectations but Nias's study shows that they are unwilling to compromise on beliefs and practices that define what she refers to as their 'substantial selves', largely driven by altruistic motives.

Questions to consider

1. How do teachers maintain a balance between meeting externally imposed requirements and guarding their substantial selves?
2. What sorts of actions and decisions as teachers define and illustrate 'the sort of person I am'?
3. What sorts of reference groups might teachers utilise and what particular role does each group play in defining them as teachers and stiffening their resistance to change?

Investigations

Protecting the self. Interview teachers to find out what sort of teacher they aspire to be, the constraints placed upon them and ways in which they conspire to protect their core beliefs.

Caring teachers. Conduct a group discussion with teachers or trainees to discuss their understanding of what it means to be a caring teacher.

Reference groups. Conduct a survey (possibly through a questionnaire) asking teachers to list the people whom they consult about educational issues, the reasons for using them and other strategies to bolster self-esteem and confidence.

Think deeper

Taylor (2002) found that over 80 per cent of a group of fifty-five experienced teachers opted for an approach that can be broadly defined as 'child centred' (Doddington and Hilton 2007), which is defined as follows (see p. 34):

- Learning comes naturally to pupils.
- Children or students learn because they want to learn and not because they are told to do so.
- Play and work are indistinguishable.
- Learning is a communal activity rather than individual.
- The main aim of teaching is to develop the whole person (academic, social, spiritual).
- The curriculum should be related to the child's or student's needs.
- The teacher should encourage children to develop their own mode of learning.

These beliefs are almost identical to those of primary teachers a generation earlier (Ashton *et al.* 1975). Only about one-fifth of the teachers in Taylor's sample group aligned themselves with the prevailing official view that (1) learning is never easy; (2) children must be made to work; (3) play is not work; (4) learning is an individual thing; (5) the main aim of teaching is to develop the intellect; (6) the curriculum should relate to societal needs; and (7) the teacher's job is to motivate and direct learning.

Ashton, P., Kneen, P. and Davies, F. (1975) *Aims into Practice in the Primary School*, London: Hodder & Stoughton.

Doddington, C. and Hilton, M. (2007) *Child-Centred Education*, London: Sage.

Taylor, P.H. (2002) 'Primary teachers' views of what helps and hinders teaching', *Education 3–13*, 31 (2), 34–9.

Think wider

Teaching relies heavily on the creation and maintenance of a bond of trust and mutual respect between adult and pupil. Paterson and Esarte-Sarries (2003) noted from their interviews with classroom teachers that rather than emphasising simple 'one–way' didactic practice, reciprocal communication was preferred, communication that relied on feedback or contributions from pupils. The attempt to 'negotiate understandings' and 'dig deeper into meaning' drew attention to 'the important link . . . between reciprocal communication and the presence of an appropriate classroom climate or environment, and thus implicitly the social and emotional needs of pupils' (p. 90). **Pupil–adult interactions: see Extracts 21 and 22.**

Paterson, F. and Esarte-Sarries, V. (2003) 'Digging deeper: a typology of interactive teaching', in Moyles, J., Hargreaves, L., Merry, R., Paterson, F. and Esarte-Sarries, V., *Interactive Teaching in the Primary School*, Maidenhead: Open University Press.

Extract 35

Source

Kelchtermans, G. (2009) 'Who I am in how I teach is the message: self-understanding, vulnerability and reflection', *Teachers and Teaching*, 15 (2), 257–72.

Introduction

Kelchtermans argues that the person of the teacher is an essential element in what constitutes professional teaching and therefore needs careful conceptualisation. Central concepts are 'professional self-understanding' and 'subjective educational theory' as components of the personal interpretative framework every individual teacher develops throughout his or her career. This personal framework results from the reflective and meaningful interactions between the individual teacher and the social, cultural and structural working conditions constituting his or her job context(s). (Based on article abstract)

Key words and phrases

Career stories, deeply held beliefs, future perspective, good education, job motivation, moral integrity, person of the teacher, self-esteem, self-image, self-understanding, task perception

Extract

"My analysis of teachers' career stories resulted in the identification of five components that together make up teachers' self-understanding: self-image, self-esteem, task perception, job motivation and future perspective . . .

The *self-image* is the descriptive component, the way teachers typify themselves as teachers. This image is based on self-perception, but to a large degree also on what others mirror back to the teachers (e.g. comments from pupils, parents, colleagues, principals, etc.) . . .

Very closely linked to the self-image is the evaluative component of the self-understanding or the *self-esteem*. Self-esteem refers to the teacher's appreciation of his/her actual job performance (how well am I doing in my job as a teacher?). Again the feedback from others is important, but that feedback is filtered and interpreted . . . Self-esteem further refers to the fact that emotions matter a great deal in teaching as well. Positive self-esteem is crucial for feeling at ease in the job, for experiencing job satisfaction and a sense of fulfilment, for one's well-being as a teacher . . . Those positive self-evaluations, however, are fragile, fluctuate in time and have to be re-established time and again . . .

The self-esteem as the evaluative component has to be understood as intertwined with the normative component of self-understanding: the *task perception*. This encompasses the teacher's idea of what constitutes his/her professional programme, his/her tasks and duties in order to do a good job. It reflects a teacher's personal answer to the question: what must I do to be a proper teacher? What are the essential tasks I have to perform in order to have the justified feeling that I am doing well? What do I consider as legitimate duties to perform and what do I refuse to accept as part of 'my job'? . . . The task perception encompasses deeply held beliefs about what constitutes good education, about one's moral duties and responsibilities in order to do justice to students. When these deeply held beliefs are questioned – and the risk that this happens is always present (see below) – teachers feel that they themselves as a person are called into question. Evaluation systems, new regulations, calls for educational change that differ from or contradict teachers' task perception will deeply affect their self-esteem, their job satisfaction . . .

The *job motivation* (or conative component) refers to the motives or drives that make people choose to become a teacher, to stay in teaching or to give it up for another career . . . It is important to note, however, that the motives for working as a teacher may develop over time. Especially with secondary school teachers, I often found shifts in their motivation. Most of them first of all got into teaching because of their love for and interest in their subject discipline. Over time, however, several of them came to understand that their work, presence, actions were also meaningful to their students for other reasons than just being a qualified source of subject matter knowledge. Meaning something as a person to youngsters who are struggling with their life project, their individual identity, with growing up – in other words, being important to them in a broader educational sense – became a very motivating factor in their careers as well as a source for job satisfaction and positive self-esteem.

Finally, self-understanding also includes a time-element: the *future perspective* reveals a teacher's expectations about his/her future in the job ('how do I see myself as a teacher in the years to come and how do I feel about it?'). This component explicitly also refers to the dynamic character of the self-understanding. It is not a static, fixed identity, but rather the result of an ongoing interactive process of sense-making and construction. It thus also indicates how temporality pervades self-understanding: one's actions in the present are influenced by meaningful experiences in the past and expectations about the future. The person of the teacher is always somebody at some particular moment in his/her life, with a particular past and future."

Summary

Kelchterman's analysis of the five components making up a teacher's self-understanding helps us to understand that the person of the teacher relies on the way that he or she is perceived by others; emotional well-being; moral integrity; motivation for becoming or remaining a teacher; and the situational context. Teaching is dynamic inasmuch as these components change and transform over time. The person of the teacher is therefore never static.

Questions to consider

1. How can a school culture affect a teacher's self-image and self-esteem?
2. What strategies can be employed to ensure that teachers' emotions are safeguarded?
3. What do you understand by the phrase 'the person of the teacher'? How would you describe your own 'person'? How has it changed over time?

Investigations

The impact of comments. Interview a number of colleagues about the way in which comments or feedback adversely or positively affected their confidence and motivation.

Tracking emotional well-being. Ask a few colleagues to keep a straightforward log or diary of their emotional condition over a period of (say) three weeks. Discuss with them the implications of the variations.

Changing states of motivation. Interview a number of younger and more experienced colleagues about their motivation for the job of teaching.

Think deeper

From the responses of 241 recently graduated teachers, Cooman (2007) concluded that teachers consider intrinsic, altruistic and interpersonal features as strong job-specific motivators, while non-teachers are more attracted by individualistic work values such as career opportunities and executive power. There appear to be a number of factors influencing a teacher's self-worth: (1) general competence and skills; (2) gaining approval from significant others (e.g. parents); (3) receiving support from colleagues; (4) being convinced that teaching makes a positive difference to children's lives; and (5) strong moral convictions, including religious faith. A contradiction exists in that teachers often complain about the unreasonable demands placed on them yet they continue to remain in the job, which suggests that altruism and motivation generally outweigh self-doubt.

Canadian researchers Beauchamp and Thomas (2009) provide an overview of the issues revealed in recent discussions of teacher identity: (1) the problem of defining the concept; (2) the place of the self and related issues of agency, emotion, narrative and discourse; (3) the role of reflection; and (4) the influence of contextual factors. Beauchamp and Thomas admit that student teachers in particular face numerous challenges as they progress through teacher education and into their first post: negotiating within shifting conceptions of what teaching is or should be; and relating to the identities of others and becoming agents of their own identity development. For these trainees, the person they aspire to be is in part constrained and shaped by the person that others (e.g. supervisors, tutors) *want* them to be. **Rite of passage: see also Extracts 28 and 32.**

Beauchamp, C. and Thomas, L. (2009) 'Understanding teacher identity: an overview of issues in the literature and implications for teacher education', *Cambridge Journal of Education*, 39 (2), 175–89.

Cooman, R.D. (2007) 'Graduate teacher motivation for choosing a job in education', *International Journal for Educational and Vocational Guidance*, 7 (2), 123–36.

Think wider

Mertler (2001) examined the current state of teacher motivation among predominantly white, female elementary, middle and high school teachers in the United States. They responded to a web-based survey that examined their overall level of job satisfaction as a teacher. Data analysis indicated that 77 per cent of teachers were satisfied with their work. Males were slightly more satisfied as teachers than females. Teachers early in their careers and near the end of their careers indicated the highest levels of job satisfaction. More teachers in their early twenties and thirties indicated that they would choose to be teachers again. Males reported knowing significantly more unmotivated teachers than did females, and 23 per cent of respondents reported knowing or working with more than ten teachers they would classify as unmotivated. **Motivation for teaching: see also Extracts 59 and 60.**

As part of an exploration of what has constituted, and presently does constitute, a 'good teacher' from an Australian perspective, Connell (2009) makes proposals for a new understanding based on the labour process and occupational dynamics of teaching; the intellectual structure of education studies; and the overall logic of education itself. She argues that education is fundamentally a process of forming a culture; an adequate concept of good teaching includes teachers' roles in the social action required to create good learning environments for pupils.

Connell, R. (2009) 'Good teachers on dangerous ground: towards a new view of teacher quality and professionalism', *Critical Studies in Education*, 50 (3), 213–29.

Mertler, C.A. (2001) 'Teacher motivation and job satisfaction in the new millennium', paper presented at the Annual Meeting of the Mid-Western Educational Research Association, Chicago, 24–27 October 2001.

Extract 36

Source

Cohen, J.L. (2008) 'That's not treating you as a professional: teachers constructing complex professional identities through talk', *Teachers and Teaching*, 14 (2), 79–93.

Introduction

Cohen claims that the notion of teacher professional identity, framed in a variety of ways, engages people across social contexts, whether as educators, parents, students, taxpayers, voters or consumers of news and popular media. The article investigates the identity talk of three mid-career teachers, Tim, Sondra and Avery, in an urban public school in the United States as a means of gaining a better understanding of how teachers use language to accomplish complex professional identities. Note the significance of teacher as collaborator.

Key words & phrases

Agents of change, collaborator, community, critical engagement, discursive strategies, multiple contexts, professional growth, social practices, talk, teacher identity, values and practices

---

Extract

"The aim of this study was to better understand how teacher identity, as a social role identity, gets defined and enacted in local contexts through talk . . . to ask how teachers use explicit and implicit meaning to accomplish a role identity as teacher in a particular context and how teacher talk functions as cultural work . . .

The analysis in this article focuses on how teachers accomplished the implicit identity claim of teacher as collaborator. I found that each of the teachers made this implicit identity claim and linked it with professional identity, but they defined it differently, using a range of discourse strategies to construct, and sometimes enact, the qualities they associated with collaboration. The teachers situated teacher identity in relation to other people and institutional practices. They used conversation as a site for negotiating existing social practices regarding teacher identity, including work structures and beliefs about teacher competence and motivation. Tim defined collaboration in terms of professional development by emphasising the need for teachers have a common sense of purpose, which they build by regularly sharing information about daily practice and vision. Sondra emphasised the need for teachers to identify with the group as a whole and collaborate in non-exclusive ways that build community. Avery argued that collaboration is at the heart of a teacher professional identity committed to praxis. In other words, a single implicit identity claim takes on differing significances in terms of professional identity. In this case, collaboration can define professional identity itself, enable professional growth, and build a community.

The implicit role claim of teacher as collaborator functioned in the teachers' identity talk as a counter-discourse emphasising teachers' professional role as knowledge producers rather than information deliverers, collaborative, rather than isolated and, for some of the teachers, as agents of change engaged in critical analysis to plan action. Awareness of how these counter discourses operate in the teachers' conversation helps us better understand teachers' identity talk as cultural work through which teachers negotiate significances for the role identity of teacher.

Within this conversation, the teachers often addressed the values and practices of others as important constraints and resources in accomplishing professional identity . . . teachers are not free to completely recreate this role identity, nor are they completely constrained by the effects of existing or prior social structures. Though they clearly responded to existing social and material constraints, the teachers used discursive strategies to make distinctions and arguments about the role identity of teacher, often locating teacher identity in multiple contexts, including graduate school, other high schools, outside organisations, classroom practice, planning meetings and institutional practices such as professional development. The teachers also located teacher identity in relation to the range of other people indexed by their discursive strategies . . .

The teachers' active, critical engagement in theorising professional identity suggests that ample opportunities to engage in identity talk should be an important part of teachers' professional environment, in order to support teachers' ability to accomplish reflective professional identities."

Summary

Cohen uses analysis of teacher discourse ('conversation') during planning sessions to identify the ways in which teachers perceive themselves and their role. He found that rather than a single form of discourse, the teachers used a number of 'discursive strategies' located in a variety of contexts. Cohen argues for teachers' implicit identities to form a more substantial part of discussions at an institutional level.

Questions to consider

1. What factors contribute towards understanding 'implicit teacher identity'?
2. What part does collaboration play in shaping and refining teacher identity?
3. In what ways might teachers play a more integral role in the institutional discourse shaping teacher identity and practice?

Investigations

Discussion of teacher roles. Initiate and record a discussion between colleagues about the nature of their roles. Take particular note of the sorts of metaphors, examples and distinctions that they use.

External influences. Interview teachers about the ways in which different external agencies influence their perceptions of their role and subsequent behaviour.

Teachers' role priorities. Draw up a list of (say) twelve different teacher roles and use the list as a basis for a survey of teachers' priorities by placing in rank order. Discuss the overall findings with a representative group of teachers.

Think deeper

Day *et al.* (2007) and Hayes (2009, chapter 2) provide an in-depth description of teachers' work and lives. The various roles occupied by teachers have many facets but are dominated by functional aspects, including curriculum implementation, planning lessons, assessing pupil progress and compiling reports. Motivating factors such as altruism, compassion, love for children and the fulfilment of working in a school environment sometimes have to be subordinated to these pragmatic concerns. A teacher also has to be influential beyond the classroom door in areas of personal relationships with support staff, contact with parents and visitors, demonstrating initiative with respect to health and safety issues and being a positive presence around the school. Six key influences appear to affect a teacher's identity: (1) the intense pace of life in school, with a lack of opportunity for thoughtful reflection; (2) coping immediately with daily occurrences such as resolving disputes between pupils; (3) offering support to colleagues in an effort to maintain harmony and promote collegiality; (4) shortage of time to achieve all that needs to be accomplished, regardless of how long and hard they work; (5) disconnection and reduced opportunities for liaison with colleagues; and (6) organisational demands.

Day, C., Sammons, P., Stobart, G., Kington, A. and Gu, Q. (2007) *Teachers Matter: Connecting work, lives and effectiveness*, London: McGraw-Hill International.

Hayes, D. (2009) *Primary Teaching Today*, Abingdon: Routledge.

Think wider

Palmer (1997, online) defines *identity* as an evolving nexus where

> all the forces that constitute my life converge in the mystery of self: my genetic makeup; the nature of the man and woman who gave me life; the culture in which I was raised; people who have sustained me and done me harm; the good and ill I have done to others and to myself; and the experience of love and suffering.

Palmer argues that *integrity* 'requires that I discern what is integral to my selfhood, what fits and what does not – and that I choose life-giving ways of relating to the forces that converge within me . . . By choosing integrity, I become more whole'; however, this form of wholeness should not be confused with perfection.

Writing from the perspective of pre-service teachers of English, Alsup (2005) insists that attention to how the teacher's identity develops from teacher education is itself an education. She emphasises that the intersection of the personal and professional in teacher identity formation is more complex than is acknowledged in typical methods classes. Alsup proposes that educating others while being educated is where the student teacher must begin the process of professional identity. The work of learning to teach and then the process of doing so in a classroom situation necessitate being part of a profession that can and should question its own authority.

Graham and Phelps (2003) suggest that when the language of reflection is applied in a superficial way, the opportunity to acknowledge, nurture and challenge the developing identity of the student ('neophyte') teacher is limited and the critically important question of 'Who am I?' is subsumed by an emphasis on 'What do I have to do?' Graham and Phelps advise that in establishing an identity as a professional, it is critical that teacher education students come to understand their identity as a lifelong learner and, consequently, their own values, attitudes and beliefs as learners. Furthermore, Graham and Phelps distinguish between *expert learners*, who notice when they are not learning and thus are likely to seek a strategic remedy when faced with learning difficulties, and *novice learners*, who rarely reflect on their own performance and seldom evaluate or adjust their cognitive functioning to meet changing task demands or to correct unsuccessful performances.

Alsup, J. (2005) *Teacher Identity Discourses: negotiating personal and professional spaces*, Mahwah, NJ: Lawrence Erlbaum.

Graham, A. and Phelps, R. (2003) 'Being a teacher: developing teacher identity and enhancing practice through metacognitive and reflective learning processes', *Australian Journal of Teacher Education*, 27 (2), 1–14.

Palmer, P.J. (1997) 'The heart of a teacher: identity and integrity in teaching', *New Horizons for Learning*, online at www.newhorizons.org/strategies/character/palmer.htm.

Professional and personal growth

Source

Hoban, G.F., Butler, S. and Lesslie, L. (2007) 'Facilitating self-study of professional development: researching the dynamics of teacher learning', *Studying Teacher Education*, 3 (1), 35–51.

Introduction

A teacher educator worked with two elementary ('primary') teachers to facilitate a self-study of their learning during a professional development programme. The programme ran for six months and was underpinned by four learning processes: reflection, sharing, action and feedback. The two teachers documented their learning experiences and were interviewed several times during and after the study. At the end of the six-month period the teachers sketched and shared models of their learning and collaborated to produce a joint model. (Based on article abstract)

Key words & phrases

Action learning project, independent learner, journal, mini-challenges, open-ended activities, own childhood, personal reflection, professional development, professional learning, questions for herself, reflect, stimulate, values system

---

Extract

"Sue had been teaching for over 30 years and had been a casual (temporary teacher) at the school for 5 years. She decided to keep a journal during the study because she often gets to the end of a professional development course and thinks, 'What did I learn?' Keeping the journal would help her to reflect on her learning. In the journal she recorded questions for herself, items that she needed to work on, issues discussed at meetings, comments on her thoughts at meetings and personal insights . . .

Sue learned that she needed to take her professional learning one small step at a time and try not to change too much. She also believed that she needed to be independent and do research using the Internet and she developed confidence to 'do it'. She also found that, in order to maintain her professional learning, it was important to set her own challenge at the beginning so that she controls what she is trying to learn . . . She found out that her professional learning is not continuous but is somewhat stop–start because of all the interruptions at school. Hence she had to set herself 'mini-challenges' to sustain her learning and change her teaching in small but ongoing ways. Another important aspect of her learning was the collaboration, especially with [her colleague] Loraine. When Sue 'hit a brick wall' she would talk to Loraine about it and Loraine would throw ideas at her and help her to move on . . .

When summarising what she had learned about herself at the end of the study, Loraine believed that she was an independent learner and reported that she liked the challenge of doing something different. She believed that she learned by trying something out and then reflecting upon what happened and why. She believed that she was a bit of a perfectionist and that she had a critical mind. She believed that 'I do a lot of mulling over and reflecting and I go back to my own values system'. She described herself as a 'visual learner and very systematic', so sketching the model of her own learning came quite easily as she had thought it through before-hand.

One particular feature that Loraine learned about herself was that the experience of getting her own Year 2 children to design and make simple machines in science reminded her of her own childhood. Her father was a motor mechanic and she remembered sitting in the family garage and watching her father make different devices . . .

Loraine's teaching of science involved many different changes in her teaching to improve her children's design-and-make skills. This involved giving her students various open-ended activities as well as encouraging her children to share the ideas that they were testing out in their designs. These changes were supported by many factors, including her personal reflection, her own professional needs, the responses of the children, and support from the facilitator, her teaching buddy [Sue] and other members of the action learning team."

Summary

Hoban *et al.* state that teachers may be interested in what the authors refer to as the methods and discourses of self-study but may not know where or how to start. They suggest that teacher educators develop collaborations with teachers to help them research their own practice with a self-study component. By doing so, Sue and Loraine clearly learned not only about their teaching practices but also about themselves as individuals.

Questions to consider

1. In what ways might the act of keeping a journal assist a practitioner's ability to reflect on practice? What are its benefits and limitations?
2. What is the validity of the claim that professional learning always comes 'one small step at a time'?
3. To what extent are teachers influenced by past experiences that lie outside their formal education? What benefits might be gained through identifying such influences?

Investigations

Keeping a journal. Maintain a journal in a similar way to that described above for a period of (say) one month using a trusted friend or colleague as a 'buddy'. Add reflective comments as appropriate.

Setting mini-challenges. In conjunction with a colleague, establish mini-challenges (i.e. challenges that are manageable without major adjustments to practice) and monitor progress over a given time.

Adjustments to practice. Adopt a more problem-solving approach to your practice in a way that involves pupils or students to a greater extent in finding solutions. Evaluate the impact on motivation levels and outcomes.

Think deeper

A common way for teachers and other practitioners to evaluate their practice is through a form of research known as 'action research'. Action researchers use a variety of research techniques that employ both quantitative and qualitative data. There are numerous publications that address the issues and practicalities associated with action research. For instance, Hitchcock and Hughes (1995, p. 27) write that the principal feature of an action research project is change (action) or collaboration between researchers and researched. They argue that action researchers are concerned to improve a situation through active intervention and in collaboration with the parties involved. In the sixth edition of their book about research methods in education, Cohen *et al.* (2007, chapter 13) argue that action research is a powerful tool for change and improvement at the local level. They suggest that this form of research can be used to explore a variety of areas in education, citing seven examples: (1) teaching methods; (2) learning strategies; (3) evaluative procedures; (4) attitudes and values; (5) continuing professional development of teachers; (6) management and control; and (7) administration.

Note that the journal *Action Learning: Research and Practice* is published by Routledge.

Cohen, L., Manion, L. and Morrison, K. (2007) *Research Methods in Education*, sixth edition Abingdon: Routledge.
Hitchcock, G. and Hughes, D. (1995) *Research and the Teacher: A qualitative introduction to school-based research*, second edition, London: Routledge.

Think wider

Arguing from a languages perspective, McDonough (1994) suggests that diary writing in an educational context has become a popular technique, with several different types of application. However, despite its reported advantages in both teaching and research, there are few diary studies available based on the writing of experienced language teachers. Her paper examines the diaries of four teachers working on the same language programme in terms of a variety of topic headings, and insists that diaries can be a useful tool for both classroom research and personal and professional development.

In similar vein, Pollard (2008) suggests that keeping a diary or journal is a valuable way of enhancing practitioners' techniques of enquiry into their practice (see chapter 3). In addition to its being an excellent way of recording classroom or school experiences, he promotes the idea that a diary can also record feelings and perspectives. Pollard further advises that even if the diary is kept private, it offers a safe space to speculate, propose, theorise and enter into a conversation with oneself. In addition to serving a cathartic (i.e. therapeutic) purpose, a diary is a useful professional development tool and can provide a useful source of data for analysis as part of a research project or course of study. **Action research: see also Introduction.**

McDonough, J. (1994) 'A teacher looks at teachers' diaries', *ELT Journal*, 48 (1), 57–65.
Pollard, A. (2008) *Reflective Teaching: Evidence-informed professional practice*, London: Continuum.

Extract 38

Source

Tang, S.Y.F. and Choi, P.L. (2009) 'Teachers' professional lives and continuing professional development in changing times', *Educational Review*, 61 (1), 1–18.

Introduction

The findings reported in this extract were elicited from studying a small sample of teachers in Hong Kong as a means of enriching our understanding of teachers' professional lives and continuing professional development (CPD) during times of rapid change in education. Data were gained through studying the professional lives and CPD of five teachers of different levels of experience who joined the teaching profession in different decades.

Key words & phrases

CPD, culture of trust, de-humanising, externally driven, fierce competition, integration and contextualisation, just and caring, managerialist, market orientated, moral agency of the teacher, moral purposes of teaching, overload of initiatives, professional knowledge, self-directed, social construction, transformative teaching profession

---

Extract

"While the conceptual distinction between self-directed and externally driven professional development enriches our understanding of how teachers make sense of CPD experiences in qualitatively different ways, caution is needed when regarding specific examples as neatly falling into a distinct type. Nevertheless, fierce competition among individuals and schools, intensification of work, [and] stress, uncertainty and alienation on the part of teachers revealed in the study evidence the de-humanising effects of the increasingly managerialist and market-oriented approach to school education. The extent to which such de-humanising effects on teachers would distance them from the moral purposes of teaching is worth paying attention to . . .

If what is reported in this paper is a widespread phenomenon then there is a need for the education community and wider society to have a deep reflection on the perils of adopting quasi-market strategies in education. While counteracting the de-humanising effects of quasi-market strategies in education is necessary, we need to address a more fundamental question: Do we need competent and 'managed' professionals to work in education with a major aim of increasing productivity in the global economic arena or do we need a transformative teaching profession dedicated to education as a public investment for the creation of a prosperous, just and caring society?

At the policy and practice levels, educational leaders need to consider the following when developing CPD policy infrastructure at the system level and practices at the school levels:

- the importance of reducing the overload of initiatives and creating time and space for genuine engagement with educational issues;
- the need to have policies and practices that restore a culture of trust in schools and within the education community; and
- the reconstruction of teacher professionalism in which the moral agency of the teacher is fully acknowledged.

While issues in the education ecology need to be examined and sustained and comprehensive support for teacher development needs to be provided, teachers at the individual and group levels need to rethink their own agency in:

- sustaining and renewing their commitment to the moral purposes of teaching;
- constructing professional knowledge through integration and contextualisation;
- shaping organisational conditions to support the social construction of professional knowledge.

It is only through the synergy of efforts at the individual, collective, school and system levels to adopt a transformative stance that the development of a transformative teaching profession is possible."

Summary

Tang and Choi's study shows that the features of teachers' self-directed professional development are driven by a commitment to the moral purposes of teaching. The increasingly market-orientated and managerialist approach to school education gradually shapes a 'performativity' culture such that professional development is more likely to become externally driven. The combined effort of everybody with a role in education is needed to transform the teaching profession.

Questions to consider

1. How do we identify and quantify self-directed and externally driven forms of professional development?
2. What are the perils of adopting quasi-market strategies in education?
3. To what extent can a performance-orientated education system result in the development of a transformative teaching profession? What other approaches are preferable?

Investigations

Self-directed and externally driven professional development. Carry out a survey among colleagues of how they view the driving force behind professional development.

Moral purposes of teaching. Convene a discussion among interested parties about the moral purposes of teaching and how a managerialist and performance-orientated education system might help to fulfil or hinder such aims.

Formulating policy. Share the first bullet point in the extract with school leaders as a stimulus for discussion about future policy and initiatives.

Think deeper

A report into CPD in schools by Gray (2005) found that ongoing career development took a variety of forms, including:

- whole-school training days;
- the induction, mentoring and assessment of individual teachers;
- peer observation;
- collaborative planning and evaluation;
- self-evaluation.

Beyond the individual school, teachers might build networks by:

- visiting other schools;
- attending conferences;
- undertaking joint training exercises with other schools;
- joining teacher networks;
- engaging with specialist subject associations.

Outside the school environment, teachers might:

- attend short courses by commercial and not-for-profit providers;
- study for higher degrees validated by universities;
- take part in examining processes (for example by becoming examiners);
- study using online courses;
- take part in secondments, sabbaticals and exchanges.

When looking towards the wider community, teachers might:

- take part in outreach activities, particularly in the case of ASTs (advanced skills teachers);
- provide opportunities for community learning.

Not all teachers took part in these different activities all the time; they tended to engage with CPD in different ways at different points in their careers. Teacher engagement depended upon personal, financial and family circumstances; the school and the local educational authority (now 'local authority') in which they worked; and government funding available that year.

Gray, S.L. (2005) *An Enquiry into Continuous Professional Development for Teachers*, London: Esmée Fairbairn.

Think wider

Alexander *et al.* (2004) present a range of approaches to understanding the role, function, impact and presence of performance in education. Their book – written from a US perspective – facilitates a discourse among theorists and teacher practitioners who are interested in understanding the politics of performance and the practices of performative social identities that intervene in the educational endeavour. Alexander and colleagues explore the relationship between performance and performativity in pedagogical practice; the nature and impact of performing identities in varying contexts; cultural and community configurations in teaching, education and schooling; and issues of educational policies and reform as performances. Further information about 'professionalism and professional development' from an international perspective can be found in the journal *Professional Development in Education*, vol. 35, issue 2.

Simmons and Thompson (2008) examine the circumstances affecting creative teaching and learning within the further education (FE; post-compulsory) system with particular reference to the concept of performativity. Drawing on a range of empirical studies and policy analyses, they argue that FE is increasingly positioned towards the bottom of a largely class-based division of post-compulsory education in England whereby meaningful creativity is difficult to achieve. **Creativity: see also Extracts 9 and 10.**

Alexander, B.K., Anderson, G.L. and Gallegos, B. (2004) *Performance Theories in Education: Power, pedagogy and the politics of identity*, New York: Lawrence Erlbaum.

Simmons, R. and Thompson, R. (2008) 'Creativity and performativity: the case of further education', *British Educational Research Journal*, 34 (5), 601–18.

Reflecting on practice

Extract 39

Source

Larrivee, B. (2008) 'Development of a tool to assess teachers' level of reflective practice', *Reflective Practice*, 9 (3), 341–60.

Introduction

Larrivee describes the development, validation process and construction of an instrument to assess a teacher's level of reflection. She discusses the need for a commonly shared language to categorise the various levels involved in becoming a critically reflective teacher. The assessment tool is to provide a way to gauge how a prospective or practising teacher is progressing as a reflective practitioner to facilitate the development of higher-order reflection.

Key words & phrases

Assessment tool, critical reflection, critically reflective teacher, higher-order reflection, level of reflection, pedagogical reflection, pre-reflection, reflective practice, surface reflection

---

Extract

"Selected participants were sent an email to request their expert judgment in establishing specific descriptors to define levels of reflective practice . . . The following level descriptions were provided.

Level 1: Pre-reflection

At this level the teacher interprets classroom situations without thoughtful connection to other events or circumstances. The teacher's orientation is reactive, believing that situational contingencies are beyond the teacher's control. Beliefs and positions about teaching practices are generalised and not supported with evidence from experience, theory, or research. The teacher's perspective is undifferentiated and general regarding the needs of learners.

Level 2: Surface reflection

At this level the teacher's examination of teaching methods is confined to tactical issues concerning how best to achieve predefined objectives and standards. Beliefs and positions about teaching practices are supported with evidence from experience, not theory or research. The teacher's view of learners is somewhat differentiated, acknowledging the need to accommodate learner differences.

Level 3: Pedagogical reflection

At this level the teacher is constantly thinking about how teaching practices are affecting students' learning and how to enhance learning experiences. The teacher's goal is continuously improving practice and reaching all students. Reflection is guided by a pedagogical conceptual framework. Beliefs and positions about teaching are specific and supported by evidence from experience, as well as being grounded in theory or research. The teacher's view of teaching and learning is multidimensional, connecting events within a broader framework.

Level 4: Critical reflection

At this level the teacher is engaged in ongoing reflection and critical inquiry concerning teaching actions as well as thinking processes. The teacher holds up both philosophical ideologies and teaching practices for continuous examination and verification. The teacher consciously considers how personal beliefs and values, assumptions, family imprinting, and cultural conditioning may impact on students. The critically reflective teacher is concerned with promoting democratic ideals and weighs the ethical and social implications of classroom practices."

Summary

The research provides a means of assessing the extent to which teachers have developed the capacity to reflect upon their practice. Descriptions for the four levels of reflection offer a starting point for a consideration of a teacher's present status but, perhaps more importantly, a means to engage with ways to enhance reflective practice to reach what the author refers to as higher-order reflection.

Questions to consider

1. Why is high-quality reflection so important for effective teaching and professional development?
2. Which of the reflective practice characteristics listed at levels 3 and 4 take place principally *during* teaching and how many take place *following* teaching?
3. What sort of evidence should be used in the process of allocating a level?

Investigations

Self-evaluation. Use the Larrivee analysis as a basis for evaluating your own reflective practice.

Evaluation of colleagues. Ask some colleagues to use the Larrivee analysis as a basis for evaluating their own practices. Convene a group discussion to compare results.

Creating a list of high-order reflective skills. In conjunction with interested colleagues, compile a list of 'high-level' reflective qualities and compare results with the characteristics listed under level 4 ('critical reflection')

Think deeper

The philosopher John Dewey concluded that there are two basic sorts of actions, the first type being *routine* action, governed by habit or expectations; the second type being *reflective* action, involving flexibility and self-appraisal, influenced by the social conditions. Dewey's original publication in 1910, *How We Think*, made a unique impact on education. He wrote this book for teachers and the first edition became the bible of progressively minded educators. In more recent years, Donald Schön's work is often quoted as seminal in stimulating interest about reflective practices. In *The Reflective Practitioner: How Teachers Think* (Schön 1983; republished 1993) he argued that professionals who receive coaching and encouragement to think carefully about what they do, while they do it, learn in a more profound way than those who fail to do so.

Taggart and Wilson (2005) suggested that one way of manifesting the characteristics of reflective thinking is through modes of delivery (see chapter 1). Referring to Van Manen (1977), they offer three modes, or levels, of reflective thinking. (1) At the *technical* level of reflection, practitioners function with minimal reference to schemata ('overall plans') from which to draw when dealing with problems, using short-term measures to get through situations. Many trainee and inexperienced teachers operate at this technical level. (2) At the *contextual* level of reflection, pedagogy is examined from a theory–practice perspective. The practitioner makes decisions with reference to the specific context – notably, interactions between the personal and the environment – and draws from competing views about consequences and actions; as a result, he or she develops routines and establishes what Taggart and Wilson refer to as 'rules of thumb'. (3) The *dialectical* level of reflection is the highest mode of reflectivity. At this level, practitioners interrogate moral and ethical issues that relate to various teaching practices. A distinctive element of dialectical reflection is risk taking, which may take the form of peer review and self-assessment. Practitioners thereby mentally reconstruct their actions and situations as a means of reviewing the 'self' as teacher and challenging previously held assumptions. **Self in teaching: see also Extracts 34 and 35.**

Schön, D. (1983, 1991) *The Reflective Practitioner: How teachers think*, New York: Basic Books.

Taggart, G.L. and Wilson, A.P. (2005) *Promoting Reflective Practice in Teachers*, Thousand Oaks, CA: Corwin Press.

Van Manen, M. (1977) 'Linking ways of knowing with ways of being practical', *Curriculum Inquiry*, 6 (3), 205–28.

Think wider

Michigan State University's website (TNE, undated) provides a summary of teachers as reflective learners, arguing that teachers must be self-reflective, as persons and professionals, understanding that their development occurs over the course of their careers. The authors argue that teachers must understand the philosophies and passions that motivate their teaching as well as how they are culturally situated and politically aligned. Thus, teachers as reflective learners are characterised by having *knowledge* about:

- their values, morals, beliefs, orientations, commitments, strengths and weaknesses in relation to accepted standards for teaching;
- how their personal philosophy of teaching and learning integrates and articulates one's own values, morals, and commitments;
- the relationship among their own learning style and pedagogical tendencies, and potential consequences for particular students;
- how positioning by social and historical forces affects their perceptions of difference and pedagogical decisions;
- their own personal life experiences and how they affect perceptions and decisions;
- their own positions relative to the cultural commitments of the community being served;
- processes, capacities and dispositions for learning as a teacher;
- how to recognise and draw upon available resources to construct a teaching persona;
- how their teaching persona affects whether and how students learn;
- systematic self-assessment and goal setting regarding all aspects of teaching, including balancing professional commitments and personal needs;
- the potential impact of individual teachers as agents of change.

Teachers as reflective learners *act* as follows:

- They articulate, justify, act on and adapt a personal philosophy of teaching and learning that is consistent with current learning theory and ethical and legal standards of the profession.
- They integrate theories, concepts and ideas from coursework, programme experiences, teaching experience and continued professional development, into their work.

- They function as teacher-researchers within their own classroom.
- They reflect on positioning and personal experiences to form responsive and sensitive relationships with students that enhance learning.
- They project an effective teacher persona (i.e. how to be who students need them to be in order for students to learn from them).
- They habitually reflect on feedback and consequences of choices and decisions made to inform future actions and decision making.
- They learn to negotiate their own identity and commitments in response to the perspectives of various stakeholders.
- They recognise and change behaviours that are inconsistent with accepted standards for teaching.
- They use multiple sources of information to form judgements about their own teaching efficacy.

See also Ghaye and Ghaye (2004), who suggest a model of the teacher as a reflective learner, with enlightenment and empowerment as central themes.

Ghaye, A. and Ghaye, K. (2004) *Teaching and Learning through Critical Reflective Practice*, London: David Fulton.
TNE (undated) 'Teachers as reflective learners', online at www.msu.edu/~tne/reflective.htm.

Extract 40

Source

Loughran, J.J. and Russell, T. (2007) 'Beginning to understand teaching as a discipline', *Studying Teacher Education*, 3 (2), 217–27.

Introduction

Loughran and Russell explore the possibility of understanding teaching as a discipline in its own right, rather than as a domain that is ancillary to the many academic disciplines. They insist that while teaching looks easy and is widely regarded as easy, the image of teaching as transmission and the perspective of technical rationality mask the many ways in which challenging and engaging teaching represents a highly disciplined view. (Based on article abstract)

Key words & phrases

Competence, delivery of information, discipline, familiar conceptions, intellectual engagement, pedagogical reasoning, personal control, powerful learning experiences, quality teaching, skilful teachers, smooth delivery, understanding of teaching, untrained observer

Extract

"Challenging familiar conceptions of what skilful teachers do to encourage quality learning is all the more difficult because student [teacher]s do not have access to a teacher's pedagogical reasoning – the thinking that underpins what teachers do, how they do it and why. Student [teacher]s and other untrained observers do not see the planning that goes into how a productive lesson is constructed, how a 'need to know' might be used to draw students into learning a new topic or how intellectual engagement might be carefully developed in the learner. What student [teacher]s do see, without much effort, are the superficial aspects of the delivery of information . . .

In sharp contrast to everyday views of teaching, sophisticated, skilful teaching practice is often confused with a good performance, a fun activity or an enjoyable experience. Unfortunately, to the untrained observer, much of what happens and how it happens in a classroom may appear to be arbitrary, left to the teacher's personal or professional whim and certainly not requiring careful analysis. While teaching is not easy, many (including some teachers) inadvertently and unintentionally assume that it is easy because the very act of teaching is still mistakenly perceived as only being about the simple delivery of information.

Attending carefully to what pedagogy really means is crucial to unpacking the relationship between teaching and learning that is at the heart of moving beyond the stereotypic notion of teaching as telling. If the observer of a pedagogic experience inadvertently overlooks, or is not sensitised to, the skilful creation of situations that enhance such things as, for example, linking, processing, synthesising and meta-cognition, then the smooth delivery that is apparent on the surface will inevitably attract most of the observer's attention. Unfortunately, in so doing, the hard work that is essential to building learning from a firm foundation is masked and the real skills, the deep thinking, the careful analysis and the pedagogic experience that shape quality practice are overlooked. Although quality teaching might unintentionally be made to look easy, the reality is something very different . . . If teaching is not understood as a discipline, it is very difficult to challenge the status quo and teaching as telling will inevitably persist as the default interpretation of practice . . .

Developing knowledge, skills and abilities and creating powerful learning experiences require high levels of competence and discipline – competence in knowing what and knowing how in ways that combine to inform intentions and actions in the practice setting, and discipline in gaining personal control over one's teaching behaviours. Such an understanding of teaching is dramatically different from a view of teaching as the delivery of information. Such an understanding can only be based on awareness that teaching is constructed on a foundation from which disciplined studies of practice lead to knowledge about the field. That knowledge matters because it is the basis on which skilful practitioners further develop, test and refine their knowledge in order to shape quality pedagogical experiences for their students."

Summary

Loughran and Russell alert us to the fact that observing lessons taught by experienced practitioners can be counter-productive for inexperienced teachers if they fail to appreciate the thinking, planning and decisions that have taken place prior to the session. They insist that a fuller understanding of pedagogy is crucial to analysing the relationship between teaching and learning. The authors assert that competence exists in knowing what to do and knowing how to go about such that it informs the teacher's intentions and actions and the discipline required to gain control over teaching behaviour.

Questions to consider

1. What are limitations of relying on observations of skilled practitioners as a means of understanding teaching?
2. How can trainee teachers be encouraged to look at the 'learning product' of teaching as well as the act of teaching itself?
3. What forms of knowledge do trainee teachers need to develop to gain personal control over their teaching behaviour?

Investigations

Observing an experienced teacher. Arrange for two trainee teachers to observe a lesson taught by an experienced teacher without discussion beforehand. In a post-lesson forum, invite the teacher to explain his or her thinking and the factors that he or she took into account in making decisions before and during the session. Invite the observers to offer their perspectives.

Rationale for teaching approach. Invite a number of qualified teachers to discuss the factors that affect their teaching approach and classroom decisions, aside from the need to cover the curriculum.

Influential teacher models. Invite teachers to share their memories of teachers who have directly influenced their present teaching approach, paying particular attention to the extent to which the influences were (1) techniques and strategies, and (2) based on educational priorities and beliefs.

Think deeper

A leading twentieth-century education writer (Jeffreys 1971) claimed that the values that teachers bring to the classroom should not be casual beliefs but the result of careful consideration and informed thinking. Eaude (2006) argues that who a person is as a teacher cannot be dissociated from who that teacher is as a person. Consequently, the values that individuals bring to the classroom, with regard to relating to others, expectations and the things they espouse, influence children at least as much as when they are directly teaching them. More recently, Richards (2009) refers to the teacher as a 'frighteningly significant person whose teaching helps to shape attitudes to learning at a most sensitive period in children's development' (p. 20). **Person of the teacher: see also Extracts 26 and 35.**

Eaude, T. (2006) *Children's Spiritual, Moral, Social and Cultural Development*, Exeter: Learning Matters.

Jeffreys, M. (1971) *Education: Its nature and purpose*, London: Allen & Unwin.

Richards, C. (2009) 'Primary teaching: a personal perspective', in Arthur, J., Grainger, T. and Wray, D. (eds) *Learning to Teach in the Primary School*, Abingdon: Routledge.

Think wider

Teaching in the sixteen to nineteen sectors of further education ('post-compulsory education') has been a neglected area for attention. Butcher (2005) insists that the sixteen to nineteen age-phase is distinctive in at least three ways. (1) There are different demands for teachers, notably the curriculum and assessment systems. (2) The sixteen- to nineteen-year-old student's college or university is likely to have selected him or her for a particular academic, vocational or pre-vocational pathway. (3) Post-sixteen students have chosen to remain in education on completion of the compulsory phase (i.e. up to sixteen years of age); consequently, their abilities, motivations, attitudes, aspirations, institutional contexts and personal circumstances are so varied that they should not be viewed as a homogeneous group (see p. 2). Huddleston and Unwin (2007) provide a comprehensive overview of recent developments in further education, including policy, legislation, organisation, student profiles and other contextual factors that are having an impact on the everyday life of colleges. The book contains a number of practical activities and case studies with reference to the increased flexibility programme, marginal groups in college, workplace learning, college–workplace links, e-learning and individualised learning, developments in e-assessment and personal records of achievement.

McQueen and Webber (2009) investigated sixteen- to nineteen-year-old students' reflections on a teaching and learning model in a further education college. A total of 374 sixth-form students individually sorted twenty-one statements into those that they viewed as very, quite or less important to their learning. In addition, nine semi-structured interviews were carried out with first-year students to gain a deeper understanding of which aspects of the model were deemed more important. Data analysis showed that first- and second-year students were united in their greater preference for explicitly exam-focused lessons within a socio-emotionally safe learning environment. Students considered that the following factors were particularly important, in order of priority: (1) being able to ask questions; (2) equality and respect for all; (3) lessons providing a good preparation for exams and coursework; (4) interesting and inspiring lessons; (5) constructive feedback; and (6) a positive working environment. By contrast, aspects of practice promoted by government policy makers – active involvement; clear ground rules; appropriate expectations; review of learning; links to other areas and to previous learning – figured less strongly. **Engaging students: see Extract 50.**

Gravells (2008) focuses on adult learning – so-called 'lifelong learning' – and suggests that it is characterised in a number of ways (see chapter 1).

- It can take place in a variety of contexts; for example, colleges, private organisations, prisons, industry, etc.
- Adults are usually motivated to learn for personal benefit or to enhance their job prospects.
- Adults tend to have a lot of practical or theoretical experiences and are more confident in asking questions, challenging views and relating new knowledge to their specific situations.
- Adults are usually not afraid to make mistakes and keen to learn from others.
- They normally arrive promptly but personal circumstances may create practical difficulties. The author suggests that tasks should be logically ordered, relating theory to practice and including summaries of key points, and kept uncomplicated.

Gravells also stresses the importance of creating a relaxed atmosphere, not least for students who have had previous unsatisfactory experiences of learning.

Butcher, J. (2005) *Developing Effective 16–19 Teaching Skills*, Abingdon: Routledge.
Gravells, A. (2008) *Preparing to Teach in the Lifelong Learning Sector*, Exeter: Learning Matters.
Huddleston, P. and Unwin, L. (2007) *Teaching and Learning in Further Education*, Abingdon: Routledge.
McQueen, H. and Webber, J. (2009) 'What is very important to learning? A student perspective on a model of teaching and learning', *Journal of Further and Higher Education*, 33 (3), 241–53.

Extending expertise

Source

O'Flynn, S. and Kennedy, H. (2003) *Get Their Attention! How to gain pupils' respect and thrive as a teacher*, London: David Fulton; see pp. 53–5.

Introduction

O'Flynn and Kennedy emphasise the importance of confidence for teaching and describe the sorts of decisions that teachers have to make in maintaining order and ensuring a settled learning environment. They also describe the tension that exists between avoiding confrontation and allowing the lesson to flow, while at the same time preventing a troublesome minority from dominating and disrupting the proceedings.

Key words & phrases

Behaviour, better nature, body posture, confidence, confrontation, courage, decisions, endless argument and confusion, eye contact, formal warning, mask of the teacher role, minor incidents, pander, sanction, self-assured, students' attention, subtle hints, troublemakers, tyranny, weakness and indecisiveness

---

Extract

"Confidence is an elusive quality that comes slowly, with experience . . . When students can sense a teacher's authority they are unlikely to challenge it . . .

The use of body posture: openness of arm position, a sideways lean, tilt of the head, forward lean, close proximity to the addressee and strong eye contact are all elements of a confident demeanour. While a confident person can amplify these, to suggest that it is easy would further undermine those who have difficulty in this respect . . .

Discretion being the better part of valour, on occasion it may be wise for the teacher to selectively ignore minor incidents in order to avoid interrupting the flow of the lesson. In other cases, subtle hints (pauses, dropping names or the use of eye contact) may be sufficient. Teachers can minimise the damage that minor trouble-makers cause by sitting them alone or at the margins of the class, which amounts to moving them off stage.

If the student does not catch on and take the hint then it will be necessary to stop the lesson and give one clear formal warning, naming the student(s) involved, stating clearly what behaviour the teacher is objecting to, suggesting a positive alternative and pointing out the consequences that will follow if the misbehaviour continues. When all attempts by the teacher to be sympathetic, to appeal to the student's better nature and to give [him or her] a chance fail to change the student's behaviour, it will be obvious that these actions are not seen by the student as kindness but as weakness and indecisiveness on the teacher's part. Confrontation between the teacher and the student will be unavoidable.

Most people find confrontation unpleasant and try, as far as they can, to avoid it. The responsibility of the teacher, however, is to teach the whole class and not to pander to the tyranny of a few disruptive students. When it comes to the 'crunch', there is a professional requirement of a subject teacher to (a) be able to assess the situation that has arisen, (b) know what to do and (c) have the courage to do it. One of the demands of teaching is the requirement to make decisions, judge situations accurately and take appropriate action when dealing with incidents of indiscipline . . .

If the student persists in misbehaving or a serious breach of discipline occurs then the teacher has no alternative but to administer a sanction as a deterrent, appropriate to and following closely on the offence. At this juncture the teacher should say and do as little as possible. The tone of voice is kept polite, short and firm. Avoid getting into excuses or getting involved in 'whys', as these lead to endless argument and confusion. The use of 'I statements' by the teacher is very effective in making the interaction with the student real and immediate. They allow the personality of the teacher to emerge from behind the mask of the teacher role."

Summary

O'Flynn and Kennedy adopt a rather defensive tone in the extract, as they anticipate behavioural difficulties and offer advice about possible strategies to combat them. The extract is replete with words such as confrontation, courage, sanctions and deterrents. The final sentence of the extract offers a strong clue about the authors' priorities.

Questions to consider

1. How might a teacher show authority and confidence in such a way that students will not challenge it? Is this a realistic expectation?
2. In what ways might a teacher 'pander to the tyranny of a few disruptive students'?
3. How do you understand the authors' comment about allowing the teacher's personality to emerge from behind the mask of the teacher role?

Investigations

Body language variations. Observe a series of lessons and note the changes in the teacher's body language when (1) addressing the class; (2) listening to a pupil speak; (3) asking questions; and (4) facing challenging behaviour. Consider the implications of your findings with respect to the prevailing levels of adult and pupil confidence generated.

Maintaining harmony. Observe a series of lessons and note the strategies that the teacher uses to maintain a calm environment and avoid confrontation. Pay particular attention to the nature of pupils' reactions and responses.

Use of 'I statements'. Record yourself for (say) 20 minutes during a lesson. Invite a carefully selected group of pupils to listen to the recording and comment on the effect that your voice has upon them and the way they interpreted your mood.

Think deeper

Wright (2006) argues that a situation can arise in which a teacher seems to be naturally popular or charismatic, with the result that pupils want to please her or him; in doing so, however, they may not assume responsibility for their own behaviour (see p. 53). Consequently, when a different teacher is in charge, pupils who were well behaved with the first teacher fail to behave well for the next. Ellis and Tod (2009) underline the fact that 'teachers are placed in a vulnerable position within the group setting of the classroom' (p. 133) for the simple reason that pupils register and remember their mistakes. However, the contrast between the experienced and regular teacher who has already built a rapport with the class, and the trainee or new teacher who has not done so, is quite marked, for whereas the established teacher can quickly repair the damage, the neophyte will struggle to do so. The authors note that although all teachers are 'in a position of designated authority', the trainees or new teachers may feel that they cannot afford to make mistakes lest these are interpreted by pupils as being the norm; as a result, inexperienced teachers tend to 'play safe' for fear of inviting behaviour problems. **Behaviour and discipline: see also Extracts 46–49.**

Ellis, S. and Tod, J. (2009) *Behaviour for Learning: Proactive approaches to behaviour management*, Abingdon: Routledge.
Wright, D. (2006) *Classroom Karma*, London: David Fulton.

Think wider

Body language is significant in education because the teacher's non-verbal communication can have an impact on pupil behaviour and conduct and thereby on the quality of learning. In his innovative and visually compelling book, Robertson (1996) argues that a teacher's gestures are valuable unless used to excess, as they constitute an integral part of the adult's relationship with the learner and help to clarify the message being conveyed. He argues that teachers are performers – not in the same way as a stage artist who aims to receive public acclaim; rather, they use their performance as a vehicle to improve their teaching. Variations in body language can increase pupil response rate, create enthusiasm and help to excite a more vibrant learning environment. It certainly seems to be true in most schools that adults with the brightest, most 'animated' personalities are the most popular. Miller (2005) provides a concise look at the non-verbal messages that take place in the classroom, including facial expressions; eye behaviour; vocal intonation; touching; body movements and gestures; use of space; and dress. **Body language: see also Extracts 25 and 41, both under 'Think wider'.**

Miller, P.W. (2005) *Body Language: An illustrated introduction for teachers*, Chicago: Patrick W. Miller.
Robertson, J. (1996) *Effective Classroom Control*, London: Hodder & Stoughton.

Extract 42

Source

Mason, J. (2009) 'Teaching as disciplined enquiry', *Teachers and Teaching*, 15 (2), 205–23.

Introduction

Mason argues that it is essential for teachers to refresh their sense of the disciplined ways in which natural human powers are employed, of the role of fundamental themes, practices and 'awarenesses' which comprise the subject and its discipline, together with the uniqueness of the learners in (1) their historical-cultural and (2) their institutional setting. He argues that teaching is fundamentally 'enquiry in the domain of human attention and awareness'. In this extract, Mason provides an 'assertion' and 'consequences for teaching' for each element of 'disciplined enquiry'.

Key words & phrases

Assertion, attention, awareness, consequences for teaching, disciplined enquiry, learners as agents, ongoing enquiry, ongoing realisation, origins of the actions, process of enrichment, the psyche, sense-making, subject-specific ways, teaching, transformations

---

Extract

"I begin with an outline of the development of my thesis that teaching is usefully seen as disciplined enquiry . . .

Agentiveness and mechanicality

Assertion: Human beings are potentially agentive even if their actions are frequently driven by automatism based on habit. Consequently, cause-and-effect as a mechanism is not useful for theorising about or informing effective teaching . . .

Consequences for teaching: This is the basis for teaching to be seen as ongoing enquiry rather than a combination of a storehouse of knowledge and a mastery of pedagogic mechanisms.

Natural powers

Assertion: Learners arrive at educational institutions having already demonstrated natural powers of sense-making. Learning involves developing those powers in subject-specific ways, combined with changes in disposition to attend, changes in what is attended to and changes in how that attention is structured.

Consequences for teaching: This assertion is based on the view that ongoing enquiry into the use of one's own powers is vital in order to develop, maintain and enrich sensitivity to others' use of their own powers. In order to direct other people's attention effectively, it is necessary to be aware of both what you are attending to, and how you are attending to it . . .

Teaching and learning sites

I do not assume that what is taught is what is learned, nor that what is learned is learned immediately or even as a result of any simple cause-and-effect mechanism initiated by teaching.

Assertion: Teaching takes place *in* time, as a succession of acts; learning takes place *over* time as a result of maturation and co-evolution of perceptions, conceptions and alterations through transformations in the structure of *attention* and *awareness* arising through experience of activity.

Consequences for teaching: Appreciation and understanding of different topics is not a binary matter: either you do or you do not understand. Rather, it is potentially an ongoing process of enrichment even if it can stagnate or remain dormant for periods of time.

Structure of topics related to structure of the psyche

Assertion: To promote learners' understanding and appreciation of topics, it is necessary to 'psychologise the subject matter' (Dewey 1902/1971), which can be seen as arranging for learners to encounter aspects of topics that relate to the human psyche.

Consequences for teaching: Understanding and appreciation of subject-specific topics is a dynamically evolving process of ongoing realisation, dependent on disposition and volition. Again, appreciation and understanding of different topics is not a binary matter: either you do or you do not. Rather, it is potentially an ongoing process of enrichment even if it can stagnate or remain dormant for periods of time.

Actions, awareness and attention

Assertion: Teaching involves provoking learners to make use of familiar actions in unfamiliar ways in order to meet fresh challenges, and supporting learners in drawing back out of activity (reflecting) in order to learn from their experience. Actions are based on awareness, which may be unconscious (as in somatic actions), semi-conscious (as in trained behavioural habits) and conscious. Awareness can be educated, whereas behaviour can be trained, and these transformations take place through learners drawing upon or 'harnessing' the flow of energies through their emotions.

Consequences for teaching: Ongoing enquiry into the actions available to learners and into ways of both triggering them and making them available for inspection involves ongoing enquiry into the origins of the actions which underpin different topics."

Dewey, J. (1902) *The Child and the Curriculum*. Reprinted as *The Child and the Curriculum and the School and Society* (1971), Chicago: University of Chicago Press, pp. 19–31.

Summary

Mason insists that teaching is fundamentally about connecting with learners in such a way that what is said and done is meaningful to them. To be effective requires sensitivity to learners' states and powers, which is only made possible through ongoing enquiry into the teacher's own attention and awareness. Teaching and learning cannot be reduced to a simplistic 'I teach, you learn' formula; rather, factors such as cultural norms, disposition, temperament and emotions are all significant.

Questions to consider

1. What is your understanding of teaching as disciplined enquiry?
2. To what extent do you subscribe to Mason's view that awareness can be educated, whereas behaviour can be trained?
3. How should we understand 'meaningful' from a learner's perspective?

Investigations

Professional development. Use the Mason thesis as a basis for in-service work with colleagues or preliminary work with trainees. Elicit their responses to the usefulness of the theory–practice links.

Identifying beliefs about education. Select what you consider to be key phrases from the Mason model and use them as a basis for a survey of colleagues.

Learning over time. Taking note of Mason's assertion that teaching takes place *in* time and learning takes place *over* time, assess the development of students' understanding of a topic over a given period.

Think deeper

Vagle (2009) asked eighteen middle school teachers during an unstructured interview or written description of a lived-experience to describe moments when they recognised and responded to a student who did not understand something during an instructional activity, with particular reference to the student's body language. The author argues that we should think seriously about how teachers come to know this 'pathic' dimension of teaching [feeling a particular way]. Teachers should be asking themselves a number of questions: How did I perceive that student's look? Can I perceive the student differently? Do I care to perceive the student differently? How are my perceptions of this particular student limiting how I see the student? Are these perceptions turning into self-fulfilling prophecies? In other words, if I perceive a student as not able to understand, will he or she continue to not understand? Did my perception prompt me to think reflectively in that particular situation? How is my perception influencing my actions and how are my actions influencing the student at this point in time and in the future? **Response to pupils' body language: see also Extract 25 under 'Think wider'.**

Vagle, M. (2009) 'Locating and exploring teacher perception in the reflective thinking process', *Teachers and Teaching*, 15 (5), 579–99.

Think wider

White (2009) argues that equipping young people for a meaningful life is a worthwhile but not all-important educational aim, so that educators should help them not only to see their lives as meaningful but also to lead lives that *are* meaningful. He concludes that to make school life more meaningful requires rethinking the traditional academic curriculum of discrete subjects and timetabling. Educators need to reconsider what schools should be for and arrange learning activities in the light of these aims rather than the reverse.

White, J. (2009) 'Education and a meaningful life', *Oxford Review of Education*, 35 (4), 423–35.

Support staff

Extract 43

Source

Wilson, E. and Bedford, D. (2008) 'New Partnerships for Learning: teachers and teaching assistants working together in schools – the way forward', *Journal of Education for Teaching*, 34 (2), 137–50.

Introduction

The research conducted by Wilson and Bedford explored the opinions of teachers as to the personal skills, attributes and training required to enhance a changing professional relationship by posing the question: What are the issues to address in enabling teachers to work in effective partnership with teaching assistants? The findings reveal the different experiences of teachers working with teaching assistants across the primary and secondary phases. (Based on article abstract)

Key words & phrases

Attributes, communication skills, good practice, inhibitors to change, lack of pay, level of education, partnerships, personal attributes, personal characteristics, professional teachers, remodelling agenda, (teaching) skills, social inclusion, teaching assistant roles, team working, variety of practice

---

Extract

"Two main themes emerged in respect of the skills and personal attributes common for both teachers and teaching assistants. First, there was an overwhelming majority (95%) who made comments related to relationships needed for team working; second, half of all respondents commented on the need for communication skills . . . In respect to respondents' views of skills required by teachers, comments overwhelmingly focused on aspects of their professional role. A number of skills were identified such as effective delegation and enabling autonomy in others, and the ability to reward and celebrate success. Other skills concerned effective organisation and management, such as the need for comprehensive planning and preparation and good time management. Respondents highlighted the view that the teacher has responsibility for all the pupils, therefore teaching assistants should not be expected to have sole charge of those they are working with. This is often the case for those working with pupils with special educational needs.

In contrast, when identifying attributes required by teaching assistants, there was considerably greater emphasis on personal characteristics such as the ability to take initiative and be proactive, punctuality, open-mindedness and conscientiousness. Achievement of 'a certain level of education', a good standard of writing and subject knowledge were identified as prerequisites. Skills identified included the ability to plan, manage time and manage behaviour. They also included aspects of the professional role such as being alert and sensitive to the needs of the teacher, particularly with respect to the role and development needs of those who were newly qualified . . .

The focus groups were asked to discuss the partnerships between teachers and teaching assistants in their schools, identifying what worked well and where change was needed. From the discussions it could be seen that there was a considerable variety of practice and this difference was particularly marked between the primary and secondary phases. These ranged from a close working partnership through to teaching assistants going into classes not having been given any indication of the sort of support that was needed . . .

In terms of major inhibitors to change outside of the school, funding issues were seen to be significant by the largest number of teachers (43%), although parental concerns also featured highly (35%), a typical comment being, 'Parents want their children to have professional teachers.' Lack of pay structures for teaching assistants (TAs) was cited by 21%, a comment being, 'If the pay structure was there, TAs would be the single most important agent for progression.' The English government's workforce remodelling agenda (6%) and lack of training for teaching assistants (6%) were also mentioned . . . The most significant theme identified was resources, with the greatest need being time for liaison and planning . . .

Another theme identified the culture of social inclusion and team working within the school. This was seen as important by over half of the interviewees. Here, again, there were comments relating to the need for mutual respect and ensuring that teaching assistants are treated as full members of the school and have access to all facilities.

The adaptability, enthusiasm and willingness of teaching assistants to undertake training and development were noted . . . Respondents wanted to see the provision of regular planned and paid meeting time for teachers and teaching assistants, as well as specific training programmes for the latter."

Summary

Wilson and Bedford argue that a key issue arising from their research is the development of training programmes that incorporate information on workforce remodelling into all programmes of initial teacher training. A second issue is the need for joint training of teachers and their teaching assistants to develop team-working skills and to share good practice from primary and special schools in the secondary sector. A third issue concerns the roles and responsibilities of TAs, and related issues of pay. Finally, the varied needs and aspirations of TAs are important. Wilson and Bedford insist that the key issue is whether the relationship between teacher and teaching assistant is a hierarchical one or a genuine partnership.

Questions to consider

1. What distinctive skills help teaching assistants to do the job effectively?
2. What distinctive personal attributes characterise the best teaching assistants?
3. What factors might assist and hinder the work and morale of a teaching assistant? How might these factors differ in various learning situations?

Investigations

Views of teaching assistants. Interview teaching assistants from a variety of school situations about their role, aspirations and frustrations in the job.

Perceptions of teaching assistants. Ask a number of TAs to keep a log or diary about key elements of their day and their feelings about what happened. Conduct a group discussion with them about the findings.

Views of teachers. Interview teachers about the way they perceive the role, aspirations and frustrations of TAs. If possible, convene an open discussion involving the teachers and participants from 'Views of teaching assistants' above.

Think deeper

Teaching assistants have long been employed in schools as 'classroom assistants' for general duties but in recent years they have gradually assumed greater responsibility for pupils' learning. Employment of TAs is intended to lead to more flexible models of teaching and learning and free teachers from more routine tasks to allow them to concentrate on the planning, preparation and assessment of pupils' learning (PPA time). The application of this strategy necessitates that assistants are suitably trained to ensure that they possess the appropriate skills to complement the work of teachers (see Kerry 2005). Many TAs are gaining considerable expertise in specific subjects or areas of the curriculum or in working with pupils diagnosed as having special educational needs (see Spooner 2010). While the roles of teachers and TAs are complementary, their salaries are widely different, which is a potential source of discontent.

Kerry, T. (2005) 'Towards a typology for conceptualizing the roles of teaching assistants', *Educational Review*, 57 (3), 373–84.
Spooner, W. (2010) *The SEN Handbook for Trainee Teachers, NQTs and Teaching Assistants*, Abingdon: Routledge.

Think wider

Increasingly, all paid assistants possess a qualification and attend additional in-service courses to develop their expertise (see Watkinson 2003; Cousins *et al.* 2004). However, for those assistants wishing to pursue further study there are career routes into teaching; indeed, it is estimated that about 10 per cent of teaching assistants are trained teachers. The need to develop expertise becomes even more essential when higher-level teaching assistants (HLTAs) take responsibility for teaching a group of children or even the whole class under the general guidance of the teacher (Rose 2005; Cullingford-Agnew 2006). Guidance for experienced TAs can be found in Watkinson (2010).

Cousins, L., Higgs, M. and Leader, J. (2004) *Making the Most of Your Teaching Assistants*, London: PfP.
Cullingford-Agnew, S. (2006) *Becoming a Higher Level Teaching Assistant: Primary SEN*, Exeter: Learning Matters.
Rose, R. (2005) *Becoming a Primary Higher Level Teaching Assistant: Meeting the HLTA standards*, Exeter: Learning Matters.
Watkinson, A. (2003) *The Essential Guide for Competent Teaching Assistants*, London: David Fulton.
Watkinson, A. (2010) *The Essential Guide for Experienced Teaching Assistants*, Abingdon: Routledge.

Extract 44

Source

Fraser, C. and Meadows, S. (2008) 'Children's views of teaching assistants in primary schools', *Education 3–13*, 36 (4), 351–63.

Introduction

The authors carried out a significantly large study of children's perceptions of the role of the teaching assistant (TA) using data collected from a self-completed questionnaire – completed by 419 junior-aged children (aged seven to eleven years) – and semi-structured interviews conducted with a sample of 86 pupils, aged from five to eleven.

Thus: 'The aim of this study is to elicit children's views of TAs and to give them a voice about a world which they are compelled to inhabit for a large percentage of their day' (p. 354). In particular, information was elicited about who 'teaches' and who is 'in charge' in the classroom, of what the TA does to 'help' in the classroom and to obtain explicit views of whether working with the TA stigmatises pupils.

Key words & phrases

Aid individual pupils, children aged 5–11, children's perceptions, cross-section of pupils, explains things, helpful, insightful views, needing help, responsibilities towards children, roles, school community, teaching assistant (TA), unique rights, wide range of jobs, withdrawn from the class

---

Extract

"Children aged 5–11, from three state primary schools . . . contributed to this study. In all schools, children aged 7–11 completed questionnaires. Due to time constraints, only children in [two of the] schools were interviewed. Interviews were conducted with children aged 5–11 from these two schools. The three schools represent a cross-section of pupils in ethnicity, ability and social background. A total of 21 TAs, all women, were employed in the three schools . . . Some of the TAs were 'brought in' to aid individual pupils with special educational needs (SEN), with the help provided ranging from help with mobility to supporting children with emotional and behavioural difficulties. None of the TAs had higher level assistant qualifications but one TA used to be a teacher and found it 'more convenient for her family' to work as a TA . . .

The wide range of jobs which children listed that a TA may carry out concurs with the current expectation that the role the TA plays has shifted from an ancillary role to one of supporting the pupil. Many children commented on the extra responsibility the teacher carries in comparison to the TA. The children's main citation of an important job performed by the TA is when they help them with their work and, more specifically, when they do not understand or are confused and the TA explains things more clearly. Children can articulate how the TA actually helps them when they are stuck with their work. The majority of the children reported that they would work equally hard for either a teacher or a TA. The majority of children perceive the TA to be in the classroom to help 'everyone' and at least one TA per class was desired. Most children do not mind being withdrawn from the class for extra help or being taught inside or outside the classroom, but a small minority of children in each class perceive themselves to be shy and quiet and feel that they are in a situation whereby they do not like asking for help. Most children viewed working individually with a TA as a positive rather than a stigmatising experience, but further consideration needs to be given to the problem of those children who were anxious about asking for help. Those children who did not themselves work with a TA nevertheless felt that the work of the TA freed up the work of the teacher and was, in turn helpful to them.

Finally, the children's clear and insightful views of the roles of their teaching assistants were impressive . . . So often adults decide what is 'best' for the children and make decisions on their behalf. This is right and proper in that parents, teachers and carers all have responsibilities towards children but it should also be remembered that children have unique rights, opinions and perspectives and need to be heard."

Summary

The research reveals a number of interesting findings, including the following: (1) TAs are important members of the school community. (2) The roles of teachers and TAs overlap but are different. (3) The vast majority of children work as hard for the TA as for the teacher, though more boys than girls work harder for the teacher. (4) TAs mainly assist pupils who are 'stuck'. (5) Children did not mind being taken out of class for extra help. (6) Older children were more likely to feel embarrassed asking for help from a TA. (7) Girls were much more willing than boys to consider the job of teaching assistant. Pupils are also able to distinguish between the role of the teacher and the TA and offer reasoned views to substantiate their distinctions.

Questions to consider

1. Why are younger children less likely to discriminate between the roles of teachers and assistants?
2. What significant issues arise from the study about stigmatisation and self-confidence in learning?
3. What significant issues arise from the study about gender?

Investigations

Perceptions of the TA role. Conduct your own investigation about pupils' perceptions of the TA role, with particular emphasis upon ways in which they view the TA and the teacher.

TAs' perceptions of their role. Conduct interviews with assistants in terms of: (1) how they perceive their role; (2) areas of the role that overlap with that of the teacher; and (3) their priorities and aspirations.

Lived experiences in a TA's work. Interview assistants about the joys, frustrations and 'critical incidents' in the job and compile a dossier of 'lived' experiences.

Think deeper

Adult assistants tend to be used in one or more of seven ways: (1) being involved as a genuine participant in pupils' activities; (2) as a detached observer of how pupils cope with tasks; (3) as a scribe for pupils who struggle with writing; (4) doing a variety of menial tasks; (5) checking what pupils are doing; (6) listening to what pupils want to read to them, tell them about and discuss; and (7) helping pupils to review their work. Teaching-Assistants.co.uk is a website dedicated to those working as TAs and those seeking to recruit and employ them: recruitment agencies, schools, nurseries and after-school clubs (www.teaching-assistants.co.uk). Cheminais (2009) provides the background to current legislation as well as information on how children learn and how teaching assistants can support their learning and promote pupil well-being. Arnold and Yeomans (2005) offer advice about different schools of psychology, the way they apply to children and ways in which TAs can help to enhance their education.

Arnold, C. and Yeomans, J. (2005) *Psychology for Teaching Assistants*, Stoke-on-Trent: Trentham Books.

Cheminais, R. (2009) *Every Child Matters: A practical guide for teaching assistants*, Abingdon: Routledge.

Think wider

Teachers have a responsibility to be specific about their expectations of TAs each day and from session to session. The need for clarity is especially relevant in early years classes, where additional adult support is often interwoven into the fabric of the teaching day. With older pupils the TA may be involved in intensive coaching of those who have fallen behind or struggling, or she may be allocated to supervise a group and guide them in task completion. Part of TAs' essential skills training is to gain more experience in behaviour management for those occasions when they are directly responsible for a group of children or the whole class (Bentham 2005). One of the quickest ways to damage a TA's dedication is to make unjustified assumptions about her capability and level of responsibility or to take advantage of her goodwill (see contributors to Hancock and Collins 2005).

Butt and Lance (2009) note that policy makers decided that workforce remodelling would decrease teacher workload and increase their job satisfaction. However, they argue that the policy makers have not necessarily given sufficient attention to the complexities of expanding the TAs' responsibilities, and insist that we should not be driven by a desire to find instant solutions to complex issues but should pay much greater attention to the views of TAs themselves. Butt and Lance conclude that teaching assistants are increasingly taking on the primary teacher's responsibilities.

Bentham, S. (2005) *A Teaching Assistant's Guide to Managing Classroom Behaviour*, Abingdon: Routledge.

Butt, G. and Lance, A. (2009) '"I am *not* the teacher!" Some effects of remodelling the roles of teaching assistants in English primary schools', *Education 3–13*, 37 (3), 219–31.

Hancock, R. and Collins, J. (eds) (2005) *Primary Teaching Assistants*, London: David Fulton.

Extract 45

Source

Simkins, T., Maxwell, B. and Aspinwall, K. (2009) 'Developing the whole-school workforce in England: building cultures of engagement', *Professional Development in Education*, 35 (3), 433–50.

Introduction

In their article, Simkins *et al.* draw from research that engaged forty-five schools in developing and implementing new strategies and approaches to the training of the whole-school workforce, focusing on nine schools that were the most successful at meeting the needs of the whole workforce. Data were used to explore two questions: (1) How did the schools conceive and implement strategies that would genuinely meet the needs of the whole-school workforce? What were their purposes and what kinds of interventions did they use to pursue these? (2) What were the characteristics of those schools that were most successful in addressing seriously the issue of training and development for the whole workforce?

Key words & phrases

Cultures, differentiated developmental activities, enhancing collaboration, genuine engagement, integration, multiple perspectives, roles, support staff, values framework, whole workforce, workforce development

---

Extract

"Support staff undertake a wide variety of roles and often bring to training and develop-ment contexts different motivations and learning histories from those of teachers . . .

The importance of values and culture: The most common cultural factors to emerge . . . can be summarised in terms of a supportive or developmental culture where:

- people trusted the vision and purpose of the leadership;
- people were open to change;
- risk-taking was accepted;
- there was generally an ethos of openness, participation and support;
- teamwork was widely observed across the school; and
- motivation and morale were high.

More specifically there were commonalities in the values and beliefs espoused by these schools. They believed in equity in the treatment for all staff, they valued staff as much as pupils, and they believed in the importance of personal development for all as well as learning from each other . . .

Orchestrating genuine engagement: In general, the cultures of the successful schools provided affordances and invitations for all members of the workforce, and especially for those other than teachers, to engage in developmental processes and activities . . . the most effective strategies did not just make the engagement of the whole staff *possible*; they also made it *meaningful* through strategies to engage them actively in various development events . . .

Holding multiple perspectives: Successful strategies did not just involve making invitations genuinely open to all staff, although this was important. They also recognised the complexity of staff needs and perspectives . . . schools implemented interventions at three distinct levels: those aimed corporately at the school as a whole; those aimed at identifiable staff groups within the workforce; and those directed at individuals . . . interventions were established that were designed to bring the whole workforce together and increase interactions among disparate groups, and policies were put in place to extend to all members of the workforce access to key processes such as induction, developmental appraisal/review and staff development courses. In these senses, *integration* was deemed to be of great significance. However, it was also recognised that particular groups of staff played their own particular roles in the school and worked in different ways and to different rhythms. Consequently it was necessary to provide *differentiated* developmental activities that were tailored to these differing needs as the examples of welfare assistants, school meal supervisors and support staff team leaders identified earlier illustrate . . .

These two dimensions – genuine engagement of all groups, and a recognition that needs and perspectives can and will differ even within a whole-school values framework – were two key characteristics of the cultures of the successful schools in our sample. Nevertheless, underlying these characteristics was a consistency of beliefs and values about the equitable treatment of staff that went deeper than mere statements of purposes and development of strategies. It meant genuinely valuing each member of the workforce, recognising the potential of all members of the organisation to benefit from developmental activities, and a commitment to the importance of enhancing collaboration across staff work groups irrespective of task and status."

Summary

As a result of their extensive research, Simkins *et al.* commend a school culture conducive to learning for all members of the school community, and approaches that promote genuine engagement rather than relying solely on invitation. Effective school development recognises the complexity of staff needs and perspectives when viewed across the workforce as a whole. Simkins *et al.* stress that recognising the potential and priorities of each group has to be set in a context of integration and collaboration supported by values that promote mutual respect.

Questions to consider

1. What sorts of assumptions (correct or incorrect) might a school's headteacher or senior management team make about different groups of staff? How can these assumptions be verified or confounded?
2. How is a balance to be maintained between genuine inclusion of all staff, while allowing for the fact that particular groups of staff play their own roles in the school and work in different ways and to different rhythms?
3. How will members of a staff group know they are genuinely valued?

Investigations

School values. Ask members of different staff groups to summarise what they perceive to be the school's aims and core values. Compare and contrast their responses with the formally documented ones.

Discovering needs of staff groups. Devise a straightforward questionnaire or set of questions to ascertain from members of different groups (1) the things they find most satisfying and unsatisfying in their role; (2) the sort of training and development they would most value; and (3) their aspirations. Show the same questionnaire or set of questions to their managers and ask them what they anticipate members of the group will say. Compare and contrast the results of the two sets of replies (managers' predicted ones; group members' actual ones).

Professional development strategies. Interview colleagues with responsibility for continuing professional development about strategies to facilitate (1) genuine engagement of group members, and (2) responding to diversity of needs across and within groups.

Think deeper

The School Workforce Development Board (SWDB) in England was established in the autumn of 2004 as the sector-wide body concerned with training and developing the wider workforce. It was dissolved in autumn 2008 and replaced by the National Advisory Group (NAG) for the professional development of the Children's Workforce. The Group's remit is posited on the fact that as about half a million support staff currently work in schools, they must be helped to realise their potential and enjoy high morale and job satisfaction. Well-trained and motivated support staffs that are fairly rewarded and clear about their distinctive contribution have a significant role in raising academic standards and enriching children's lives. The professional development strategy for the children's workforce in schools (2009–2012) sets out the government's vision to embed a learning culture within, and across, all schools to maximise the potential of the whole workforce and enable children and young people to achieve success. Three priorities underpin the work: (1) embedding a learning culture; (2) increasing coherence and collaboration; and (3) improving quality and capacity. For further information, consult the website at www.tda.gov.uk/partners/cpd/pds_cwds.aspx.

Think wider

Southworth (2004) argues that collaborative cultures are characterised by high levels of trust and interaction that he refers to as 'interactive networks', allowing members of staff to learn with and from one another. Sharing ideas, talking openly, planning together and supporting one another create learning enriched environments. He goes on to say that collaborative cultures allow staff to talk openly and feel sufficiently secure to share professional concerns and to seek help and advice from one another. Southworth emphasises his belief that the real power of such workplaces is that they facilitate and nurture professional learning. Collaborative cultures not only make schools better places to work in but also help individuals to grow and develop their expertise.

It is important that collaboration is authentic and not contrived (Hargreaves and Dawe 1990; Hargreaves 1994), conducted within agreed professional boundaries and pedagogically sound; that is, it must be manageable and beneficial for teaching and learning. Much of what passes for collaboration may lack rigour and lapse into low-level debate when it has the potential to enhance the educational provision within the school. Collaboration has to be seen alongside 'collegiality', which implies a 'flat' rather than a hierarchical staff structure. **Pupil collaboration: see also Extracts 3 and 4.**

Hargreaves, A. (1994) *Changing Teachers, Changing Times: Teachers' work and culture in the postmodern age*, London: Cassell.

Hargreaves, A. and Dawe, R. (1990) 'Paths of professional development: contrived collegiality, collaborative culture, and the case of peer coaching', *Teaching and Teacher Education*, 6, 227–41.

Southworth, G. (2004) *Primary School Leadership in Context: Leading small, medium and large sized schools*, London: RoutledgeFalmer.

Class management

Establishing boundaries

Extract 46

Source

Wragg, E.C. (2004) 'The two Rs: rules and relationships', in Wragg, E.C. (ed.) *The RoutledgeFalmer Reader in Teaching and Learning*, London: RoutledgeFalmer; see pp. 60–1, 64–5.

Introduction

Wragg writes from a perspective of rules and relationships, which he refers to as 'the two Rs'. He begins by explaining the importance of rules in society before describing three different types of rule that are relevant to a school situation. While recognising the essential nature of establishing rules, Wragg argues that it is important to take account of pupils' ideas and beliefs when framing them.

Key words & phrases

Case law, consistency, legal and contractual obligations, national rules, negotiating rules, rule conventions, school rules, self-discipline, sensible proposals, take responsibility, teachers' rules, understand the need

---

Extract

"Rules in school are of several kinds. There are national rules, many incorporated in Acts of Parliament, which govern such matters as pupil attendance, parental rights, use of punishments; there are local authority rules, such as the code of laboratory safety, or what teachers must do on field trips; there are also school rules, which may be similar to or different from those of other schools, and these can concern dress, behaviour in the playground or use of facilities. Finally, there are teachers' rules on matters such as talking, movement, the setting out of work or disruptive behaviour.

The question of rules is closely bound up with, but also distinct from, that of relationships. The relationship between two or more people is to some extent affected by the rule conventions under which it operates . . . [Teachers] also have legal and contractual obligations, to act as a parent, *in loco parentis*, which means that, to some extent, their relationship with children is affected by what a court might require of them. Should there be an accident, teachers can avoid legal action for negligence by acting as a responsible parent would, summoning help, checking that the child is in good hands, communicating with those who need to know. When sour relationships develop, it is sometimes because rules are perceived to be unfairly or inconsistently applied or because there is dissent or uncertainty about the rules themselves.

Within the first few days of the school year, dozens of rules are established or reaffirmed in some form or another by teachers . . . Given the many rules and conventions governing behaviour in schools, it is hardly surprising that teachers do not attempt to read them all out on the first morning – it would be too much to recall and would suggest that the school is solely about rules . . .

One of the most frequent findings in our own research is the importance of *consistency*. Teachers who are consistent seem to have fewer difficulties that those who are inconsistent or erratic, tolerating misdemeanours on certain occasions or from some pupils but becoming cross about identical matters at other times . . .

Rules are usually imposed on children by adults. The idea of negotiating rules with them is not as widespread as one may believe . . . There are many other ways in which pupils themselves can take more responsibility for their own and their colleagues' behaviour and progress, without the teacher abdicating responsibility . . .

One important fundamental question about negotiation is not merely what is or what should be negotiable, but how children can understand the need for rules . . . This does not negotiate away teachers' legal responsibilities; it actually makes them more meaningful. Adolescents need to face up to matters such as self-discipline and respect for others because these are necessary in families and communities, as well as in schools. Teachers in the end must take responsibility for rules, even if they sometimes endorse sensible proposals from pupils."

Summary

Wragg recognises that society cannot do without rules but stresses that the key factor is the way that they are established, managed and interpreted. He points out that teachers have the difficult task of accepting responsibility for what happens in the classroom – notably discipline and learning – while actively encouraging pupils to participate in the decision-making process and exercising self-responsibility.

Questions to consider

1. What factors and practicalities need to be considered to allow teachers individual flexibility in their own teaching situations while ensuring that school-wide rules are observed?
2. To what extent is the process of negotiating rules more a case of interpretation than agreeing the rule itself?
3. How, in practice, do teachers take account of pupil perspectives when framing rules, especially when those perspectives vary?

Investigations

School without rules. Discuss with pupils what school would be like without rules. If appropriate, ask them to write about, draw or otherwise represent the situation.

Explicit and implicit rules. Observe a colleague teaching and note the number of (1) explicit and (2) implicit rules that govern the conduct of adults and pupils.

Pupil perceptions. Talk to several groups of pupils from the same class or cohort about their perceptions of the rule system that operates within the class or school. Compare and contrast their responses.

Think deeper

Pollard (2008) refers to 'rule frames' that vary in strength according to different situations. Thus, a strong rule frame is required at the start of a lesson when the teacher is sharing information and explaining what will be happening; on the other hand a less strong rule frame is needed (say) during a pupil-initiated session, and a weak rule frame may be applied during a 'wet break' when pupils are kept indoors to read, play board games and draw. Pollard goes on to say that teachers influence the nature of the rule-framing by the way they act and behave; for instance, entering the room in a brisk, purposeful manner indicates 'down to business and no messing', with an accompanying tightening of the rule frame.

As a result of tracking 111 boys aged between eleven and twenty-one as they tried to make sense of the messages they heard from home, school, the law and peer culture, Walker (2007) suggests that boys see the life experience of figures such as teachers and parents as being too dated and irrelevant. Perhaps more surprisingly, the glamorous lifestyles of famous sportsmen and stars from the entertainment industry were seen as too far removed from their own life experiences. Although messages from society encourage boys to be hardworking, ambitious and law-abiding, the boys cited examples of people who had conformed in these ways yet achieved little. The boys appeared to draw their role models from those whose life experience and future goals were similar to their own. The author concluded that boys tend to evaluate the positive and negative examples offered by local, 'older brother' role models to the exclusion of more traditional figures. From an education perspective, choice of 'peer educators' need not only be from a similar age range (ideally a little older) but also those who had similar social lives, socio-economic circumstances and future goals.

Pollard, A. (2008) *Reflective Teaching*, London: Continuum.

Walker, B.M. (2007) 'No more heroes any more: the "older brother" as role model', *Cambridge Journal of Education*, 37 (4), 503–18.

Think wider

In 2005 the Innovation Unit (then called the DfES Innovation Unit) in England funded a project led by Geoff Whitty, Emma Wisby and Anne Diack (University of London Institute of Education) to produce materials for schools to set up and run school councils. This project was part of the Innovation Unit's programme of work on so-called personalised learning. A document was published called *Real Decision Making? School councils in action* (Whitty *et al.* 2008), which contained examples of good practice and an invitation for schools to share ideas. The authors made a number of recommendations, including the following (amended) list:

- Schools need to have a clear understanding of why they are introducing provision for pupil voice in general and establishing a school council in particular.
- Schools need to be willing to change their ethos and structures where necessary.
- Teacher support for pupil voice is crucial if its influence is to move beyond environment and facilities issues to the heart of teaching and learning.
- Schools must endeavour to include all pupils in their provision for pupil voice, not just those actually on the school council or who are most comfortable expressing their views in a school context.
- Pupils with special educational needs may require particular support to participate in school councils.
- Training and support for pupils are essential if they are to contribute effectively to decision making.

Whitty, G., Wisby, E. and Diack, A. (2008) *Real Decision Making? School councils in action*, London: The Innovation Unit, Institute of Education University of London for the DCSF.

Extract 47

Source

Galton, M. (1989) *Teaching in the Primary School*, London: David Fulton; see pp. 162–3, 170.

Introduction

Maurice Galton was the director of a major observational study about primary classrooms in the 1980s, usually referred to by its acronym ORACLE, which stands for 'Observational Research And Classroom Learning Evaluation'. Galton draws from this highly influential study and numerous classroom experiences to offer a view of effective teaching and learning but also to explain why things happen as they do. In this extract he focuses on rules, behaviour and control, notably the significance of relationships and the importance of involving pupils in decisions. He concludes by presenting a number of dilemmas for student teachers and their mentors.

Key words & phrases

Acceptable behaviour, behaviour modification process, conflicts, crack down, exercises power, explanations, firm control, freedoms, independent learning, lose status, negotiated approach, rules of behaviour, shared decision-making, temporary expedient

---

Extract

"Teachers who wish children to engage in independent learning require pupils who are unafraid, self-reliant and self-disciplined, but it is precisely pupils with these kinds of qualities who are likely to react badly to the teacher's imposition of control over their behaviour. If the teacher continually exercises power . . . pupils will conform either out of fear of embarrassment or fear that they will lose status and therefore self-esteem. This strategy of avoidance requires them to be dependent upon the teacher for clues about what constitutes acceptable behaviour and this dependency transmits itself to their work.

The alternative approach involves, whenever necessary, shared decision-making, with consideration given to both the teacher's and pupils' needs. This differs from the behaviour modification process where the emphasis is on the teacher's wants. Initially, this negotiated approach requires teachers to face their pupils with explanations of their needs so the children can accept their share of responsibility . . .

It cannot be said too often that the negotiated approach does not hand over control to the children. Children need to exercise their freedoms within a framework, so they need to know which solutions to problems that they suggest are unacceptable to the teacher because they do not meet the teacher's needs. Nor does the approach mean that teachers should never tell children what to do . . .

When teachers use their authority to control the class and are unable to resolve the conflict at their first attempt, the only recourse is to increase the power. This process can be stressful because the individual is on trial in the eyes both of the pupils and of the other teachers. Negotiating rules of behaviour has one great advantage. Although it may take time to agree the rules, the rules are everybody's, so that if they are broken it is no longer a defeat in personal terms for the teacher . . .

If we accept the argument in this book that children will only risk taking responsibility for their own learning if they are also encouraged to take responsibility for their behaviour, then what should we demand of [student teachers], particularly in classrooms where such a system does not operate? Many tutors argue that it is unreasonable to ask a student [teacher], in so short a time, to try to change the existing system. Student teachers are therefore encouraged to be firm, as a temporary expedient, even to shout and . . . to use tricks (hands on head, finger on lips, etc.) . . . As tutors we comfort ourselves that during their first year of employment, as the students gain more confidence and have their own class, they will put our theories into practice. There is little evidence from the research to suggest that this happens in the majority of cases . . . In promoting the ideas of independent learning among student teachers, while at the same time telling them to 'crack down' on the pupils until they are in firm control, we may unwittingly be providing messages for the future that this strategy is reasonable and effective."

See also Galton, M., Hargreaves, L., Comber, C., Wall, D. and Pell, A. (1999) *Inside the Primary Classroom: 20 years on*, London: Routledge.

Summary

Galton insists that the imposition of rules and regulations from adults without involving pupils in the decisions and giving them a degree of ownership and responsibility is undesirable. Although student (trainee) teachers may be limited in the extent to which they can influence existing practices, the use of techniques to exert control is flawed. Good teaching habits need to be established early.

Questions to consider

1. How should power be distributed and authority exercised during a teaching session?
2. What are the key issues for consideration in agreeing classroom rules and procedures? With whom does the ultimate responsibility lie?
3. How do teachers reach a workable balance between imposition and negotiation?

Investigations

Naughty or nice: Find out how pupils view power and authority in the classroom. Use group interviews to discover what pupils are really thinking about issues of discipline, control and behaviour.

Rules and regulations: Ask a class to write down (say) five rules that they think should apply to every pupil. Collate the responses into a 'top ten' and ask the same pupils to list them in order of priority. Discuss the results with them.

Using sanctions: Present five scenarios to a group of pupils in which there is a clear transgression of rules in each case. Discuss with them an appropriate response or sanction. Repeat the process with a different group. Compare and contrast the different reactions.

Think deeper

Roffey and O'Reirdan (2001) argue that children need to be provided with an enforceable rule framework, sensibly but consistently applied, within which they can gradually strengthen their own self-control. The need for clarity and patience is most acute when teachers deal with new entrants, some of whom do not possess the self-control or social graces to conform. Newell and Jeffery (2002) emphasise the importance of teachers modelling good behaviour to children. Strategies include being prepared to say sorry; explaining that teachers as well as children have rights; taking a keen interest in learning; demonstrating a strong sense of purpose in teaching; and showing that even difficult behaviour can be overcome.

It is a common experience that high-achieving children tend to dominate learning interactions, while underachievers are more likely to be passive, daydream or behave inappropriately. Passivity does not create a climate for deep learning unless accompanied by opportunities for pupils to grapple with issues and concepts in subsequent tasks and activities (Coultas 2007).

Hofer (2007) offers a perspective on pupils' misconduct as a result of changing from on-task to off-task behaviour. The change of emphasis entails a switch from the current learning priority to an activity that the student finds more appealing but is viewed as a discipline problem by the teacher. In such a situation a tension is created between academic and non-academic goals. The author employs motivational conflict theory in exploring the premise that a discipline problem is a consequence of a student's goal shift. Off-task behaviour is thereby interpreted as a failure to coordinate academic and non-academic goals.

Coultas, V. (2007) *Constructive Talking in Challenging Classrooms*, Abingdon: Routledge.

Hofer, M. (2007) 'Goal conflicts and self-regulation: a new look at pupils' off-task behaviour in the classroom', *Educational Review Research*, 2 (1), 28–38.

Newell, S. and Jeffery, D. (2002) *Behaviour Management in the Classroom: A transactional analysis approach*, London: David Fulton.

Roffey, S. and O'Reirdan, T. (2001) *Young Children and Classroom Behaviour: Needs, perspectives and strategies*, London: David Fulton.

Think wider

In stark contrast to Galton's view of power relations in the classroom (see the extract above), Piekara (2009, online) argues that teaching depends on the teacher's ability to motivate, lead, manage and coerce. He claims that teachers' and students' fates are intimately interwoven, as the students' failure to behave and interact is based on the teacher's failure to control and communicate. Just as each student learns differently, he or she also behaves differently and responds to different methods of control; consequently, teachers must be aware of what Piekara refers to as 'power dynamics' and be able to modify their actions appropriately by using five methods of power collectively 'to exert their dominion over the classroom': (1) *Reverent power*, which is defined as the star quality and celebrity status that every teacher must possess in the classroom. Energy, confidence and aspirations reinforce that the teacher is the rightful leader and controls each student's destiny. (2) *Coercive power*, whereby expectations and consequences are established and punishments are given consistently when rules are broken. (3) *Reward power*, displayed by bestowing recognition on those who demonstrate progress, appropriate behaviour or achievement. (4) *Legitimate power*, which is the formalised power exhibited in a hierarchical structure, exhibited by being able to respond appropriately to situations without recourse to help from senior staff, thereby reaffirming to students that the teacher is the supreme authority in the classroom. (5) *Expert power*, expressed by exuding confidence, showing mastery and understanding, and invoking personal anecdotes. Piekara's approach to power and authority also differs markedly from that advocated by writers such as Noblit (1993), who argue that power also contains a caring perspective when it is viewed as moral authority. He distinguished between the concept of power – often linked with oppressive measures – and 'moral authority', the ethical use of power in the service of others. **Managing behaviour: see also Extracts 48 and 49.**

Noblit, G.W. (1993) 'Power and caring', *American Educational Research Journal*, 30 (1), 23–38.
Piekara, E. (2009) 'Power and classroom control', *The Unbearable Lightness of Teaching*, online at http://theulot.wordpress.com/category/evan-piekara.

Managing behaviour

Source

Furlong, J. and Maynard, T. (1995) *Mentoring Student Teachers*, London: Routledge; see pp. 80–2.

Introduction

Furlong and Maynard endeavour to trace the stages of student teacher development. The extract is taken from the section about 'personal survival' and 'dealing with difficulties' and the way in which student teachers struggled to cope with the multiplicity of demands. Note the way that the authors build the tension by using quotations from the subjects to highlight the difficulties and dilemmas – but also the positive final sentence. For the sake of clarity, the word 'students' has been replaced by 'student teachers' in the extract.

Key words & phrases

Anger, attention, battling, behaviour, confusion, constrained, fear, frustration, heading for disaster, interaction, lack of control, lesson plans, misbehaved, out of control, performance, rushed, sheer panic, student teachers, survival

Extract

"Lack of control not only influenced the content of student teachers' activities, it also influenced their actual practice – their 'performance'. Several student teachers maintained that, at this stage, all their effort was put into keeping the class quiet, and when they did have the children's attention, it was a case of 'quick, tell them everything I know'. Many student teachers recognised that they had left the pupils bewildered and confused, as they rushed through instructions or explanations . . . Most student teachers agreed with the comment, 'I didn't have time to stop and think what I was doing' and that often they felt 'out of control, out of your depth' . . .

Quite often, student teachers who felt particularly uncomfortable about control and were 'battling to get attention' tended to try to maintain a one-to-one interaction with the pupils. Student teachers were seen scuttling around classrooms, repeating the same instructions on thirty different occasions to thirty different pupils rather than, as one student teacher maintained, 'competing against the children' to get their attention . . . When things did go wrong, student teachers appeared to become consumed by a mixture of fear, anger, frustration and exhaustion. In particular, the feeling of being ignored seemed to cause real stress and indignation. One student teacher commented, 'At the end of the lesson I felt out of control as the children were packing away at their own speed and in their own way, rather than being told what to do.' Another said, 'The children started calling out suggestions. I tried to stamp on this behaviour but as soon as I turned my back to write a suggestion on the board, they started to call out again.'

While student teachers appeared to be able to rationalise both the children's and their own behaviour outside of the classroom, this appeared not to be the case inside the classroom when faced with children who did not conform to their expectations. As one student teacher humbly reflected, 'I believe that the children misbehaved because the work was not demanding enough for them.' Her real feelings may have been more clearly revealed, however, by her next comment, 'I must ask about what punishments are available to give children.'

Not only did the student teachers appear to be constrained by the class teacher, the pupils and their own lack of knowledge and skill but also, in a sense, by their lesson plans . . . One class teacher commented that she had noticed that student teachers, in their first few weeks in the classroom, would pursue discussions, explanations and activities even when it was painfully obvious to all concerned that it was heading for disaster – rather like 'holding onto the back of a runaway horse'.

Fortunately, the confusion and sheer panic brought about by their first taste of teaching did not, in most cases, last more than a week or so. Slowly, the 'survival' stage gave way to a second stage where student teachers could at least start to identify some of the difficulties they faced."

Summary

Furlong and Maynard offer a realistic view of early encounters with a new group of pupils. They argue that people charged with helping them to negotiate this difficult period need to be aware of the considerable pressure under which student teachers labour. Without these insights, mentors and tutors and even other teachers in the situation may mistakenly believe that the student teacher is incompetent or (worse still) uncooperative. The rest of the chapter describes how new teachers gain confidence and learn to prosper.

Questions to consider

1. How can mentors, tutors and resident teachers assist new student teachers to adjust to and cope with the demands of initial encounters?
2. What factors underlie inexperienced student teachers' unwillingness or inability to deviate from their lesson plans?
3. What professional and personal changes take place in student teachers as they establish themselves in the classroom?

Investigations

Pre-school placement emotions. Interview student teachers during their preliminary visits to ascertain the sorts of concerns and anxieties that dominate their thinking.

Survival strategies. Observe student teachers teaching a number of lessons at the start of their school experience, taking special note of the survival strategies they employ. Discuss the findings with the student teachers, encouraging them to offer their own perspectives.

Experienced student teachers. Interview more experienced student teachers about ways in which they have adjusted mentally, emotionally and practically to the demands of teaching.

Think deeper

Malm (2009) insists that teacher training programmes need to focus more on objectives such as promoting 'conflict literacy', self-awareness, empathy, leadership and collaborative skills; that is, taking into account not only the cognitive but also the social and emotional aspects of human development. She asserts that emotions are at the heart of teaching and comprise its most dynamic qualities. The psychic rewards of teaching and the power to make independent judgements, as well as exercise personal discretion, initiative and creativity through their work, are essential to sustaining teachers' sense of self. Malm concludes that there is a need to heighten the awareness of what it means to be a teacher, with both the personal 'being' and the professional 'becoming' as essential and interrelated dimensions of career development. The person that the student (trainee) teacher *is* becomes of the utmost relevance to how he or she develops professionally. Research by Smithers and Robinson (2009) found that more than a quarter of all trainee teachers never work in the classroom and may experience a 'culture shock' of such intensity that 40 per cent leave after just a few years, citing poor behaviour among pupils and excessive workload as the main reasons. Neill and Caswell (1993) claim that strategies that appear to work with one group of pupils may be less successful with a different set, even in an almost identical situation. The challenges are particularly acute when a teacher begins teaching in a new school, where codes of conduct and accepted procedures are taken for granted by the existing staff and pupils but have yet to be learned by the new teacher.

Malm, B. (2009) 'Towards a new professionalism: enhancing personal and professional development in teacher education', *Journal of Education for Teaching*, 35 (1), 77–91.

Neill, S. and Caswell, C. (1993) *Body Language for Competent Teachers*, London: Routledge.

Smithers, A. and Robinson, P. (2009) *Good Teacher Training Guide 2008*, Buckingham University's Centre for Education and Employment Research.

Think wider

Sewell *et al.* (2009) used a questionnaire and interviews to discover from primary and secondary trainee teachers the extent to which other adults had bullied them during the training course. They found that most bullying took place in the school rather than in the higher education institution; younger trainees and female trainees were particularly vulnerable. This study also indicated that the primary school trainees were more reluctant to tell someone they were being bullied than their secondary school counterparts. Bullying incidents were often characterised by a breakdown in communication between the trainee teacher and the school mentor. Sewell *et al.* conclude that bullying can cause both physical and psychological effects, which might be causal in influencing the numbers of trainees subsequently declining to pursue a career in teaching. **Pupil bullying: see Extracts 17 and 18.**

Sewell, K., Cain, T., Woodgate-Jones, A. and Srokosz, A. (2009) 'Bullying and the postgraduate trainee teacher: a comparative study', *Journal of Education for Teaching*, 35 (1), 3–18.

Extract 49

Source

Haydn, T. (2007) *Managing Pupil Behaviour: Key issues in teaching and learning*, Abingdon: Routledge; see pp. 2–4.

Introduction

Haydn claims that his book is an attempt to develop understanding of the factors that influence the working atmosphere in the classroom. To achieve this goal he uses a wide range of quotations from headteachers, teachers and pupils as they grapple 'to manage the very difficult tensions that arise from attempting to educate all pupils without allowing some to hinder the learning of others'. The scale in the extract was devised by Haydn to encourage teachers to think about: (1) the factors influencing classroom climate; (2) the influence of climate on teaching and learning; and (3) equal opportunities.

Key words & phrases

Authority, calm, chaotic, class control, confrontation, continuum, escalate problems, factors that influence, friendly, harassed, lesson activity, levels, purposeful, relaxed and comfortable, rowdy, scale, transgressions, working atmosphere

Extract

"One of the instruments used in the research that went into this book is a 10-point scale that attempts to describe this [working atmosphere in the classroom] continuum . . .

Level 10: You feel completely relaxed and comfortable; able to undertake any form of lesson activity without concern. Class control not really an issue – teacher and pupils working together, enjoying the experiences involved.

Level 9: You feel completely in control of the class and can undertake any sort of classroom activity, but you need to exercise some control/authority at times to maintain a calm and purposeful working atmosphere. This can be done in a friendly and relaxed manner and is no more than a gentle reminder.

Level 8: You can establish and maintain a relaxed and cooperative working atmosphere and undertake any form of classroom activity, but this requires a considerable amount of thought and effort on your part at times. Some forms of lesson activity may be less calm and under control than others.

Level 7: You can undertake any form of lesson activity, but the class may well be rather 'bubbly' and rowdy; there may be minor instances of a few pupils messing around on the fringes of the lesson but they desist when required to do so. No one goes out of [his or her] way to annoy you or challenge your authority. When you address the class, they listen in silence, straight away.

Level 6: You don't really look forward to teaching the class; it is often a major effort to establish and maintain a relaxed and calm atmosphere. Several pupils will not remain on task without persistent surveillance/exhortation/threats. At times you feel harassed, and at the end of the lesson you feel rather drained. There are times when you feel it is wisest not to attempt certain types of pupil activity in order to keep things under control. It is sometimes difficult to get pupils to be quiet while you are talking or stop them calling out or talking to each other at will across the room, but in spite of this, no one directly challenges your authority and there is no refusal or major disruption.

Level 5: There are times in the lesson when you would feel awkward or embarrassed if the head/a governor/an inspector came into the room because your control of the class is limited. The atmosphere is at times rather chaotic, with several pupils manifestly not listening to your instructions. Some of the pupils are, in effect, challenging your authority by their dilatory or desultory compliance with your instructions and requests. Lesson format is constrained by these factors; there are some sorts of lessons you would not attempt because you know they would be rowdy and chaotic, but in the last resort there is no open refusal, no major atrocities, just a lack of purposefulness and calm. Pupils who wanted to work could get on with it, albeit in a rather noisy atmosphere.

Level 4: You have to accept that your control is limited. It takes time and effort to get the class to listen to your instructions. You try to get onto the worksheet/written part of the lesson fairly quickly in order to 'get their heads down'. Lesson preparation is influenced more by control and 'passing the time' factors than by educational ones. Pupils talk while you are talking; minor transgressions (no pen, no exercise book, distracting others by talking) go unpunished because too much is going on to pick everything up. You become reluctant to sort out the ringleaders as you feel this may well escalate problems. You try to 'keep the lid on things' and concentrate on those pupils who are trying to get on with their work.

Level 3: You dread the thought of the lesson. There will be major disruption; many pupils will pay little or no heed to your presence in the room. Even pupils who want to work will have difficulty doing so. Swearwords may go unchecked; pupils will walk around the room at will. You find yourself reluctant to deal with transgressors because you have lost confidence. When you write on the board, objects will be thrown around the room. You can't wait for the lesson to end and be out of the room.

Level 2: The pupils largely determine what will go on in the lesson. You take materials into the lesson as a matter of form, but once distributed they will be ignored, drawn on or made into paper aeroplanes. When you write on the board, objects will be thrown at you rather than around the room. You go into the room hoping that they will be in a good mood and will leave you alone and just chat to each other.

Level 1: Your entry into the classroom is greeted by jeers and abuse. There are so many transgressions of the rules and what constitutes reasonable behaviour that it is difficult to know where to start. You turn a blind eye to some atrocities because you feel that your intervention may well lead to confrontation, refusal or escalation of the problem. This is difficult because some pupils are deliberately committing atrocities under your nose for amusement. You wish you had not gone into teaching."

See also Haydn, T. (2002) 'The working atmosphere in the classroom and the right to learn', *Education Today*, 52 (2), 3–10.

Summary

Teachers reading Haydn's working atmosphere continuum will inevitably find themselves determining where their experiences lie on the scale between 1 and 10. Those who have endured particularly difficult experiences will doubtless be challenged and pained by recollecting their personal and professional failings. The scale is, however, intended to assist practitioners to realistically evaluate their class management skills and not, as the author emphasises, to be unhelpful and corrosive of teacher morale and solidarity.

Questions to consider

1. In what sense can teachers be said to 'control' pupils? What behavioural challenges are particular to (a) early years; (b) primary; and (c) secondary phases of education?
2. What kind of advice would you offer to a teacher whose class control is most aptly described by level 4 or 5?
3. What sort of issues and practicalities probably need to be addressed with teachers operating in the top three levels?

Investigations

Usefulness of the scale for staff development. Discuss Haydn's scale with a group of experienced colleagues to gain their impressions about its usefulness and potential for staff development.

Experiences of trainee or inexperienced teachers. Interview a number of new teachers with reference to the Haydn scale and accumulate case study material.

The impact of challenging behaviour on teacher morale. Ask a carefully selected group of colleagues (or trainee teachers) to describe some of their worst teaching moments, the impact upon their personal well-being and the way that they coped with them. (Note the powerful emotions that are likely to be evoked in such research.)

Think deeper

Hayes (2010) suggests that 'discipline' describes the means by which teachers try to ensure that the environment is orderly and conducive to learning. The term 'misbehaviour' is often preferred to 'bad behaviour' because the latter involves a moral judgement about the individual concerned, whereas the former is simply a descriptor. Nelson (2006) insists that the key to positive discipline is mutual respect, not punishment. He argues that pupils of all ages can be taught creative cooperation and self-discipline without loss of dignity. Trainee teachers have special challenges, for although they may begin to think, dress, walk and talk like a 'real' teacher, it takes time and perseverance to convince the pupils. The prospect of indiscipline affects teachers, assistants and pupils: adults, because they want to avoid being humiliated and remain 'in control'; pupils, because they do not always possess the life skills or strategies to avoid confrontation, steer clear of trouble or helpfully influence the behaviour of their peers (Hayes 2009, see chapter 5). Although a teacher may speak of a class as being 'difficult', it is often the case that the problems are confined to a very small number whose influence in the classroom gradually becomes pervasive. The vast majority of learners are desperate for the security that comes through effective discipline. **Positive learning climate: see also Extracts 21 and 60, both under 'Think wider'.**

Hayes, D. (2009) *Learning and Teaching in Primary Schools*, Exeter: Learning Matters.
Hayes, D. (2010) *The Encyclopaedia of Primary Education*, Abingdon: Routledge.
Nelson, J. (2006) *Positive Discipline*, New York: Ballantine Books.

Think wider

The labyrinth of responsibilities that comprise the teacher role mean that the successful management of the multiplicity of demands requires teachers to be vigilant in evaluating and adjusting each day's differing priorities, while maintaining the regular timetable of teaching and associated duties. Robertson (1996) claims that it is in such skills as organising, presenting, communicating and monitoring that teachers' true authority rests, as without these attributes it is almost impossible to gain pupils' interest and respect. The variety of demands has also reduced some teachers to a state of permanent exhaustion and stress, exacerbated by studies that strongly point to the teacher him- or herself as the chief factor governing pupil progress. Cosgrove (2001) looks at what is happening in teaching today and offers reasons why breakdowns have become so common; what it means to suffer a breakdown; and the consequences of this epidemic for schools and children. The author offers suggestions about strategies that teachers can use to help themselves; what schools should do to help their staffs; and the ways in which local authorities can offer practical support. For further perspectives, see Carlyle and Woods (2002) and Woods and Jeffrey (2002).

Carlyle, D. and Woods, P. (2002) *Emotions of Teacher Stress*, Stoke-on-Trent: Trentham Books.
Cosgrove, J. (2001) *Breakdown: The facts about teacher stress*, London: RoutledgeFalmer.
Robertson, J. (1996) *Effective Classroom Control*, London: Hodder & Stoughton.
Woods, P. and Jeffrey, B. (2002) 'Teacher identities under stress: the emotions of separation and renewal', *International Studies in Sociology of Education*, 23 (1), 89–106.

Pupil perspectives

Extract 50

Source

Goodman, J.F. (2007) 'School discipline, buy-in and belief', *Ethics and Education*, 2 (1), 3–23.

Introduction

Goodman begins her article by claiming that it is generally acknowledged that school discipline in the United States is failing. She advances the argument that if discipline is to succeed, students must believe in and identify with the rules and goals it is designed to support. She raises questions as to just how embracing (pervasive throughout school life), lofty (transcending the classroom) and moralised (emphasising social over personal) such goals should be.

Key words & phrases

Alienated students, authority, collectively endorsed values, common beliefs, conform, discipline, group purpose, listless conformists, mastery of the curriculum, moral code, moral component, moral mandates, rational explanation, routines, rule-conformity, rules, transcendent school goals, well-functioning disciplinary system

Extract

"Schools expect children to conform to rules-in-general. Discipline, though generally exercised over a single incident, should broadly remind them to obey prohibitions against disrupting those conditions and procedures deemed necessary for instruction. If one instance of discipline is not a stand-in for a wide category of rules, then the teacher has not advanced their agenda of conformity and has not decreased the probability of endless sanctioning . . . However, most educators, I assume, are not purely instrumental in their disciplinary objectives; they want more than rule-conformity. They would like the aggressive child, sanctioned for fighting, to have a change of heart, to believe there are better ways to handle disagreements. They would like the whispering child to see the class from a broader perspective, to realise that it is in everyone's interest if all refrain from distracting classmates . . .

Many conditions promote successful discipline – fairness, proportionality, consistency, rationality, goodwill, relatedness, etc. I have argued, however, that none of these conditions are sufficient. The backbone to a well-functioning disciplinary system is authority premised on and sustained by collectively endorsed values, rules that directly express those values and teachers who are conduits of them. The more moralised and idealised the values, the greater the likelihood of winning over children's commitment as they come to unite their sense of self with the moral mandates . . .

When all members of a group are aligned with a compelling ethic, self-worth approaches oneness with group purpose. In theory this would be the base condition for a perfect disciplinary system. Students are willing to work hard for the collective good, subjugating personal desires and disagreements that destroy the group ethos – 'it's not about me', they may say. Their common beliefs generate loyalty to one another and a willingness to make personal sacrifices for the collectivity. There is no motive to resist group norms, for resistance not only ignites criticism from others, it lowers personal self-esteem. They feel that in letting others down they have been unworthy . . .

Those highly resistant to imposing values may argue that as long as children go to school without objection, are habituated to the routines and authority and comply with instruction and rules – their real life occurring between classes and after school – nothing further is required . . . I have argued that in the absence of a more compelling purpose, engagement is likely to be minimal and frequently unstable, so that the rules will be undermined by increasingly alienated students. Further, and most importantly, a value void, rather than stimulating student thinking in the political, social, and personal realms, creates indifference . . .

If schools are to avoid becoming institutions of listless conformists or over-disciplined resistors, the academic mission must be supplemented with something more . . . When values are hidden and replaced by free-floating, poorly justified rules, children lose the chance to understand, examine, embrace, or reject the presumptive standards supporting them; they lose, in short, the chance to become possessors of their own morality."

Summary

Goodman's key argument is that authority should be premised on and sustained by collectively endorsed values among students and adults. She insists that there must be a moral component to decisions about conduct; the alternative is to impose a collection of routines, instructions and rules upon pupils, whereby they lose the chance 'to become possessors of their own morality' leading to 'value disagreements' and adult–pupil confrontations.

Questions to consider

1. What are the alternatives to expecting students to conform to rules-in-general? To what extent is the author (a) being unrealistic; (b) being pragmatic?
2. What are the advantages and disadvantages of adopting an instrumental approach to discipline objectives? Do these apply equally to all teachers, regardless of age, gender and experience?
3. What moral imperatives drive the behaviour policy in your institution? How are these manifested?

Investigations

Values–driven discipline. Conduct a survey among colleagues in school about the principles that underpin their approach to discipline.

Pupil perspectives. Read a short story, appropriate to the age group, about children or young people being naughty or behaving badly. Ask for responses about the issues that emerge, the way they perceive the actions and what it means for their own situations. You may also wish to encourage groups to write, draw, design comic strips or use the computer to represent their ideas.

Exploring the purpose of rules and regulations. Invite groups of pupils to envisage 'a day without rules' and the impact on behaviour. Note that you will probably have to allow for a period of excitement before the discussion settles. Again, you may also wish to encourage groups to represent their ideas in a variety of ways.

Think deeper

Chaplain (2006) notes that 'rules alone do not guarantee good behaviour; they need to be linked to consequences – which means *consistently* rewarding pupils who follow the rules and applying sanctions as a deterrent to those who do not' (p. 110, author's emphasis). Wragg (2004) categorises rules that commonly govern school life under nine headings: movement, talking, work-related, presentation, safety, space, materials, social behaviour, clothing/appearance. He argues that the problem with strictly applied rules and sanctions is that they fail to take account of specific circumstances. Thus, a normally placid pupil who throws a tantrum and bursts into tears requires a different response from the regularly troublesome pupil who tries to manipulate a situation by contrived fits of temper. Wise teachers regularly discuss and clarify with pupils the importance and implications of self-control and do not allow themselves to be emotionally blackmailed by defiant or devious pupils. **Rules and relationships: see also Extract 46.**

Kyriacou *et al.* (2007) administered a questionnaire to secondary student (trainee) teachers in England and Norway at the start and at the end of their course about (1) their views regarding the factors accounting for pupil misbehaviour; (2) the frequency of pupil misbehaviour; (3) the strategies for dealing with pupil misbehaviour; and (4) their confidence that as a full-time teacher they would have the skills needed to keep pupils engaged in their work and to deal with pupil misbehaviour. The responses from the student teachers indicated that the major factor accounting for pupil misbehaviour was reported to be parents failing to instil pro-school values in their children. The most frequent pupil misbehaviour reported was talking out of turn (e.g. calling out, interrupting, inappropriate remarks or distracting chatter during the lesson). The strategy rated most positively was to establish clear and consistent school and classroom rules about the behaviours that are acceptable and that are unacceptable. **Establishing boundaries: see also Extracts 46 and 47.**

Chaplain, R. (2006) 'Managing classroom behaviour', in Arthur, J., Grainger, T. and Wray, D. (eds) *Learning to Teach in the Primary School*, Abingdon: Routledge.

Kyriacou, C., Avramidis, E., Hole, H., Stephens, P. and Hultgren, A. (2007) 'The development of student teachers' views on pupil misbehaviour during an initial teacher training programme in England and Norway', *Journal of Education for Teaching*, 33 (3), 293–307.

Wragg, E. C. (2004) 'The two Rs: rules and relationships', in Wragg, E.C. (ed.) *The RoutledgeFalmer Reader in Teaching and Learning*, London: RoutledgeFalmer.

Think wider

Kohlberg (1981) was interested in children's reasons for making moral choices and established a theory based on six stages, the first four of which are most applicable to primary children:

1. *Obedience and punishment.* The earliest stage of moral development is especially common in young children, who see rules as fixed and absolute. Obeying the rules is important because it is a means to avoid punishment.
2. *Individualism and exchange.* At this stage of moral development, children account for individual points of view and judge actions based on how they serve individual needs.
3. *Interpersonal relationships.* This stage of moral development is focused on living up to social expectations and roles with an emphasis on conformity, being nice and how choices influence relationships.
4. *Maintaining social order.* The focus is on maintaining law and order by following the rules, doing one's duty and respecting authority.
5. *Social contract and individual rights.* People begin to account for the differing values, opinions and beliefs of other people.

6.   *Universal principles.* People follow their own principles of justice, even if they conflict with laws and rules.

Kohlberg, L. (1981) *Essays on Moral Development 1*, San Francisco: Harper & Row.

Extract 51

Source

Ellis, S. and Tod, J. (2009) *Behaviour for Learning: Proactive approaches to behaviour management*, Abingdon: Routledge; see pp. 140–2.

Introduction

Ellis and Tod are concerned with the identification and difficulties attached to 'relationship with self'. They provide examples of behaviour that are influenced by relationship with self as follows:

- reluctance to try new things;
- being easily frustrated from lack of immediate success or understanding;
- attitudes that are hypercritical, negative, sarcastic and cynical;
- withdrawal, depression and unwillingness to communicate;
- blaming behaviour outside themselves;
- dependency on others to tell them what to do, what is good, what is acceptable;
- lying;
- non-compliance with authority.

Ellis and Tod stress the importance of emotions in affecting the way individuals think and behave (see pp. 119–20).

Key words & phrases

Academic achievement, collaborative learning, emotional, facets of self, individual pupil, interdependence, management of behaviour, negative effects, physical, relationships, self, self-concept, self-esteem, social, strategy choice

---

Extract

"Relationship with self is particularly relevant to this book as it helps us to understand how the *individual* pupil interprets and experiences the teaching approaches and management of behaviour that have been designed for the *group* setting of their school . . . The literature . . . refers to both self-esteem and self-concept as key explanatory constructs relevant to the understanding of what we refer to in the behaviour for learning conceptual framework as 'relationship with self' . . . Self-esteem has been shown to share a mutually reinforcing relationship with academic achievement such that prior academic self-esteem influences subsequent achievement, and prior achievement influences subsequent self-esteem . . . Faced with the task of improving a pupil's learning and behaviour in school, we can either focus on directly improving their relationship with the curriculum or we can focus on improving their relationship with self.

Developments in research into an individual's relationship with self reflect a move away from the acceptance of a unidimensional notion of self-esteem to one that recognises the many facets of self through the use of multidimensional models . . . the pupil may have many facets of self, both positive and negative, that are influencing his/her behaviour. These multidimensional models involve not just academic and non-academic components of self-esteem but also propose further divisions into subject specific academic facets of self . . . and various non-academic social, emotional and physical components of self . . . From these models we have a framework for understanding why the behaviour makes sense from the pupil's perspective and the purpose it serves for them. For example, it may not make sense to us if a pupil will not persist with a task when we know that they need to get a qualification in order to improve their life chances . . . However, they may have experienced academic failure in the past and not believe that any action on their part can change the 'fact' that they are not going to achieve any success with academic learning. The pupil's behaviour makes sense to them and serves the purpose of confirming their academic self-esteem. The same pupil may, however, work hard and persist with a non-academic activity, as they may well have a relatively favourable social or physical self-esteem.

Strategy choice in this case might . . . challenge the pupil's academic self-esteem by promoting learning behaviours that allow increased academic success and/or getting them to reconsider the evidence that led them to the conclusion that they were never going to succeed in any academic areas. Other strategy choices might seek to use the pupil's relatively good social self-esteem to increase their academic interest and success by increased use of collaborative learning activities . . .

Influences on relationship with self are many and varied and some are likely to have been long-term. As such, teachers may be limited in the extent to which they can effect change to this relationship. They can, however, through the interdependence of relationship with curriculum, relationship with others and relationship with self, promote appropriate learning behaviours that support the individual to reduce the negative effects of any damaging relationship with self."

Summary

Ellis and Tod argue that a pupil's relationship with self and with others is of greater immediate significance than relationship with the curriculum. All pupils need to have a belief in the worthwhile nature of academic endeavour before engaging fully with lesson content. Teachers have an important role to play in the process by being sensitive to individual needs and motivation, especially with those who have had unhappy experiences of learning and have lost confidence owing to low self-esteem.

Questions to consider

1. What do you understand by the concept of self-esteem and its impact on social, emotional and cognitive development?
2. How realistic and manageable are the strategy choices outlined above? What are their implications for practice?
3. To what extent can teachers compensate for the long-term impact on relationship to self that is caused by 'persistent environmental influences'?

Investigations

Literature search. Research the different definitions and beliefs about (1) self-esteem; (2) self-concept; and (3) self-efficacy.

Teachers' ideas about pupil behaviour. Interview at least one teacher about his or her beliefs regarding the underlying causes for pupil behaviour. Conduct a similar process with pupils. Compare and contrast their responses.

Attitudes towards self-esteem. Carry out a survey of colleagues' attitudes towards, and understandings of, the concept of self-esteem.

Think deeper

One definition of self-esteem is a state of mind controlled by what a person believes about the way that others view him or her. The associated terms 'self-belief' and 'self-concept' and 'self-efficacy' indicate a state of mind controlled by how a person views him- or herself and are considered by some educationists to be more useful terms than self-esteem as they can be linked to verifiable achievement rather than opinion (Maclellan 2005). Nevertheless, high self-esteem contributes to a state of what is referred to as 'relaxed alertness' in learning, which in turn allows pupils to evaluate their strengths and weaknesses and increases the likelihood that learning will be deep rather than superficial. **Teachers' self-identity: see Extracts 34–36.**

American educationist Lilian Katz (1995) suggests that parents and teachers can strengthen and support a healthy sense of self-esteem in children in at least seven ways: (1) help them to build healthy relationships with peers; (2) clarify their own values and those of others that may differ; (3) offer them reassurance that support is unconditional; (4) appreciate rather than merely praise their interests; and avoid flattery; (5) offer them opportunities to face challenges as well as to have fun; (6) treat them respectfully, take their views seriously and offer meaningful feedback; and (7) help them to cope with setbacks and use the information and awareness they gain to future advantage.

Katz, L.G. (1995) 'How can we strengthen children's self-esteem?', University of Illinois, Urbana, IL, ERIC Clearinghouse on Elementary and Early Childhood Education, online at www.kidsource.com/kidsource/content2/Strengthen_Children_Self.html.

Maclellan, E. (2005) 'Should we raise pupils' self-esteem?', *Education 3–13*, 33 (1), 7–12.

Think wider

In the introduction to a comprehensive text about student motivation, Brophy (2004) focuses on motivational principles rather than motivational theorists or theories, which leads into a consideration of specific classroom strategies. Brophy suggests that educators tend to divide into two distinct groups: first, those with overly romantic views of human nature, who claim that all learning can be fun and exciting if the curriculum is well matched to students' interests and abilities, especially if learning incorporates a lot of practical 'hands-on' activities; and second, those who claim that school is inherently boring and frustrating as we attempt to teach students things in which they have little or no interest and find meaningless. Brophy dismisses the need for constantly creating intrinsic motivation in students, claiming that a more balanced and fruitful way of considering motivation should be based on the notion of gradually socialising students' motivation to learn.

Barrow *et al.* (2001) offer support and guidance for teachers who are dealing with issues of behaviour and offer suggestions for building creative relationships in school. They suggest that a major factor in our communication and relationship with others is how we 'contract' with them, and whether we do this implicitly ('indirectly') or explicitly ('directly'). Transactional analysis is founded on the principle that 'I am okay with myself and you are okay with me; I respect and accept myself and you, and trust you to do the same to me' (p. 6).

Barrow, G., Bradshaw, E. and Newton, T. (2001) *Improving Behaviour and Raising Self-Esteem in the Classroom: A practical guide to using transactional analysis*, London: David Fulton.

Brophy, J. (2004) *Motivating Students to Learn*, New York: Lawrence Erlbaum.

Education policy and practice

Shaping education thinking

Source

Shor, I. (1993) 'Education is politics', in McClaren, P. and Leonard, P. (eds) *Paulo Freire: A critical encounter*, London: Routledge; see pp. 25–8.

Introduction

Paolo Freire was one of the twentieth century's great thinkers on education and the politics of liberation, notably in Latin America and Africa. The editors of this volume, McClaren and Leonard, suggest that he dared to tread where even Karl Marx refused to walk. Shor begins his chapter by quoting from Freire when he told a group of literacy teachers that above all they needed to have faith in human beings and to love them. Shor points out that the principles of 'liberation' can and should be readily applied to teaching and learning.

Key words & phrases

Banking method, critical knowledge, intellectual centres, justice, liberating classroom, lifeless bodies of knowledge, political, political alienation, problem-poser, social change, social consequences, social pedagogy, transformative relationship

---

Extract

"Freire's passion for justice, for critical knowledge, and for social change stand out when you meet him or read his work. For Freire, teaching and learning are human experiences with profound social consequences. Education is not reducible to a mechanical method of instruction. Learning is not a quantity of information to be memorised or a package of skills to be transferred to students. Classrooms die as intellectual centres when they become delivery systems for lifeless bodies of knowledge. Instead of transferring facts and figures from teachers to students, a Freirean class invites students to think critically about subject matter, doctrines, the learning process itself, and their society.

Freire's social pedagogy defines education as one place where the individual and society are constructed, a social action which can either empower or domesticate students. In the liberating classroom suggested by Freire's ideas, teachers pose problems derived from student life, social issues, and academic subjects, in a mutually created dialogue.

This pedagogy challenges teachers and students to empower themselves for social change, to advance democracy and equality as they advance their literacy and knowledge. His critical methods ask teachers and students to question existing knowledge as part of the questioning habits appropriate for citizens in a democracy. In Freirean critical classrooms, teachers reject the methods which make students passive and anti-intellectual. They do not lecture students into sleepy silence. They do not prepare students for a life of political alienation in society. Rather, Freirean educators pose critical problems to students, treat them as complicated, substantial human beings, and encourage curiosity and activism about knowledge and the world.

A Freirean critical teacher is a problem-poser, who asks thought-provoking questions and who encourages students to ask their own questions. Through problem-posing, students learn to question answers rather than merely to answer questions. In this pedagogy, students experience education as something they do, not as something done to them. They are not empty vessels to be filled with facts or sponges to be saturated with official information or vacant bank accounts to be filled with deposits from the required syllabus. Freire's famous metaphor for traditional education, the 'banking' method, focused on the stifling of creative and critical thought in mass education . . .

The critical teacher must also be a democratic one. If the critical teacher criticises inequality and the lack of democracy in society and then teaches in an authoritarian way, she or he compromises her or his credibility. The empowering education Freire suggests is not a new data bank or doctrine delivered to students; it is, instead, a democratic and transformative relationship between students and teacher, students and learning, and students and society . . .

Freirean critical education invites students to question the system they live in and the knowledge being offered them, to discuss what kind of future they want, including their right to elect authority and to remake the school and society they find. Education is politics because it is one place where individuals and society are constructed."

Summary

Freire's philosophy is strongly critical of systematic teaching and learning approaches that create passivity in the learner and supremacy (intellectually and authoritatively) in the person of the teacher. Shor stresses the importance of student engagement in learning, the need to challenge, ask questions and eschew conformity. The implications for the classroom, schooling in general and meeting examination targets are, therefore, profound and extensive.

Questions to consider

1. Evaluate the claim that 'classrooms die as intellectual centres when they become delivery systems for lifeless bodies of knowledge' and that education is 'one place where the individual and society are constructed'.
2. What strategies might be employed to ensure that 'the teacher and students develop co-intentionality'?
3. In what ways might methods of teaching incline to make students passive and anti-intellectual? What approaches are likely to produce the opposite effect?

Investigations

Teachers' verbal dominance. Record a number of lessons during the interactive phase (pupil–adult) and estimate the proportion of time for which teachers speak and pupils speak. Discuss the implications with the teachers concerned.

Pupil questions. Observe a number of lessons and note the questions that pupils ask. Categorise questions into: (1) those that ask for clarification; (2) those that relate to instructions; (3) those that interrogate a statement that the teacher has made; and (d) other types. Discuss the implications of your findings with the teachers concerned.

The education philosophy of school or college leaders. Share all or a selected part of the extract with senior colleagues, highlighting some of the more explicit statements. When they have had opportunity to absorb the points – perhaps after a few days – invite them to respond.

Think deeper

John Dewey (1859–1952) approached education as part of a broader project that encompassed an exploration of the nature of experience, knowledge, society and ethics and was a leading representative of the progressive movement in school education during the first half of the twentieth century. Dewey argued that much of education failed because it neglected the fundamental principle of the school as a form of community life.

He believed that school should be a place where certain information is to be given, where certain lessons are to be learned and where certain habits are to be formed (see

Infed, online, and a re-released edition of Dewey's *Democracy and Education* (1997)). **John Dewey: see also Extract 53.**

Dewey, J. (1997) *Democracy and Education*, New York: Simon & Schuster/Free Press.
Infed (undated) 'Education for democracy', www.infed.org/biblio/b-dem.htm.

Think wider

In 1998, Professor Bernard Crick reported to the UK government on education for citizenship and the teaching of democracy in schools. He defined citizenship education as having three main strands: (1) social and moral responsibility; (2) political literacy; and (3) community involvement. Leading researchers and expert teachers worked for over two years in seminars and in debate with Bernard Crick to produce a book edited by Audrey Osler, called *Citizenship and Democracy in Schools* (2000), which provides a framework for citizenship education in the context of cultural diversity underpinned by an understanding and practice of human rights. The rationale is that human rights principles can be used by schools to challenge structural inequality, discrimination and exclusion and to support young people in developing confident identities in contexts of diversity.

Kelly (1995) argued that one of the major tasks that education must perform in a democratic society is 'the proper preparation of young citizens for the roles and responsibilities they must be ready to take on when they reach maturity' (p. 101). Contributors to Lee and Fouts's edited collection (2005) who employ teachers' perceptions from the United States, Australia, England, Russia and China about education for social citizenship remind us that the things that teachers see as important in citizenship education – and how their perceptions facilitate or hinder the preparation of good citizens – vary across the globe according to prevailing social norms and political influences. The Institute for Citizenship (www.citizen.org.uk/about.html) is an independent charitable trust that aims to promote informed, active citizenship and greater participation in democracy and society through a combination of community projects, research, education and discussion and debate.

Crick, B. (1998) *Education for Citizenship and the Teaching of Democracy in Schools*, London: QCA Publications.
Kelly, A.V. (1995) *Education and Democracy: Principles and practices*, London: Paul Chapman.
Lee, W.O. and Fouts, J.T. (eds) (2005) *Education for Social Citizenship: Perceptions of Teachers in the USA, Australia, England, Russia and China*, Hong Kong: Hong Kong University Press.
Osler, A. (ed.) (2000) *Citizenship and Democracy in Schools: Diversity, identity, equality*, Stoke-on-Trent: Trentham Books.

Extract 53

Source

Dewey, J. (1922/2009) 'Education as engineering', *Journal of Curriculum Studies*, 41 (1), 1–5.

Introduction

John Dewey's short essay 'Education as engineering' was first published in 1922. It is followed by four commentaries (see 'Think deeper', below) discussing the contemporary relevance of its argument that a science of education cannot advance education in the absence of pioneering developments on the ground of the schools. (From article abstract)

Key words & phrases

Ambiguity, collective experience, conventional, courageous disposition, mental pattern, new concepts, new personal attitude, new type of education, old things with new names, prior experimentation, voice of authority

---

Extract

"There is an ambiguity in referring to a 'mental pattern' in connection with schools. The pattern is not mental, if we mean a pattern formed *by* mind. There is doubtless a pattern *in* our minds, but that signifies only a sense of a comfortable scheme of action which has been deposited by wont and use. The pattern is so deep-seated and clearly outlined that the ease of its recognition gives rise to a deceptive sense that there is something intellectual in the pattern itself . . . New conceptions in education will not of themselves carry us far in modifying schools . . .

There is no question that would-be pioneers in the educational field need an extensive and severe intellectual equipment. Experimentation is something other than blindly trying one's luck or messing around in the hope that something nice will be the result. Teachers who are to develop a new type of education need more exacting and comprehensive training in science, philosophy and history than teachers who follow conventionally safe lines . . .

The most optimistic soul, if candid, will admit that we are mostly doing the old things with new names attached. The change makes little difference – except for advertising purposes. We used to lay out a course prescribed by authority for the improvement of the minds of the young. Now we initiate them into their cultural heritage . . .

I am not insinuating that there is personal insincerity in this state of affairs. In part it is due to the fact that docility has been emphasised in education, plus the fact that in the main the most docile among the young are the ones who become teachers when they are adults. Consequently they still listen docilely to the voice of authority . . .

In short, at present, both students and teachers of education are excessively concerned with trying to evolve a body of definite, usable, educational directions out of the new body of science . . . But it is pathetic . . . It retards the creation of a new type of education, because it obscures the one thing deeply needful: a new personal attitude in which a teacher shall be an inventive pioneer in use of what is known, and shall learn in the process of experience to formulate and deal with those problems which a premature 'science' of education now tries to state and solve in advance of experience.

I do not under-estimate the value of the guidance which some time in the future individuals may derive from the results of prior collective experience. I only say that the benefit of such an art cannot be had until a sufficient number of individuals have experimented without its beneficial aid in order to provide its materials. And what they need above all else is the creatively courageous disposition."

See also Austin, M. (1922) 'The need for a new social concept', *New Republic*, 31, 298–302.

Summary

Dewey expresses concerns that too much education is based on a passive acceptance by each generation of teachers that previous methods and approaches are appropriate. He advocates that teachers be more adventurous in developing their classroom practice creatively rather than relying on the opinions and preferences of older practitioners. Dewey stresses that he is not anti-intellectual but insists that nothing substitutes for hard-won experience. **John Dewey: see also Extract 9 under 'Think deeper' and Extracts 39, 42 and 52.**

Questions to consider

1. How much of our school system and ways of working are the result of habit and repetition? Is it fair to claim that 'we are mostly doing the old things with new names attached'?
2. How much scope do teachers have to be inventive pioneers?
3. What qualities and insights might be a help, or a hindrance?

Investigations

Changing pedagogy. Interview a number of more experienced colleagues about ways in which their pedagogy has been modified over time and what factors influenced the changes.

Experienced teachers as models. Interview experienced and inexperienced teachers separately about (1) the ways in which the experienced teachers believe that they influence less experienced ones; and (2) the ways in which less experienced teachers claim that they are influenced by more experienced ones. Contrast the two sets of views.

Creating an ideal education system. Ask a group of pre-service teachers (or any other distinctive group) to identify ways in which they would organise the education system 'from scratch', taking particular note of how their own experiences of education appear to influence their decisions.

Think deeper

The following four authors offer a response to Dewey's article in the same edition of *Journal of Curriculum Studies*, vol. 41, issue 1:

Hopmann, S.T. ('Mind the gap: Dewey on educational bridge-building')
Biesta, G. ('Building bridges or building people? On the role of engineering in education')
Garrison, J. ('The art and science of education')
Schrag, F. ('Is there progress in education? If not, why not?')

Think wider

Loughran *et al.* (2005) suggest that teacher education design may be seen as a combination of four key links: (1) conceptual links across the university curriculum; (2) theory–practice links between school and university settings; (3) social–cultural links among the participants; and (4) personal links that shape the identity of teacher educators. In a linked publication, Loughran (2006) argues that teacher educators demonstrate scholarship when they offer student teachers insights into how they might anticipate and deal with uncertainty in their practice and respond to the associated contradictions and constraints. He indicates that in so doing, the educator can offer what he refers to as a 'window of opportunity' for student teachers to consider the value of adopting such a critical approach (see p. 164).

Loughran, J.J. (2006) *Developing a Pedagogy of Teacher Education*, Dordrecht, the Netherlands: Springer.
Loughran, J.J., Berry, A. and Tudball, E. (2005) 'Developing a culture of critique in teacher education classes', in Hoban, G.F. (ed.) *The Missing Links in Teacher Education Design*, Dordrecht, the Netherlands: Springer.

Values in education

Extract 54

Source

Arthur, J., Davison, J. and Lewis, M. (2005) *Professional Values and Practice: Achieving the Standards for QTS*, Abingdon: Routledge; see pp. 161–3.

Introduction

As a basis for their book about values and practice, Arthur and his colleagues insist that 'a profession can be defined by the recognition of the social and moral context of its work' (p. 2). The role of the teacher is therefore not merely to transfer knowledge but to address issues about human development and the purpose of education. The extract below is taken from the concluding chapter of the book.

Key words & phrases

Beginning teachers, ethical systems, highly complex, improvisation and risk-taking, non-routine, professional judgement, questioning and refining, reflection, reflective practitioner, researching your own practice, routine, taking risks, teaching, theory

---

Extract

"Teaching is a highly complex business. It combines much that is routine with a very great deal that is non-routine, calling for the exercise of professional judgement time after time every day, often in tricky and pressured situations. Dealing with what is routine – or appears to be routine – is helped by reference to previous experiences of similar situations. Our responses in such cases tend to acquire something of the status of precepts or rules through habit or regular rehearsal. Dealing with the non-routine – the unexpected, the problematic, the new and unfamiliar, the paradoxical – is never straightforward precisely because of the absence of close specific parallels on which to base responses. While experience can point us in certain directions, there must always be improvisation and risk-taking in such situations.

It is at such moments that professional judgement is most tested and heavily dependent on the existence of value and ethical systems which direct us towards making sound decisions. Professional judgement is at its most fragile and insecure at such moments, especially for beginning teachers whose professional value and 'belief' systems are more likely to be emergent than established . . . That is why such importance attaches to reflection and why the goal of being a 'reflective practitioner' is so currently pervasive in professional discourse . . .

There are different things to be reflective *about*; reflection can take different *forms*; and it can operate at different *levels* . . . The natural tendency with beginning teachers to be most concerned with technical features of their personal teaching practice has been noted. At a deeper level, however, is the need to *reflect on the activity of reflection itself*, in which the practice of reflection itself becomes the subject of scrutiny and development. This is just as important in the process of being a reflective practitioner as deliberately engaging learners in 'learning about learning' is to the learning process . . . It is through reflection at deeper levels that we refine those personal and professional value systems which help us to handle non-routine and problematic situations which do not lend themselves to simple technical solutions . . . [N]ow more than ever we need teachers who are prepared to engage in questioning and refining their own personal and professional values and, from this position, to assert their voices and practice in the educational system. Part of this involves being prepared to take risks and to experiment and to question orthodoxies of policy and practice from whatever sources they emanate . . .

Theory is not, as it has sometimes been pejoratively characterised, something that exists separately from practice. It arises from development in practice, through efforts to conceptualise and organise understandings that emerge from practice. Conversely, new kinds of practice take life from efforts to implement theoretical perspectives . . . Being a 'reflective practitioner' involves, essentially, researching your own practice. But we need to understand this in two ways: using your own practice as the site of your own research; and using the research into practice elsewhere to expand your vision of possibilities and to authenticate your own ideas."

Summary

Arthur *et al.* emphasise that teaching is not a mechanical occupation involving the mastery of techniques and strategies. True professionalism is rooted in practice that stems from personal integrity and conviction about the most appropriate means of educating.

Progress as a teacher necessitates a constant evaluation of your own and others' teaching, reciprocally linking theory and practice.

Questions to consider

1. What sorts of 'professional judgements' do teachers regularly make during lessons? To which areas of teaching and learning do they relate?
2. To what extent is 'reflection' a helpful concept in terms of improving practice and preventing stagnation?
3. What makes a good theory and how should its usefulness be evaluated?

Investigations

Identifying professional judgements: Use a series of structured lesson observations to categorise when the teacher made key judgements. Discuss with the teacher the guiding principles or beliefs behind those decisions.

Aims of education: Conduct a survey of teachers' views about the key aims of education. Ask them to select from a list of statements that you provide for them and to add written comments or other significant aims. Contrast your findings with those of previous studies (see below under 'Thinking deeper').

Reflecting in and on practice: Ask a number of trainee teachers whose lessons you are observing to keep a log of reflections about their teaching – they will probably be required to do so anyway as part of their school experience – and discuss with them the decisions they made during the lesson and the values or beliefs that underpinned them.

Think deeper

Larrivee (2008) reviews the research on creating a learning climate conducive to facilitating the development of teachers as reflective practitioners. She concludes that the process of emerging as a reflective practitioner involves a willingness to be an active participant in a growth process. Thus, reflective practice involves teachers questioning the goals, values and assumptions that guide their work and entails critical questions about the means, ends and contexts of teaching and learning. Larrivee insists that it is important for teachers to become critically reflective teachers who pose important questions of practice because the aim of reflective practice is to think critically about one's teaching choices and actions. **Self-directed professional development: see Extract 38.**

Bold (2008) describes how two tutors and a group of foundation degree students explored the establishment of peer support groups to support students' reflection on practice, based on the ten principles of reflective practice described by Ghaye and Ghaye in 1998. She concluded that regular peer group activities appeared to support deeper learning approaches and an increase in the students' reflective capacity. The students appeared to be engaged in deeper learning approaches, and some of their evaluations of the impact of their work with the tutor indicated that they recognised that their professional practice was supported by academic studies. The challenge for the tutor was to manage the situation in such a way that the students engaged with misunderstandings and misconceptions at some point during the session. Many students found that peer support group activities improved their critical reflection on practice and encouraged a deeper approach to learning.

Bold, C. (2008) 'Peer support groups: fostering a deeper approach to learning through critical reflection on practice', *Reflective Practice*, 9 (3), 257–67.
Ghaye, A. and Ghaye, K. (1998) *Teaching and Learning through Critical Reflective Practice*, London: David Fulton.
Larrivee, B. (2008) 'Meeting the challenge of preparing reflective practitioners', *The New Educator*, 4 (2), 87–106.

Think wider

Teachers have long held that the job is a profession in much the same way as (say) a lawyer or a doctor; however, primary teachers have had more of a struggle than secondary teachers to be accepted as 'professionals' for two principal reasons: (1) They deal with young children, who are viewed as 'easier' to educate than older pupils. (2) There is a blurring of subject boundaries in the primary curriculum, and teachers are not identified as 'subject experts' in the same way as, for instance, a specialist geography teacher in a secondary school might be. Ornstein (1977) suggests that for a job to be called a profession it requires a defined body of knowledge that is beyond the grasp of people outside the job; control over licensing standards and/or entry requirements; autonomy in making decisions about selected spheres of work; and high prestige and economic standing. There are still anomalies existing in terms of status and promotion opportunities but governments of all persuasions have been keen to foster the belief that all teachers are professionals. Sceptics claim that such enthusiasm is a means of exercising control, expressed through the dictum that a professional must conform to the status quo, which effectively suppresses individuality and silences dissent (see, for example, Richards 2001; Silcock 2002). **Teacher professionalism: see Extracts 36 and 38.**

As part of the Primary Review, White (2008) suggests that since the turn of the new century there has been an emphasis on the promotion of personal well-being as a key aim of education, as it is seen as a more inclusive concept than the personal autonomy that characterised the twentieth century. He also notes that aims in respect of both 'well-being' and 'autonomy' have been more explicitly connected to the educational requirements of a liberal democratic society than was formerly the case. Issues associated with the place of civic responsibilities and the rights of religious and other communities found within it have been the focal point for close scrutiny and debate. Contemporary issues have highlighted the importance of education for sustainable development and global awareness, which have influenced the school curriculum in the form of environmental education 'green' issues.

Ornstein, A.C. (1977) 'Characteristics of the teaching profession', *Illinois Schools Journal*, 56 (4), 12–21.

Richards, C. (ed.) (2001) *Changing English Primary Education: Retrospect and prospect*, Stoke-on-Trent: Trentham Books.

Silcock, P. (2002) 'Under construction or facing demolition? Contrasting views on English teacher professionalism from across a professional association', *Teacher Development*, 6 (2), 137–55.

White, J. (2008) *Aims as Policy in English Primary Education* (Primary Review Research Survey 1/1), Cambridge: University of Cambridge.

Extract 55

Source

Eaude, T. (2009) 'Happiness, emotional well-being and mental health: what has children's spirituality to offer?' *International Journal of Children's Spirituality*, 14 (3), 185–96.

Introduction

Eaude's article largely consists of a discussion about what children's happiness, emotional well-being and mental health entail. Eaude argues that seeing these three elements through the 'lens' of children's spirituality can help to avoid an individualistic and introspective approach. He further claims that for happiness and emotional well-being to be seen as ends in themselves, and searched for explicitly, is potentially counter-productive and even dangerous.

Key words & phrases

Challenges, cope with adversity, emotional responses, flourishing, gratification, immediate and long-term happiness, mental health, protecting children, search for meaning and connectedness, short-term pleasure, spirituality, therapeutic education, types of response, well-being, worth living

---

Extract

"Happiness is an active state, not simply the absence of pain. Nor is it the same as pleasure. We may not know whether we are happy or not; and will in practice often be happy in some respects but not in others . . . So, self-reporting of happiness is difficult for adults; and even more so for young children less capable of placing immediate sensations into a longer perspective . . . One of Aristotle's conceptions of a life truly worth living was that it leads to *eudaimonia*, usually translated as happiness . . . I shall argue that teachers and parents should be concerned with enabling children to develop a longer-term happiness in the sense of flourishing, with the pursuit of short-term pleasure often a barrier to this . . .

Goleman (1996) is the most popular and influential author to promote emotional intelligence, emotional literacy and emotional well-being. Such terms are left deliberately vague, but are usually associated with feeling good about oneself, self-esteem, being aware of one's own and other people's emotions and, in particular, being able to regulate one's own. These are often encouraged through explicit programmes and activities, an approach that Ecclestone and Hayes (2008) call 'therapeutic education' and regard as profoundly dangerous. They do not define therapeutic education, but their key argument, in this context, is that educators have become too concerned with emotional well-being, as opposed to critical engagement with knowledge. This emphasises feelings over knowledge, creating a belief that everyone is vulnerable and needs support, rather than challenge . . . By promoting particular types of response, often on the basis of simplistic notions of well-being, adults discourage children from engaging with the complexity and ambiguity of emotional responses and how these are affected by the child's specific circumstances . . .

While adults have a role in protecting children from what may really harm them, children must be given the chance, and enabled, to develop these attributes . . . a strong sense of self, often within the context of feeling part of a family or a group, helps children believe that they can overcome adversity. More practically, if children, when upset, seek adult support as the first (or only) step, rather than one level of a range of strategies, their sense of agency – and the sense that having coped previously they can do so again – will not develop. Mental health is undermined by a sense of helplessness . . . By making happiness, especially immediate pleasure, an end in itself, adults may make longer-term happiness harder to achieve. By concentrating on emotional well-being, adults may create a sense of vulnerability. And by focusing too much on possible problems, adults may prevent children from learning to cope with adversity on their own . . .

The discourse on spirituality emphasises the search for meaning and connected-ness, and less concern with oneself. This does not involve turning inwards or avoiding difficulty but meeting, and making sense of, challenges. This leads towards a view of happiness in the sense of flourishing, rather than the immediate gratification associated with what is external and transient. Emotional well-being does not just involve feeling good, being happy or having fun . . .

So, a balance has to be struck between protecting children and providing them with the challenges implicit in learning. For children to flourish requires the chance to explore, to search, and to reflect. Paradoxically, many of the activities which promote this are what children most enjoy, so that happiness and well-being flow from these, rather than being sought directly or provided by adults."

Ecclestone, K. and Hayes, D. (2008) *The Dangerous Rise of Therapeutic Education*, Abingdon: Routledge.
Goleman, D. (1996) *Emotional Intelligence: Why it can matter more than IQ*, New York: Bloomsbury.

Summary

Eaude's article argues that an explicit focus on children's emotional well-being, happiness and mental health may be counter-productive and that these three elements are best seen as by-products of other activities, rather than as ends in themselves. The discourse on spirituality emphasises the search for meaning and connectedness, rather than concern with the self to meet and make sense of life's challenges. Eaude concludes that happiness is more appropriately viewed in terms of flourishing, rather than the immediate gratification associated with what is external and transient. (Based on article conclusion)

Questions to consider

1. To what extent do you agree that educators have become overly concerned with pupil well-being?
2. How much moral responsibility do, and should, teachers have for ensuring pupils' happiness?
3. To what extent do you agree with Eaude that children are happy and contented when they are offered the chance to explore, to search and to reflect on their learning?

Investigations

Teachers' views on pupil well-being. Send out a short questionnaire to colleagues inviting written responses and/or interviewing a number of them to elicit their views about the teacher's role in pupil well-being. Use questions such as: (1) How much is pupils' happiness your responsibility? (2) What are the advantages and disadvantages of praise and encouragement? (3) How can adults best help pupils to be confident and autonomous? (4) What are your views about a trend towards 'teaching happiness'?

Pupils' views on happiness. Ask as many pupils as possible to provide a written or verbal response to the questions: (1) What makes you happy today? (2) What will make you happy for ever?

Adults' views on pupil happiness. Ask as many adults as possible to provide a written or verbal response to the questions: (1) What makes you happy today? (2) What will make you happy for ever? Contrast the results with those you obtained when posing the same questions to pupils.

Think deeper

Ivens (2007) has created what he claims to be a psychometrically valid and reliable measure for schoolchildren aged between eight and fifteen, piloted and developed against existing measures of self-esteem, affect and depression, which he calls the 'School

Children's Happiness Inventory' (SCHI). Ivens argues that the SCHI can be especially useful in assessing the effect of school-based interventions and influences on school-children's well-being.

A three-year study by the Children's Society (2007), *Good Childhood Inquiry: Happiness*, concluded that an aggressive pursuit of personal success by adults is now the greatest threat to the well-being and happiness of children. The research team argued that a preoccupation with self was taking a lot of joy out of children's lives, out of their family lives, out of their school and even out of their leisure life and consumption. It was essential that the next generation of children recognise the importance of contributing to the welfare of others rather than themselves and putting human relationships higher than the accumulation of possessions and acquiring societal status. Noddings (2004) argues that the narrow curriculum found in most classrooms helps shape a culture with misguided priorities, whereas the idea that happiness and education not only can but should coexist must be taken seriously by everyone concerned about preparing children and young adults for a truly satisfying life in our democratic society. **Happiness: see also Extract 15.**

Children's Society (2007) *Good Childhood Inquiry: Happiness*, London: Church of England Children's Society.
Ivens, J. (2007) 'The development of a happiness measure for schoolchildren', *Educational Psychology in Practice*, 23 (3), 221–39.
Noddings, N. (2004) *Happiness and Education*, Cambridge: Cambridge University Press.

Think wider

The end result of making children over-reliant on adults and negative about their own abilities is often referred to as 'learned helplessness' (LH), a term attributed to Martin Seligman (1975). The concept of 'locus of control' is important in understanding learned helplessness and relates to whether an individual believes that events depend on his or her behaviour and personality – the so-called internal locus of control – or on luck, chance, fate or the actions of other people – the so-called external locus of control (Rotter 1975). Children who are 'helpless' believe that they are powerless to prevent failure and subject to the decisions and actions of others. Gordon (2006) grimly summarises such a condition as 'it hurts too much to try'. **Failure: see also Extract 47 under 'Think wider' and 'Extract'.**

Gordon, M. (2006) 'The turned off child', *Oregon LDA Newsletter*, online at www.ldaor.org/Newsletter-Fall2006.html.
Rotter, J. (1975) 'Some problems and misconceptions related to the construct of internal versus external control of reinforcement', *Journal of Consulting and Clinical Psychology*, 43, 56–67.
Seligman, M. (1975) *Helplessness: On depression, development and death*, San Francisco: Freeman.

Extract 56

Source

Claire, H. (2006) 'Education for cultural diversity and social justice', in Arthur, J., Grainger, T. and Wray, D. (eds) *Learning to Teach in the Primary School*, Abingdon: Routledge; see pp. 310–11, 315.

Introduction

Claire refers to every person belonging to 'a common humanity' but argues strenuously that such a claim does not mean that all pupils should be treated 'the same'. Indeed, the author is adamant that being 'colour blind means ignoring people's cultural and ethnic identities' (p. 308). She also warns against tokenism and roots her arguments for multicultural education in education for social justice that acknowledges and tackles stereotypes, prejudice, racism and wider inequalities. The extract that follows focuses on the practicalities attached to teachers' attitudes and expectations.

Key words & phrases

Attitudes, behaviour in class, celebrating diversity, culture, equal opportunities, equality, faith, good relationships, inclusive activity, languages, minority children, prejudices, racism, social justice, stereotypes, white majority

---

Extract

"Most minority children (apart from refugees) are born in Britain, and to ask 'where do you come from?' implies that they are not British and don't belong. Instead, you could plan an inclusive activity in which everyone tells each other where they have family connections or have visited, and what languages they speak and understand. Mark this up on a world map and you could find that many white English children also have connections around the world or understand languages other than English. If you are part of the white majority, don't talk about 'us' and 'them', implying that minority groups are not part of 'us'. In fact, get out of the habit of 'us' and 'them' thinking on the way to being inclusive . . .

Don't target individual representatives of a minority group to 'teach' the rest of the class, or inadvertently suggest that you are particularly concerned with one individual by looking directly at [him or her] when you talk about their culture or faith. This is embarrassing for the children who don't want to stand out as different. Parents may be willing to come and talk about specific customs but this will depend on existing attitudes towards minorities in the school and community. Good relationships are essential, in which all parents already feel quite comfortable and welcome in school to talk about their children's progress, or attend assemblies . . .

Teachers' rather than children's attitudes are unfortunately sometimes at issue. Teachers are part of wider society; it can take courage to look hard at one's own attitude and acknowledge one's own prejudices. Sadly, a variety of stereotypes about minorities co-exist in the majority white society. Where such attitudes are played out in negativity to some children, for example in being more punitive, expecting them to behave in certain ways or having lower expectations, children are denied equal opportunities and their entitlement . . . In my own research, white as well as black children reported that some playground supervisors were harder on black kids than whites, that they didn't wait to find out what had actually happened, but pounced on a few black kids who they had already decided were to blame . . .

Some white [student teachers] fear that minority children (or their parents) might accuse them of racism if they find it necessary to discipline them. Remember that the statistics show that black children, particularly Caribbean boys, *are* more prone to negative discipline or exclusion than others and that the accusations are sometimes warranted. Children from minority communities are well aware of how racism has worked against them . . .

Your strength is to show you have been taking care with the curriculum approaches . . . not only 'celebrating diversity', but promoting social justice and equality. If you are genuinely fair, just, even-handed in all situations, and it is as plain as it can be that you do not discriminate or have favourites you will be able to deal with accusations of racism."

Summary

Claire is clearly passionate about promoting fairness and avoiding unfair discrimination. In doing so, she offers unequivocal advice about strategies to ensure that all pupils are offered respect and equal opportunity to benefit from their education. The extract suggests that she has had unsatisfactory experiences of white teachers working with ethnic minority pupils.

Questions to consider

1. Is there any place for positive discrimination? What form might this take? What are the benefits and pitfalls attached to such an approach?
2. What is your understanding of the ubiquitous terms 'racism' and 'minority'? How does your view compare with other people's with whom you work or have close contact?
3. How can a teacher determine whether he or she has successfully 'celebrated diversity' and promoted social justice and equality?

Investigations

Pupil backgrounds. Use Claire's suggestion to 'plan an inclusive activity in which everyone tells each other where they have family connections or have visited, and what languages they speak and understand. Mark this up on a world map and you could find that many white English children also have connections around the world or understand languages other than English'.

Stereotypical attitudes. By discussing the extract with colleagues, evaluate the author's claim that a variety of stereotypes about minorities coexist in the majority white society.

Parental perspectives. Discuss the issues raised in the extract with friends and acquaintances from different ethnic groups.

Think deeper

At one time, boys were steered towards skills and subjects that would provide them with a foundation for working life; girls were expected to become homemakers and were taught accordingly (see Myers 2000 for an historical perspective). Today, teachers have to be aware that both girls and boys have an important role in the workplace and in the home and it is important to treat each child as an individual, rather than make blanket assumptions about temperament, ability and life chances based solely on gender. Teachers also have a considerable responsibility to use teaching approaches that appeal to lively children, as well as to the compliant ones. Conscientious teachers interrogate the ways in which their own attitudes towards pupils might affect learning, such as whether their reactions, body language and voice tone change significantly when dealing with different pupils under similar conditions. A useful antidote to discriminatory attitudes is for adults to develop a positive attitude towards achievement and to adopt a 'you can do it' working atmosphere in which all children can fulfil their potential. **Teachers' reactions: see also Extract 42.**

Myers, K. (ed.) (2000) *Whatever Happened to Equal Opportunities in Schools? Gender Equality Initiatives in Education*, Maidenhead: Open University Press.

Think wider

Stereotyping on the basis of race or religion influences the way in which educators determine their expectations about academic achievement and pupil behaviour. For instance, there are various studies showing that black ('African American' in the United States) boys in particular may suffer as a result of teachers' low expectations. Majors (2001) addresses the fact that exclusion and expulsion of black children from schools are endemic in the United States and the United Kingdom. A survey by the *Times Educational Supplement* (Ward and Stewart 2008) noted that expectations about the examination success of minority ethnic groups varied considerably from area to area across English regions. Adams *et al.* (2009) provide a comprehensive annotated bibliographical review of the preceding year's publications (largely US-based) in the field of social justice education, with particular emphasis on issues of oppression.

Adams, M., Brigham, E., Cook Whitlock, E.R. and Johnson, J. (2009) 'Review of the year's publications for 2008; social justice in education', *Equity and Excellence in Education*, 42 (4), 525–66.

Majors, R. (2001) *Educating Our Black Children: New directions and radical approaches*, London: RoutledgeFalmer.

Ward, H. and Steward, W. (2008) 'Divided on the setting of targets', *Times Educational Supplement*, 27 June.

Teachers and the education system

Extract 57

Source

Comber, B. and Nixon, H. (2009) 'Teachers' work and pedagogy in an era of account-ability', *Discourse: Studies in the Cultural Politics of Education*, 30 (3), 333–45.

Introduction

Comber and Nixon discuss the work of middle school teachers in low-socioeconomic communities from the teachers' own perspectives. Using reflective interviews, meeting transcripts and an electronic reporting template, they examine how teacher participants in a school reform project describe their work – what they emphasise and what they minimise or omit completely.

Key words & phrases

Caring relations, customised curriculum, democratic progressive student performance, designers of curriculum and pedagogy, disciplinary discourses, educational policy, ever-responsive, pedagogic processes, pointless bureaucratic demands, professional autonomy, punitive and therapeutic modes, teacher participants

---

Extract

"A great deal of educational policy proceeds as though teachers are malleable and ever-responsive to change. Some argue they are positioned as technicians who simply implement policy. However, how teachers go about their work and respond to reform agendas may be contingent upon many factors that are both biographical in nature and workplace related . . .

When teachers are told repeatedly that student performance is contingent upon the quality of their teaching and when no excuses will be brooked for low standards, how and where can they ethically voice the challenges of their lived experiences in working with young people growing up in poverty? . . . While we read daily of the failures of public schooling and low literacy standards in a relentless attack by the media, at the same time when teachers talk about their work in these times, they speak little about pedagogy, student learning and academic achievement, and more about seemingly pointless bureaucratic demands and trying to work with students who are hungry and violent, poorly clothed and mentally ill, and who may be hoping for brighter futures but are still alienated from schooling . . .

Teachers working in disadvantaged schools describe their work in terms of democratic progressive discourses and disciplinary discourses associated with caring, managing and reporting . . . For other teachers, there is a loss of professional autonomy, responsibility and judgment as the work of reporting increasingly is done through a particular software program, which curtails what can be written. The teachers' work is reorganised and regulated around a new standardised and mediated textual template. The act of reporting fundamentally changes in ways that mean it is less responsive to the differences between students; nor does it allow teachers space to document performance against their customised curriculum designed to connect with their students . . . the absence of teacher articulation about pedagogic processes as part of their work – can at least partly be explained by constraints and inducements of prevalent corporate-managerial discourses and associated practices. Still, this does not explain teacher emphasis on 'caring relationships', which might also seem outside prevalent discourses of the current policy climate . . . the current policy climate includes disciplinary discourses in both punitive *and therapeutic* modes. We suggest that the therapeutic disciplinary modality sustains an articulated ethos of caring relationships, as a residual trace of democratic progressive discourses that once had more room for expression. At the same time, the punitive disciplinary modality converges with corporate-managerial discourses that inhibit teacher senses of *agency as designers* of curriculum and pedagogy. We thus have teacher discourse about caring relations as *prerequisite* for teaching-and-learning, yet oddly divorced from thinking about teaching-and-learning as a key process dimension of teachers' work that builds from this prerequisite . . .

Teachers repeatedly told us that designing responsive, inclusive and engaging curriculum and pedagogies was very difficult to maintain in their schools. While many were exhilarated by what they and their students accomplished under the special conditions of the project, some teachers also talked about high levels of exhaustion and the difficulty of sustaining extra energy levels, the extra administration requirements and sometimes extra funds required to make possible the *extraordinary* work they undertook as participants in the research . . . And of course in the meantime, teachers' ordinary work continues . . .

Talk about, and work on, pedagogy, needs to be situated and cannot be pursued in isolation from teachers' everyday working lives . . . Teachers' working conditions need to be altered in order for them to participate in education as scholars and as researchers, not merely as the technicians and implementers of someone else's curriculum and pedagogy."

Summary

Comber and Nixon's article is written from an Australian perspective but the key messages are relevant to teaching situations in most nations. The imposition of externally imposed regulation, with the associated high levels of exhaustion and extra administrative requirements, severely constrains the need and right of teachers to 'participate in education as scholars and as researchers, not merely as the technicians and implementers of someone else's curriculum and pedagogy'. **Early years curriculum design: see also Extract 2 and Extract 6 under 'Think deeper'.**

Questions to consider

1. How valid is the assertion that student performance is contingent upon the quality of teaching? What other factors should be taken into consideration?
2. To what extent is it fair to claim that pointless bureaucratic demands on teachers detract them from the democratic progressive discourses and disciplinary discourses associated with caring, managing and reporting?
3. How might the punitive disciplinary modality and corporate-managerial discourses inhibit teachers' ability to be agents of curriculum design and pedagogy?

Investigations

Prevailing discourses. Monitor the sorts of discussions taking place formally and informally among teachers, categorising them under (1) democratic progressive discourse, and (2) corporate and disciplinary discourses.

Changes in degree of autonomy. Interview experienced teachers about the changes in their role that they have experienced over time with respect to (1) agents of designers of curriculum and pedagogy, and (2) caring relationships.

Researching, designing and enacting curriculum and pedagogy. Interview teachers about their time use, the things that drain their energies and developmental opportunities of which they feel deprived because of implementing externally imposed directives.

Think deeper

Moore (2000) notes that a fragmented subject-based curriculum, official edicts insisting on how students should 'develop' and external prescriptions about how certain skills (e.g. learning to read) should be taught lead teachers to emphasise the development of basic skills and memorising of a very narrow range of what he refers to as 'validated knowledge'. He warns that such an approach is at the expense of more sophisticated creative and reasoning skills and overactive engagement with the physical and social world. As a result, there is a mismatch between the officially cited purposes of formal education – with its hidden implications for pedagogic style – and the models of learning development favoured by teachers (see chapter 2). **Child development: see also Extract 13.**

Day (2002) suggests that as a consequence of imposed changes in the control of curriculum and assessment and increased measures of public accountability, teachers in most countries now work within cultures in which their careers are ever more dependent upon external definitions of quality, progress and achievement for their success. Under such circumstances, attention to teachers' identities – arguably central to sustaining motivation, efficacy, commitment, job satisfaction and effectiveness – has been limited.

Balarin and Lauder (2008) argue that many of the key issues arising from the current model of governance concern 'standards' and the associated batteries of tests by which pupil and school performance are judged. They suggest that the new system of governance needs to be judged with reference to two issues: (1) the way the system impacts on children's learning, while embracing economic efficiency; and (2) the learning outcomes desired by the government and imposed upon schools through the National Curriculum, national tests, national strategies and other initiatives. Balarin and Lauder conclude that the machinery of surveillance and accountability makes it difficult for schools to deviate from focusing on test performance but query whether the outcomes represent the sum of children's education or merely their ability in taking tests.

Teachers in the United States face similar challenges to those in the United Kingdom and elsewhere in attempting to implement a raft of externally imposed requirements. For example, Bérci (2007) argues that since it is popularly held that teachers are directly responsible for their pupils' educational outcomes, national policy makers attempt to impose 'teacher-proof strategies' on them. Teachers and other educators defend the quality of their preparation and level of care and blame the difficulties they encounter in managing the constraints imposed by 'No Child Left Behind' policy and the weight of standardised testing. The issue is so serious that Bérci refers to the fact that some teachers feel that they are being turned into 'teaching machines' that have to follow a scripted curriculum, mandated lesson plans and a restricted set of textbooks and to use formulaic patterns of teaching. She concludes that external requirements create problems more than they provide solutions. **Impact of regulation on teachers: see also Extract 38.**

Balarin, M. and Lauder, H. (2008) *The Governance and Administration of English Primary Education* (Primary Review Research Survey 10/2), Cambridge: University of Cambridge Faculty of Education.

Bérci, M.E. (2007) 'Constraints on teaching: notes from the classroom', in Yurichenko, L.B. (ed.) *Perspectives on Teaching and Teacher Issues*, New York: Nova Science Publishers.

Day, C. (2002) 'School reform and transitions in teacher professionalism and identity', *International Journal of Educational Research*, 37 (8), 677–92.

Moore, A. (2000) *Teaching and Learning: Pedagogy, curriculum and culture*, London: RoutledgeFalmer.

Think wider

McNess *et al.* (2003) claim that teachers are deeply committed to the affective dimension of teaching and learning. They argue that in the complex and difficult task that teachers undertake, there are many dimensions for practitioners to consider and negotiate. These include mastery of a curriculum area, the organisational and pedagogic skills needed to plan and assess children's learning and, crucially, social and emotional factors. The authors suggest that social and emotional factors have great significance for primary teachers. Thus, the affective dimension of teaching 'relied heavily upon joint negotiation and a close personal relationship between the teacher and the learner' (p. 248).

Katz (1995) insists that teachers are among the groups of professions that 'identify the goals of their work with the good of humanity at large' (p. 223). Nias (1996) argues that without personal commitment, teaching becomes 'unbalanced, meagre, lacking fire and in the end, therefore, unsuccessful' (p. 306) and that to take close account of its impact on staff is ultimately to safeguard children's education. In similar vein, Acker (1999) comments that 'the unguarded demonstration of a child's affection for the teacher, the emotional attachment between teacher and class, the sense that one is doing a job that counts, give teachers a sense of purpose to sustain them' (p. 4). **Teacher motivation: see Extracts 59 and 60.**

Acker, S. (1999) *The Realities of Teachers' Work*, London: Cassell.

Katz, L.G. (1995) *Talks with Teachers of Young Children*, Norwood, NJ: Ablex.

McNess, E., Broadfoot, P. and Osborn, M. (2003) 'Is the effective compromising the affective?', *British Educational Research Journal*, 29 (2), 243–57.

Nias, J. (1996) 'Thinking about feeling', *Cambridge Journal of Education*, 26 (3), 296–306.

Extract 58

Source

O'Quinn, E.J. and Garrison, J. (2004) 'Creating loving relations in the classroom', in Liston, D. and Garrison, J. (eds) *Teaching, Learning and Loving: Reclaiming passion in educational practice*, New York: RoutledgeFalmer; see pp. 62–4.

Introduction

O'Quinn and Garrison don't pull their punches in the extract below, in which they provide a serious and vehement critique of the standards agenda and test-driven agenda that characterise the United States and, to a lesser extent, the United Kingdom. They argue that loving relations are essential to a full and satisfactory education. They forcefully claim that education as presently conceived is failing both learners and teachers. Note, however, the ray of hope that emanates from the final two sentences in the extract.

Key words & phrases

Accountability, alienate, conformity, courage, democratic, docility, human relationship, loving recognition, loving relation, moral equality, political agenda, standardised curriculum, technocratic ethos, trust, unique individuality, uniqueness

---

Extract

"The current ethos in the institution of schooling is driven, as it has been for far too long, by the idea of accountability, an excessively cognitive knowing relation that, we believe, fails students and teachers in the most meaningful ways. Accountability depends on a standardised curriculum that is aligned to immutable standards of learning, fixed in advance of any human relationship and measured by standardised tests. Ultimately, it reduces people to numbers, relationships to ratios, and unique selves to mere ciphers. The goal of the standards movement in education seems to be to reduce students to standardised, interchangeable parts for the machine of economic production. There is little or no room for reflection or criticism, much less cooperation or creativity, on the part of either students or teacher. Instead the emphasis is on docility; conformity; and, in its most destructive sense, rivalry. The technocratic–economistic ethos is one that reduces all uniqueness, difference and individuality to a uniform but false image of caring and loving relation that has no respect for the inventions of play; prompts dishonest rather than honest relations in that it is about performance, not growth; and shrinks the boundless dimensions of loving relation to fit its own selfish needs . . .

When we talk about education in a democracy, we can never simply talk about differences in cognitive ability; how we perceive moral equality and unique individuality is of greatest concern to democratic citizens. Moral equality means everyone has an equal right to have [his or her] *unique* potential actualised, so that [he or she] might make [his or her] unique contribution to the democratic community. It eschews all classification, uniformities, and statistical averages; there are no quantitative standards common to all democratic individuals . . .

Empathy, compassion, commitment, patience, spontaneity, and an ability to listen are all closely connected to the trust necessary for creating the conditions for loving relations in the classroom community. A teacher's simple passion for her subject matter alone will not make students learn, nor will it teach them the value of learning. An institutionalised manipulation of what it means to be 'the best' will not insure that students and teachers give their best, no matter how strong the commitment to making such a thing happen. Shaming students, teachers, and schools into what a particular political agenda, moral righteousness, or work ethic believes to be the essential 'truth' will not educate; it will only indoctrinate and alienate . . . The tensions it incites between teachers and students leak into the larger community, pitting students against schools; schools against schools; and, finally, citizen against citizen . . . By determining to nurture loving recognition and response rather than instil thoughtless habits, by having the courage to take risks and exhibit their own vulnerabilities, teachers can create the loving relations in their classrooms that may convey to the larger society. We believe that is what an education can do, what a democratic education should do, and what a loving education must do."

Summary

O'Quinn and Garrison are clearly enraged that government involvement in education has created what they perceive as a 'monster', suppressing creativity and reducing teaching to success in tests. It is interesting that they refer to what they call a 'technocratic' approach as the antithesis of democracy. By contrast, an education based on a loving relation has implications for the good of society as a whole. **Educating lovingly: see Extract 5.**

Questions to consider

1. To what extent are the authors being unrealistic in hoping to reduce government involvement in publicly funded education? What are the alternatives?
2. What evidence exists to support the view that the present education system tends to indoctrinate and alienate?
3. What can teachers actively do to promote loving relations in their classrooms?

Investigations

Handling government missives. Interview in depth at least one headteacher or principal to find out how much information is received from official sources, how they manage it and the impact it has on their decisions.

Responding to external requirements. Interview teachers to get a picture of the different ways in which they incorporate external requirements while avoiding capitulation.

Fostering loving relations. Hold a group discussion with teachers and support staff to identify measures that help to create loving relations and the implications for teaching, learning and maintaining discipline.

Think deeper

The notion that a good education is to prepare pupils to pass public tests and examinations has been promoted by politicians but has failed to satisfy many educators, who view the task as far greater (see, for example, Kohn 2004). The truly educated person is someone with the skills and ability to continue development or building upon his or her physical, social, mental and emotional well-being in all aspects of life during and beyond formal schooling.

Goodson (2007) concludes that the personal missions that people bring to their employment are largely frustrated in the micro-managed and re-regulated regimes of the public sector. Consequently, the sense of vocation, public duty and caring professionalism is diminishing, as an increasing number of people withdraw their 'hearts and minds' while complying with their responsibilities by implementing the mandates and missions imposed on them by others.

Furedi (2009) insists that since the mantra 'education, education, education' was introduced in 1997 by the then Prime Minister of Britain, Tony Blair, it has remained at the forefront of political agendas and received considerable attention. Yet despite addressing the alleged problems associated with education, so many of the solutions proposed seem to have made matters worse rather than improved them. Furedi claims that the more education is talked about, the clearer it becomes that it is valued for its potential contribution to economic development, as a central instrument for encouraging social inclusion and mobility, rather than being considered to have value in its own right. As a result, the promotion of education has increasingly little to do with what ought to be the primary purpose of learning. **Pupil learning: see Section 1.**

Furedi, F. (2009) *Wasted: Why Education Isn't Educating*, London: Continuum.
Goodson, I. (2007) 'All the lonely people: the struggle for private meaning and public purpose in education', *Critical Studies in Education*, 48 (1), 131–48.
Kohn, A. (2004) *What Does It Mean to Be Well Educated?* Boston: Beacon Press.

Think wider

The concept of 'welfare' seems to have grown beyond the mere *in loco parentis* concept to incorporate issues of law and criminal responsibility. Nixon (2007) is among many writers who warn that as parents and carers become more aware of their rights under law, teachers, school governors' and local authorities' actions will be tested for negligence should a serious incident occur that results in a pupil's injury or worse. Depending on the age of the children, the person or persons with a primary duty of care must ensure that all reasonable precautions have been taken to protect and safeguard children's welfare, though defining how this concept operates is far from easy. Berry (2007) offers a concise guide suitable for teachers at every level who need to know their rights and responsibilities under the law.

Berry, J. (2007) *Teachers' Legal Rights and Responsibilities: A guide for trainee teachers and those new to the profession*, Hatfield: University of Hertfordshire Press.
Nixon, J. (2007) 'Teachers' legal liabilities and responsibilities', in Cole, M. (ed.) *Professional Attributes and Practice: Meeting the QTS standards*, London: David Fulton.

Source

Addison, R. and Brundrett, M. (2008) 'Motivation and demotivation of teachers in primary schools: the challenge of change', *Education 3–13*, 36 (1), 79–94.

Introduction

Addison and Brundrett introduce their work by stating that motivation is crucial to both individual and organisational performance, such that even a very able and well-trained member of staff will not perform effectively unless he or she is motivated to do so. They claim that it is essential to be clear about the factors affecting motivation and demotivation, for three reasons: (1) A school can be truly effective only if its staff are well motivated. (2) Hiring new teachers is time-consuming and costly. (3) School leaders need reliable evidence about teacher motivation.

Key words & phrases

Behaviour, demotivators, ethnographic, heavy workload, individual needs of staff, leadership, long hours, management, motivators, positive responses, sense of achievement, supportive colleagues, teacher motivation, workforce

Extract

"The research consisted of an initial questionnaire to gather factual details from the 69 teachers working in the six sample schools, a diary completed daily for a week and in-depth one to one interviews conducted with a cross–section of 18 staff . . .

The information gathered in this study indicates that the principal motivators for teachers in primary schools include positive responses from children, that is, 'children being well-motivated, interested or well-behaved' and 'seeing them making progress', and staff experiencing a sense of achievement from 'a completed or enjoyable task' and from having 'supportive colleagues'. This reassuringly reflects the traditionally held view of why teachers teach, that is, because they want to work with children and to see them achieve. Conversely, the two principal demotivators are poor responses from children, that is, 'children behaving badly or showing a lack of interest' and having to 'work long hours with a heavy workload' . . .

The data were reclassified using a third domain: school-based factors, in light of the findings of the literature review about the problems of classification. This reclassification reinforced the importance of intrinsic factors in relation to motivation, and extrinsic factors in relation to demotivation, and also highlighted the relatively significant influence of school-based factors in relation to both teacher motivation and demotivation, that is, those areas of school life over which the leadership and management of the school exercise a significant degree of influence.

Whilst sources of motivation and demotivation were found to be linked, in order to achieve an optimally motivated workforce, the leaders of schools need to consciously manage them separately. A greater emphasis, however, needs to be placed on the latter, as the findings would suggest that individual demotivators have a greater impact on a teacher's motivational state than any single individual source of motivation.

A review of the data collected in relation to the ethnographic characteristics of the sample indicates, at the 99 per cent significance level, that marital status, the age and number of children living at home, role within the school, the length of teaching experience, length of time in current school, qualifications, ethnicity and religion are all contributory factors in the levels of motivation and demotivation of teachers. At the 95 per cent significance level, age is a factor in relation to motivational issues . . .

The main conclusion was that the differences which arose related to the strengths and weaknesses in the leadership and management of the schools themselves and that although there are many decisions over which a school has no control, much can be done locally to manage the motivational and demotivational impact of the challenges facing schools at the beginning of the twenty-first century. School leaders need to be aware of how the individual needs of their staff vary, and how they may change as their circumstances outside school change and as an individual makes progress through [his or her] career."

Summary

The key research findings were that the principal motivators are: (1) pupils being well motivated, interested or well behaved; (2) staff experiencing a sense of achievement from a completed or enjoyable task; (3) supportive colleagues; and (4) pupils making good progress. The two principal demotivators were: (1) having to work long hours with a heavy workload; and(2) pupils behaving badly or showing lack of interest.

Questions to consider

1. To what extent are motivating factors gender related?
2. What externally imposed requirements might motivate more than demotivate teachers?
3. What are the key messages from the research for school leaders?

Investigations

Motivating factors for teachers. Ask teacher colleagues to tell you about their best and worst moments in teaching. Afterwards, use the findings from the Addison and Brundrett study as a stimulus for discussion. See also 'School leaders' perceptions', the third item in this list of topics for investigation.

Motivating factors for school leaders. Ask school leaders to tell you about the things that give them greatest pleasure and greatest angst in the job. Afterwards, use the findings from the Addison and Brundrett study as a stimulus for discussion.

School leaders' perceptions. Ask school leaders to disclose the things that they believe motivate and demotivate those for whom they have management responsibility. If possible, contrast the findings with those for 'Motivating factors for teachers', above.

Think deeper

In their study of teacher commitment in six primary schools, Troman and Raggi (2008) found that the mission to teach is still strongly evident, together with a desire to nurture expressed as 'love' and 'caring'. These altruistic desires do not mean that teachers are uninterested in good working conditions, a respectable salary and opportunities for career enhancement, but rather that nothing can match the satisfaction that comes from making a significant difference to the life of each child.

While acknowledging the significance of altruism as an incentive to teach, Pop and Turner (2009) found that for some pre-service teachers in the United States, their previous experiences and beliefs about teaching generated negative emotions. This sceptical group perceived teaching as a demanding, challenging and overwhelming job that offered few rewards; they did not see themselves as being adequately prepared for teaching and expressed a lack of confidence in their knowledge and instructional skills. By contrast, the previous teaching experiences and beliefs about teaching of other pre-service teachers triggered positive emotions that caused them to perceive teaching as a desirable career; in this case, their knowledge and skills in teaching were seen to enhance confidence. Positive emotions were expressed using words such as 'excited', 'love', 'relaxed', 'feel good' and 'feel right'. Negative emotions were revealed through words such as 'panic', 'overwhelming', 'shock' and 'uncomfortable'.

Pop, M.M. and Turner, J.E. (2009) 'To be or not to be a teacher? Exploring levels of commitment related to perceptions of teaching among students enrolled in a teacher education programme', *Teachers and Teaching*, 15 (6), 683–700.
Troman, G. and Raggi, A. (2008) 'Primary teacher commitment and the attractions of teaching', *Pedagogy, Culture and Society*, 16 (1), 85–99.

Think wider

Research shows that many of the key factors that provide the initial spur for becoming a teacher are rooted in caring, self-fulfilment and the positive impact it has on young people's lives (e.g. Spear *et al.* 2000). Studies of the views of trainee teachers reveal that their motivation rests on a belief that they can not only contribute to children's academic progress but also influence their social and moral development (Moran *et al.* 2001; Thornton *et al.* 2002). **Values in education: see also Extracts 54–56.**

Moran, A., Kilpatrick, R., Abbott, J., Dallat, J. and McClune, B. (2001) 'Training to teach: motivating factors and implications for recruitment', *Evaluation and Research in Education*, 15 (1), 17–32.
Spear, M., Gould, K. and Lee, B. (2000) *Who Would be a Teacher? A review of factors motivating and demotivating prospective and practising teachers*, Slough: National Foundation for Educational Research.
Thornton, M., Bricheno, P. and Reid, I. (2002) 'Students' reasons for wanting to teach in primary school', *Research in Education*, 67, 33–43.

Extract 60

Source

Day, C. (2004) *A Passion for Teaching*, London: RoutledgeFalmer; see pp. 11–14.

Introduction

Day argues that passion is not an optional extra for teachers but essential for effective teaching. Passion should not be confused with mere 'well-doing' but is represented by qualities and attitudes that cement good adult–pupil relationships and encourage learners to strive hard in their work. Day warns, however, that maintaining passion is more than a semantic notion; it demands courage and perseverance to translate it into action.

Key words & phrases

Caring, commitment, effective teachers, engage students, enhanced vision, enthusiasm, excitement to learn, fairness and understanding, good teachers, hope, make a difference, passion into action, passionate self, relating learning to experience, responsibility for their own learning, student as a person, teachers who care, values–led

Extract

"Passion . . . is a driver, a motivational force emanating from strength of emotion. People are passionate about things, issues, causes, people. Being passionate generates energy, determination, conviction, commitment and even obsession in people. Passion can lead to enhanced vision (the determination to attain a deeply desired goal) but it can also restrict wider vision and lead to the narrow pursuit of a passionately held conviction at the expense of other things. Passion is not a luxury, a frill or a quality possessed by just a few teachers. It is essential to all good teaching . . .

To be passionate about teaching is not only to express enthusiasm but also to enact it in a principled, values-led, intelligent way. All effective teachers have a passion for their subject, a passion for their pupils and a passionate belief that who they are and how they teach can make a difference in their pupils' lives, both in the moment of teaching and in the days, weeks, months and even years afterwards. Passion is associated with enthusiasm, caring, commitment and hope, which are themselves key characteristics of effectiveness in teaching. For teachers who care, the student as a person is as important as the student as a learner. That respect for personhood is likely to result in greater motivation to learn . . . Passion is also associated with fairness and understanding, qualities constantly named by students in their assessment of good teachers and with the qualities that effective teachers display in everyday social interactions – listening to what students say, being close rather than distant, having a good sense of playfulness, humour, encouraging students to learn in different ways, relating learning to experience, encouraging students to take responsibility for their own learning, maintaining an organised classroom environment, being knowledgeable about their subject, creating learning environments that engage students and stimulate in them an excitement to learn . . .

Bringing a passionate self to teaching every day of every week of every school term and year is a daunting prospect. Having a good idea about what to do in the classroom is only the beginning of the work of teaching. It is the translation of passion into action that embodies and integrates the personal and the professional, the mind and the emotion, that will make a difference inn pupils' learning lives."

Summary

Day insists that passion cannot be artificially generated. It emerges from a heart-felt desire on the part of educators to create a learning environment that engages pupils and stimulates in them an excitement to learn that will make a difference in their lives.

Questions to consider

1. Does passion matter, as long as teachers get results?
2. What happens when teachers don't feel passionate about their work?
3. What does the author mean when he refers to the process of 'translating passion into action'? What are the implications for your own practice?

Investigations

Motivating factors. Interview a number of teachers about aspects of their work about which they feel passionately. Ask them to reflect on ways in which their passion has changed over the years.

Adult–pupil interactions: Ask a teaching assistant or colleague to observe several lessons and note the occasions when you were and were not enthusiastic about an aspect of the lesson or subject area or interaction with learners.

Emotional labour: Keep a straightforward diary about your feelings immediately following a lesson for a period of at least one week. If possible, ask a trusted colleague to follow the same procedure. Compare and contrast the entries at the end of the period of time.

Think deeper

Day *et al.* (2005) refer to the claim that teacher commitment has been found to be a critical predictor of teachers' work performance, absenteeism, retention, burnout and turnover, as well as having an important influence on students' motivation, achievement, attitudes towards learning and being at school. On the basis of interviews about their understandings of commitment with experienced teachers in England and Australia, they concluded that teacher commitment may be understood as what they describe as a 'nested phenomenon', at the centre of which is a set of core, relatively permanent values based upon personal beliefs, images of self, role and identity subject to challenge by socio-political change.

Day and Saunders (2006) reveal the dynamic, emotional nature of the professional life phases and identities of teachers. They argue that managing the emotional demands of classroom life is fundamental to effective teaching, and an investment of emotional energy in the workplace is essential. Effective teachers will strive to engage with all of their students and this necessitates reserves of emotional energy. The implication of these ongoing demands is that teachers' effectiveness is reduced when their emotional energy is depleted through negative personal, workplace or policy experiences. Day and Saunders conclude that being a teacher is so highly complex that schools need to devote far more attention to creating policies and strategies to ensure that professional development is tailored to the staff's different life phases.

Namblar (2008) is adamant that good teachers do not ply their trade for the money or because they have to, but because they truly enjoy it and genuinely want to do so. The majority of teachers cannot imagine doing any other job, because they see teaching as a powerful influence for social change and making the world a better place to live in. They don't view education as simply feeding young minds with facts and figures but rather as assisting in the creation of a fully rounded person.

Day, C. and Saunders, L. (2006) 'What being a teacher really means', *Forum: for Promoting 3–19 Comprehensive Education*, 48 (3), 265–74.
Day, C., Elliot, B. and Kington, A. (2005) 'Reform, standards and teacher identity: challenges of sustaining commitment', *Teaching and Teacher Education*, 21 (5), 563–77.
Namblar, S. (2008) 'Teaching is a passion', online at www.razz-ma-tazz.net/2008/04/09/teaching-is-a-passion.

Think wider

Buck (2007) argues that the creation of a positive climate for learning is a prerequisite to success, as pupils learn more effectively in schools with good behaviour. If teachers and assistants have to spend too much time trying to maintain discipline, the school will not be as effective in attracting and keeping the best staff. Buck also insists that placing student responsibility at the heart of policy decisions is essential. The creation of a successful climate for learning involves a complex mix of policies to promote a positive general ethos, with some very specific shared concrete systems to underpin and facilitate the smooth running of a school. The approach must be shared, understood and seen as fair, while supporting of all members of the school and its wider community as they seek to fulfil their goals. Systems must be manageable, have appropriate administrative support and build in personal time for students. Buck accepts the need to work with other agencies, provided that the school does not assume responsibility outside its remit. **Every Child Matters: see Extracts 24 and 30.**

Osguthorpe and Osguthorpe (2008) claim that education becomes exciting and successful when both learners and teachers accomplish what they previously thought to be impossible. Educators have the responsibility of creating new expectations for learners and infuse them with new energy and motivation by encouraging individuals to go beyond familiar goals and take manageable risks.

Buck, A. (2007) *Making School Work*, Billericay: Greenwich Exchange Publishing.
Osguthorpe, R.T. and Osguthorpe, L. (2008) *Choose to Learn*, Thousand Oaks, CA: Corwin Press.

Author list

The name of each author and the extract in which the name occurs is listed below. Numbers in brackets refer to the extract in which the author's name appears. In the case of a multiple authorship, only the first author's name is used. In the case of a chapter taken from a book, the first-named author of the chapter and that of the book's first-named editor have both been included.

Acker, S. (57)
Adams, M. (56)
Addison, R. (59)
Ahn, J. (2)
Alexander, B.K. (38)
Alexander, R. (23)
Alsup, J. (36)
Arthur, J. (4, 40, 50, 54, 56)
Ashton, P. (34)
Attard, K. (27)
Austin, M. (53)
Baines, E. (3)
Balarin, M. (57)
Barnes, A. (29)
Barnett, J.E. (33)
Barratt, P. (14)
Barrow, G. (51)
Barton, E.A. (18)
Beauchamp, C. (35)
Bentham, S. (44)
Bérci, M.E. (57)
Berk, R.A. (20)

Berry, J. (58)
Biesta, G. (53)
Black, L. (4, 22)
Black, P. (5, 27)
Blatchford, P. (11)
Bloom, B. (26)
Bold, C. (53)
Bond, L. (16)
Boyd, P. (33)
Broadhead, P. (1)
Brock, A. (2)
Brooker, L. (1)
Brophy, J. (51)
Bubb, S. (27, 32)
Buck, A. (60)
Burke, L.A. (8)
Butcher, J. (40)
Butt, G. (44)
Call, N.J. (2)
Capel, S. (16, 18, 21)
Carlyle, D. (49)
Carrington, B. (19)

Casey, B. (12)
Casey, T. (2)
Central Advisory Council (9)
Chaplain, R. (50)
Cheminais, R. (44)
Child, D. (16)
Children's Society (55)
Claire, H. (56)
Clark, A. (13)
Cohen, D. (1)
Cohen, J.L. (36)
Cohen, L. (37)
Colcott, D. (10)
Cole, M. (23, 58)
Coltman, P. (2)
Comber, B. (57)
Connell, R. (25, 35)
Cook, S.L. (7)
Cooman, R.D. (35)
Corriveau, K.H. (13)
Cosgrove, J. (49)
Costello, P.J.M. (8)
Coultas, V. (21, 47)
Cousins, L. (43)
Cowan, E.M. (6)
Cramp, A. (11)
Crick, B. (52)
Cropley, A. (9)
Cullingford, C. (7, 15, 21, 25)
Cullingford-Agnew, S. (43)
David, J.L. (27)
Davies, I. (30)
Day, C. (36, 57, 60)
Dean, J. (21, 28)
De Boo, M. (11)
Deuchar, R. (14)
Dewey, J. (42, 52, 53)
DfES (3, 14)
Doddington, C. (34)
Doherty-Sneddon, G. (25)
Drummond, M.J. (5)
Duffy, B. (2)
Duncan, D. (29)
Eaude, T. (40, 55)

Ecclestone, K. (55)
Edgar, D. (12)
Eilam, B. (29)
Ellis, S. (41, 51)
Elstgeest, J. (11)
Fisch, S.M. (12)
Fisher, R. (10)
Fonagy, P. (17)
Fraser, C. (44)
Furedi, F. (22, 58)
Furlong, J. (48)
Galton, M. (4, 47)
Gannerud, B. (19)
Garner, P. (18)
Garnett, S. (13)
Ghaye, A. (39, 53)
Gipps, C. (5)
Given, B.K. (7)
Glasser, W. (29)
Gmitrova, V. (1)
Goleman, D. (55)
Goodman, J.F. (50)
Goodson, I. (58)
Goouch, K. (2)
Gordon, M. (3, 55)
Graham, A. (36)
Gravells, A. (40)
Gray, S.L. (38)
Hagger, H. (29)
Hale, L. (32)
Hall, K.M. (31)
Hallam, S. (3, 14)
Hancock, R. (44)
Hardy, I. (31)
Hargreaves, A. (45)
Hargreaves, E. (4)
Harris, A. (27, 30)
Harris, K. (19)
Hart, S. (21)
Hartley, D. (16)
Hastings, W. (33)
Haydn, T. (26, 49)
Hayes, D. (25, 26, 28, 33, 36, 49)
Haynes, J. (8)

Ornstein, A.C. (54)
Osguthorpe, R.T. (60)
Osler, A. (52)
Palmer, P.J. (36)
Parton, C. (14)
Paterson, F. (34)
Pecora, N. (12)
Perry, L. (29)
Piekara, E. (47)
Pollard, A. (37, 46)
Pop, M.M. (59)
Porter, J. (15)
Pritchard, M. (8)
Quinn, V. (20)
Raymond, J. (14)
Rex, L.A. (22)
Richards, C. (40, 54)
Riddell, S. (19)
Rigby, K. (18)
Robertson, J. (41, 49)
Robinson, K. (10)
Roffey, S. (47)
Rogers, K.M.A. (7)
Rose, R. (43)
Rotter, J. (55)
Rowe, F. (16)
Sanders, C.E. (18)
Schön, D. (39)
Schrag, F. (53)
Scott, C. (25)
Seldon, A. (15)
Seligman, M. (55)
Sewell, K. (48)
Sharman, C. (2)
Shor, I. (52)
Silcock, P. (54)
Simister, J. (10)
Simkins, T. (45)
Simmons, R. (38)
Singer, D.G. (2)
Siraj-Blatchford, I. (23)
Slavin, R. (3)

Smedley, S. (23)
Smidt, S. (13)
Smith, M.K. (9, 24)
Smithers, A. (48)
Southworth, G. (45)
Spear, M. (59)
Stephens, P. (24)
Stott, D. (14)
Taggart, G.L. (39)
Tang, S. (38)
Taubman, D. (23)
Taylor, P.H. (34)
TES (56)
Thornton, M. (19, 59)
TNE (39)
Troman, G. (59)
Trout, M. (33)
Tunnard, S. (10)
Vagle, M. (42)
Van Evra, J. (12)
Van Manen, M. (39)
Varnava, G. (17)
Vitto, J.M. (16)
Walker, B.M. (46)
Walker–Gleaves, A. (13)
Wallace, B. (7)
Watkinson, A. (43)
Webb, M. (5)
Wenger, E. (32)
White, J. (42, 54)
White, K.R. (29, 33)
Whitebread, D. (2, 28)
Whitty, G. (46)
Wilson, E. (43)
Wolke, D. (18)
Wood, D. (13)
Wood, E. (1)
Woods, P. (7, 20, 49)
Wragg, E.C. (46, 50)
Wright, D. (41)
Yurichenko, L.B. (57)

Title key words

The Title Key Words list identifies the words that occur in the *titles* of the extracts. Singular and plural forms of the word are put together; for example, 'relationship/relationships' and 'child/children'. Similarly, closely related words are placed together; for example, 'learn/learning'. Numbers refer to the extracts.

Accountability: 57

Adolescence: 16

Assess(ing)/Assessment: 1, 5, 6, 39

Attention: 41

Behaviour: 1, 11, 18, 49, 51

Belief: 50

Break time: 11

Bullying: 17, 18

Change: 59

Child/Children: 13, 14, 15, 18, 30, 44

Classroom: 3, 11

Conflict resolution: 1

Cooperative play: 1

Creative/Creativity: 9, 10

Cultures/Cultural: 45, 56

Curriculum: 2

Demotivation: 59

Developing: 13

Dialogue: 3

Discipline/Disciplined: 40, 42, 50

Discourse analysis: 22

Diversity: 56

Early years: 1, 2, 8

Education/Educational: 6, 8, 33, 52, 53, 56

Emotional: 14, 55

Emotional welfare: 14

Emotions: 33

Engagement: 45

Enquiry: 42

Every child matters: 30

Gender: 19

Group work: 3, 4, 14

Happiness: 15, 55

Health: 16, 55

Humour: 20

Interaction: 3, 19

Intervention: 3, 14

Justice: 56

Learn/Learning: 16, 27, 37, 43, 46, 51, 58

Loving: 58

Managing: 49

Mental health: 55

Mentor/Mentoring: 31, 48

Motivation: 59

NQT: 23

Partnerships: 43

Passion: 60

Pedagogy: 23, 24, 57